The early Church in

the Acts of the Apostles
and in their writings

The early Church in

the Acts of the Apostles
and in their writings

Enrico Galbiati
and
Paolo Acquistapace
Angelo Albani
Massimo Astrua
of the MIMEP Association

Photographs by Paolo Acquistapace

Translated by Kent White

EDIZIONI **ISG** ISTITUTO S. GAETANO

STRADA MORA - TELEFONO 31912 - C.C.P. 28/6534 · 36100 VICENZA

**Edizioni: Istituto S. Gaetano - Strada Mora, 12
36100 VICENZA (Italy) - Tel. 31912/22094**

ACTS OF THE APOSTLES
Preface to the Italian Edition

This book, published in Italy by the MIMEP, with the slightly complicated title of 'The Early Church in the Acts of the Apostles and in their Writings', has a dual purpose:

1. To make known the history, life and teaching of the primitive Church of the Apostolic Age.

2. To explain in their historical context the teachings of the Apostles, particularly those contained in their Letters, which today are once more being offered to the faithful in the biblical readings of the Liturgy.

For this reason the plan and contents of the book include:

1. A historical sketch with the material divided into three periods, and with link-sections (in italics) inserted at salient points in the story.

2. The complete book of the Acts of the Apostles with short notes at the ends of the sections.

3. An anthology drawn from all the Letters and the Apocalypse. All the Apostles' writings are thus represented by passages most useful for the understanding of the story itself and most important for their doctrinal content. These extracts, sometimes difficult, are clarified by explanations in italics preceding each Letter and following each extract.

4. The insertion of each Letter at the point in the narrative at which it was written. However, so as not to interrupt too often the thread of the story in the Acts of the Apostles, the Letters written by St Paul during the second missionary journey are inserted at the end of that journey, and similarly the Letters written during the third journey are inserted in one section between the end of the third journey and the sequence of events which was to bring St Paul as a prisoner to Rome.

The Introduction should be read particularly by those who do not already possess some knowledge of Roman history. It will in fact help them to understand several matters which, in the course of the book, will be mentioned only briefly or taken for granted.

This volume is produced as the third of a trilogy of which the two earlier books have received a welcome beyond all expectation; they are the **Gospel of Jesus** and the **History of Salvation in the Old Testament.** The same method of illustrating the facts and writings with photographs of the places and with little maps is followed. The large amount of ground covered by the travels of St Paul has required great sacrifice of time and energy by those who work for MIMEP, but they are happy to provide a complete documentation. No more than some small illustrations for ornamental and doctrinal purposes have been copied from ancient examples of Christian art.

The main purpose of the work is pastoral. Yet, by remaining faithful to the text, particularly in St Paul's Letters, it inclines to a more direct and complete treatment.

For whom is the book intended? First of all for Christian people who, as a consequence of liturgical reform, so often have heard in church extracts from St Paul's Letters and have no clear idea who were these Galatians, Thessalonians, Philippians, etc. to whom the Apostle addressed them. In this book we shall see, standing out from the grey background of the past, the historical reality of those lively Christian communities, enthusiastic and sometimes unruly, who were experiencing the 'newness of life' of Christ's message, while still attending to their daily tasks, slaves or free, merchants or aristocrats, in the teeming capitals or typical provincial cities of the Roman Empire.

But the book has also been thought of for use in schools. On the level of the lower forms of grammar schools it can be understood and followed with interest in the story of events and in the actual circumstances which make the framework for the doctrinal message. This latter is more suitable for upper classes. Indeed, under the guidance of a good teacher, it would be possible to supplement or even to substitute for the set religious text, for here are to be found all the passages of theological importance which, when more or less co-ordinated, make up biblical theology in the New Testament.

This book is not intended as a substitute for editions of the New Testament. It is written for the service of God's word, of which it offers a copious exposition, and for the service of God's people who, given thereby a first taste of His word, will be encouraged to seek a more complete exposition of it.

Mgr. Enrico Galbiati
Doctor in Biblical Sciences

Contents

Introduction   page   11

    I. The Environment   14
    II. The People   26
    III. The Books   37
    IV. The Expansion of Christianity   40

First Period

    The Church in Jerusalem
    From Pentecost to the Persecution
    under Agrippa I (30-44 A.D.)   page   45

    I. The Birth of the Church   nos.   1-6
    II. The First Persecution and the Martyrdom of
    St Stephen   7-19
    III. The Missions of Philip and of Peter in Judea
    and Samaria   20-32
    IV. The Persecution under Agrippa I   33-35

Second Period

    The Mission of Paul to the Gentiles
    From the establishment of the Church
    in Antioch to the beginning of the
    Persecution under Nero (44-64 A.D.)   page   117

    I. St Paul's first two missionary journeys
    The First Journey   nos.   36-43
    The Second Journey   44-53

II. St Paul's Letters written during the second missionary journey: 1 & 2 Thessalonians — nos. 54-60

III. St Paul's third missionary journey — 61-69

IV. St Paul's Letters written during the third missionary journey: 1 & 2 Corinthians, Galatians, Romans — 70-100

V. The Arrest of St Paul and his trials in Jerusalem, to Caesarea and Rome — 101-116

VI. St Paul's Letters written during his captivity in Rome: Philippians, Colossians, Ephesians, Philemon — 117-129

Third Period

The Apostolic Writings from the Persecution under Nero till the death of St John

(64-104 A.D.) — page 325

Historical summary — 327

I. St Paul's Pastoral Letters: 1 Timothy, Titus and 2 Timothy — nos. 130-139

II. The Letter to the Hebrews — 140-144

III. The Apostles' Seven Letters called Catholic: James, 1 & 2 Peter, Jude, 1, 2 & 3 John — 145-165

IV. The Apocalypse — 166-180

Indexes — page 423

INTRODUCTION

INTRODUCTION

THE NEW TESTAMENT

The New Testament is that part of the written Revelation (i.e. the Bible) which covers the historical period from the birth of Jesus Christ till the death of St John, the last of the Apostles, at the end of the first century. It is called the New Testament because it presents to mankind the 'New Covenant' (Testament here means Covenant) offered by God to men through the sacrifice of his Son, Jesus Christ.

Its contents are:
The Gospels, the personal teaching of Jesus, handed down by the Evangelists,
The Acts (or History) of the Apostles, written by St Luke,
The Apostles' Letters written by them to various Christian communities,
The Apocalypse, a revelation about the future of the Church and the world, addressed by St John the Apostle to the churches of Asia Minor.

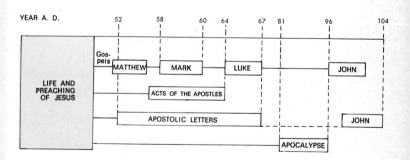

The diagram shows the origin of all the writings of the New Testament, from the life and teaching of Jesus, according to their chronological order.

I - THE ENVIRONMENT

THE HISTORICAL SETTING

The setting in which the Apostles begin the preaching of the Gospel is the Roman Empire, i.e. the Mediterranean Basin. Their work begins about the year 30 A.D. and lasts till the early years of the second century, that is from the Emperor Tiberius (14-37) to Trajan (98-117).

In the first century of the Christian era the Roman Empire was at the height of its splendour and prosperity and was also beginning to reach its greatest territorial expansion. Yet that vast Empire, politically Roman, was culturally Greek. In Rome itself many people no longer spoke Latin but

Rome, Via dei Trionfi. Marble map of the Roman Empire in the time of Augustus. Christianity first found room to spread in the area of the Roman Empire.

Greek, which had become the international language of the time. Palestine, annexed to the Province of Syria, was a part of the Roman Empire, but enjoyed a special administration under Herod and his successors, and the Roman Procurators.

A great network of roads joined all the most important places with each other and with Rome. This network made travel easy and so aided the commercial and cultural development of the peoples.

Rome. The 'Altar of Augustan Peace', consecrated in 9 B.C. in the Field of Mars, as a symbol of the peace which reigned in the whole Empire.

GAUL

SPAIN

ILLYRIA

ITALY

MALTA

MEDITERR

The basin of the Mediterranean at the time of Christ
origins and history, was unified for political a

the Apostles, though including peoples of differing
administrative purposes by the Roman Empire.

ROMAN EMPERORS AT THE TIME OF THE NEW TESTAMENT

YEAR

14 *Tiberius Caesar* succeeded Augustus, who had adopted him as a son, as ruler of the Empire. The crucifixion of Christ and the birth of the Church occurred in the last years of his reign.

37 He was succeeded by his grandson *Caligula* who, towards the end of his reign, indulged in acts of folly and ferocity. He was the first of the emperors to claim divine honours for himself.

The Emperor Tiberius
(14-37 A.D.)

41 After him came *Claudius*, who was in a sense the victim of the corruption of his court. It was his edict of 48-50 which banished the Christians from Rome.

54 *Nero* became emperor at the age of seventeen, and blotted his record quite soon with a dreadful series of crimes. He blamed the Christians for the burning of Rome; in the persecution which followed the Apostles Peter and Paul perished.

The Emperor Nero
(54-68 A.D.)

68

After the death of Nero there were in the short space of one year, four emperors chosen by the army in different provinces: *Galba, Otto, Vitellius* and *Vespasian.*

68

Vespasian was acclaimed by the soldiers who were besieging Jerusalem in the campaign against the rebellious Jews. He was an emperor of simple and honest habits. In his reign Jerusalem was razed to the ground by the Roman armies under the command of his son Titus.

79

The Emperor Vespasian
(69-70 A.D.)

He was succeeded by *Titus* who, because of his wise rule, was called the 'darling of the human race' by the Roman historian Suetonius.

81

Under *Domitian* the bloody persecutions against the Christians were resumed.

96

98

Nerva was wise and gentle. Under *Trajan* the Empire reached its greatest territorial expansion. It was in his reign that the historical cycle of the written Revelation ended, with the death of St John the Evangelist.

The Emperor Trajan
(98-117 A.D.)

19

THE EMPIRE OF ALEXANDER THE GREAT

Alexander the Great (336-323 B.C.)

Some centuries before the birth of Christ, Alexander the Great (336-323 B.C.) conquered an enormous empire which comprised the whole of the then-known Eastern world, Macedonia, Greece, Syria, Persia and Egypt, of which he became the great Monarch, venerated as a god. But the peoples he governed were quite different in habit, customs, language and religion. In order to rule them better, he dreamed of merging them into one people with one culture, that of Greece. But it was only in the time of his successors, the Seleucids in Syria and the Ptolemies in Egypt, that Greek culture spread through the whole East with the exception of Judea, whose people, though subjected to its influence, preserved their own ancient culture (see *The Old Testament*, pp. 429 ff.).

HELLENISM

The best men of Greece were thus scattered throughout the kingdoms of Asia Minor, the Middle East and Egypt, bringing a new impetus to the cultures and economic activities of the vast empire. The whole eastern basin of the Mediterranean saw the flowering of a new civilization which had common features in as much as each people kept to the same Greek culture as if to a pattern.

This was characterized by the pursuit of art and by a special interest in philosophical reflexion, particularly with regard to moral and religious problems. This civilization was appropriately called *Hellenistic*.

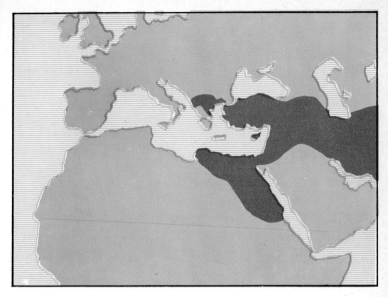

The empire of Alexander the Great.

In 144 B.C. the Romans conquered Greece, but the civilization and culture of the vanquished country conquered the conquerors. It was thus that Hellenistic civilization was extended to Rome itself and illuminated also those western regions which were under Roman rule.

Political unification favoured religious unification also, bringing about the 'mingling' of the various cults, a phenomenon which was given the name of 'Syncretism'. The gods and rituals of the different peoples became confused or integrated by them into a single national religion. For example, the Greek Zeus was identified with the Roman Jove (Jupiter) and the Egyptian Amon; Hera became Juno, Aphrodite corresponded to Venus... But, with the coming of Hellenism, religion acquired a more intimate and profound character also: men felt more intensely the problems of their moral life and their fate after death; and their minds were therefore prepared to welcome the teaching of Jesus, propagated by the Apostles.

21

Ankara. Temple of the goddess Rome.

The Roman Empire usually respected local cults and supported them by contributing to the building of temples and by subsidizing them. The most tangible result of this religious policy was the easy acceptance of the Imperial idea by the different peoples, and the installation everywhere in the Empire of the worship of the goddess Rome and of the Emperor. This worship ended by being taken as a sign of civic loyalty.

Greece. Mount Olympus.

The imagination of the ancient Greeks had deified the forces of nature and the feelings of man, peopling their creeds with a multitude of *divinities*. These had their abode on Mount Olympus, whose peak, often shrouded by clouds, seemed to merge into the sky. We list here the principal ones, at least those necessary for understanding the Acts.

PAGAN DIVINITIES MENTIONED IN THE ACTS

Jove (or *Zeus*), father of the gods and lord of all men. From Olympus he exercized power over time, yet he did not disdain to visit men on earth in human guise (see no. 39).

Jove - Zeus.

Mercury (or *Hermes*) was the god of eloquent speech, and the messenger of the gods (see no. 39).

Artemis of Ephesus, was an oriental goddess, patroness of fertility, whose widely diffused cult had already reached Rome in the third century B.C. Her ancient statue at Ephesus was believed to have fallen from heaven.

Artemis of Ephesus.

THE DIASPORA

The long series of catastrophes which had afflicted Palestine for several centuries before Christ had induced many Hebrews (also called 'Jews') to emigrate. At the beginning of the Christian era they were already to be found scattered throughout the Graeco-Roman world in great numbers. They all continued to regard Jerusalem as their true home and their only religious centre.

In the most important cities which they reached they organized communities centred in the synagogue, in which the faith of their fathers kept alive their consciousness of belonging to the people of God's abundant promises.

This historical phenomenon, which took many Hebrews far from their native land, with which they still maintained ethnic and religious bonds, was called the 'Diaspora' from a Greek word meaning 'dissemination'.

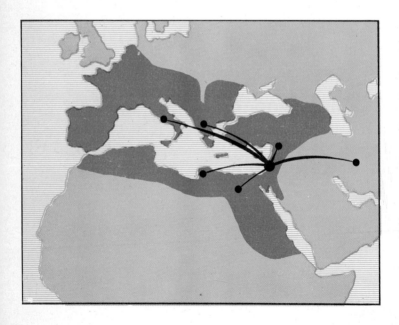

The dispersion (or Diaspora) of the Hebrews among the pagan nations.

It was to these communities of the Diaspora that the Apostles' preaching was first directed. Many Jews accepted the new teaching and became disciples of Christ, at the cost of being renounced by the Jewish community and expelled from the synagogue. So were born the first Christian communities, which were at once opened to Gentiles also. In these very early communities good relations between converted pagans and Jews were disturbed by the fact that, in the minds of many, it was not yet clear whether or not Judaism was an obligatory gateway into Christianity. That problem was to be resolved at the first Apostolic Council of Jerusalem (see no. 42).

THE DIASPORA AND THE SPREAD OF CHRISTIANITY

There is something marvellous about the rapidity of the spread of Christianity, from the historical point of view also. It was certainly assisted by particular historical circumstances like the 'pax romana', the relative ease of communications, the diaspora of the Jews and the inhuman state of the slaves and the poor to whom the 'Good News' was addressed. Against this there were very great obstacles such as divergent traditions, ancient social divisions and profound differences on the cultural level. To this was added the decline in religious beliefs which, in the great cities, had deteriorated considerably. In spite of all this, the Roman historian Tacitus tells us, only thirty years after the death of Christ, that Nero put to death 'an enormous number of Christians'.

Corinth. Marble fragment from the Synagogue with an inscription. Corinth was an important centre of the Jewish Diaspora.

II - THE PEOPLE

THE APOSTLES

Simon Peter. Jesus changed the name of Simon, a native of Bethsaida on the Lake of Galilee, to Peter. The Lord was often his guest when he was in Capernaum. After Pentecost, by command of Jesus himself, he became the visible head of the new community. From Jerusalem he moved to Antioch, and thence to Rome, where he suffered martyrdom under Nero about 67 A.D.

The field of the Apostles' action may have extended the then known world. The universality of Christianity ha

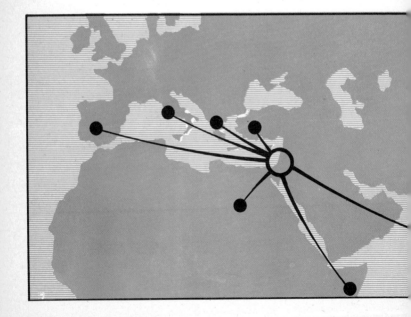

He is the only Apostle who has today a direct successor, the Pope. The other apostles are instead succeeded by the college of bishops en bloc.

John the Evangelist, of Galilean origin, was in his early days a disciple of John the Baptist, as were Andrew and Philip. With them he joined Jesus' followers and he was always specially attached to the Master. In the Acts he, Peter and James are described as 'pillars of the Church'. According to an old tradition, when he left Jerusalem he preached Christianity in Asia Minor and became head of the church in Ephesus. Exiled to Patmos, he there wrote the Apocalypse (see p. 391). He also wrote the fourth Gospel and three Letters (see p. 381). He died at a great age at Ephesus probably in 104 A.D.

Spain to far off India, thus embracing the whole of s a historical confirmation from the very beginning.

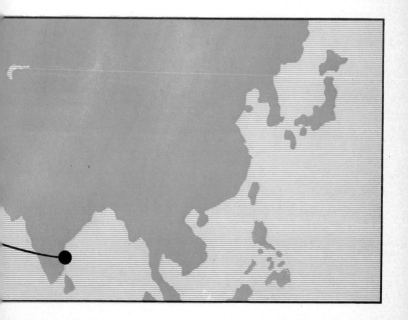

James, called the Great, was the brother of John the Evangelist and one of Jesus' three special friends (the others were Peter and John). He was the first of the Apostles to suffer martyrdom and died under Agrippa I who had him beheaded in 42 A.D.

Andrew, a native of Bethsaida in Galilee, was a fisherman with Simon Peter his brother. Originally a disciple of John the Baptist, it was he who brought his brother to Jesus. After the dispersal of the Apostles he preached the Gospel in Asia Minor and in Scythia, the region between the Danube and the Don. He went thence to Achaia (i.e. the Peloponnese) where he suffered martyrdom on the cross at Patras.

Philip who also came from Bethsaida was a disciple of John the Baptist and one of the first to be called by Jesus. For the period after Pentecost our only source of information is tradition, according to which he preached in Asia Minor and was possibly crucified at Ephesus at the age of about 87.

Thomas, called Didymus (the Twin) also came from Galilee. His early disbelief in the Resurrection of Jesus is what is best remembered about him. We have very uncertain information about him. We have very uncertain information about the field of his apostolate after Pentecost. A fairly reliable tradition assigns to him the

East: Syria, Persia and India, where he seems to have suffered martyrdom and where the oldest Christian community, the Syro-Malabar church, venerates his tomb.

Bartholomew. We find his name only in the lists of Apostles in the Gospels and the Acts. He was a native of Cana in Galilee and in St John's Gospel he is called Nathanael (see *The Gospel of Jesus* p. 81 for the account of his call). After Pentecost tradition says that he made very long missionary journeys and was martyred in Armenia.

Matthew, a tax-contractor in Capernaum, was called by Jesus to be his apostle (see *Gospel of Jesus*, p. 101). After Pentecost he preached the Gospel to the Jews in Palestine, and wrote for them the first of the four Gospels, in Aramaic. He also evangelized other countries, among which was probably Abyssinia.

James, called the Less and also the 'brother' (i.e. cousin) of Jesus, is named among the 'pillars of the Church' at Jerusalem, as are Peter and John. He was later the 'Head', that is the Bishop, of the Jerusalem Church and is the author of a Letter (see page 357). His apostolate was directed mainly towards the converted Jews and he was martyred under the High Priest Hanan II in 62.

Simon, called the Canaanite or the Zealot. About him we know very little, but he is often coupled with Judas Thaddaeus in the Liturgy. For the time after Pentecost, tradition is very confused and uncertain about where he exercized his apostolate. He may be the same Simon, related to Jesus, who presided over the church in Jerusalem after James the Less.

Judas Thaddaeus, brother of James the Less, is not often mentioned. He is the author of the Letter of Jude among the New Testament writings. He seems to have preached the Gospel in Palestine and the neighbouring regions and finally to have suffered martyrdom near the present Beirut.

Matthias was a disciple of the Lord and, after the Ascension, was chosen by the Eleven to be an apostle in the place of Judas the traitor (see page 51). He preached the Gospel in Palestine and then went to Abyssinia. According to another ancient tradition he suffered martyrdom by stoning, in Palestine itself.

Madras (India). Tomb of the Apostle Thomas.

Ephesus. Ruins of what, according to tradition, was the Tomb of St Luke.

To the list of the Twelve Apostles we add other people who played a prominent part in early Christianity.

Luke, author of the third Gospel and the Acts (see page 37).

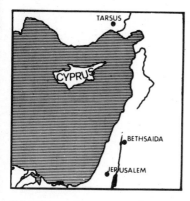

Palestine, with some places of interest in the life of the Apostles.

John Mark is the author of the second Gospel. His proper Jewish name, John, was almost always supplanted by the Greek name, Mark. Very probably, while still a boy he knew our Lord personally (see 'Gospel of Jesus', p. 322). From the account in the Acts we know that his house in Jerusalem had become the meeting-place of the Christians. He later joined the Apostles and was first with Paul and then with Peter, with whom, in Rome, he wrote his Gospel in Greek for Gentile converts. Tradition speaks of him next as founder of the Church in Alexandria in Egypt, where he is said to have suffered martyrdom. In 828 A.D. Venetian merchants took his remains to Venice.

Paul of Tarsus, called the 'Apostle of the Gentiles' because of his tireless and very extensive missionary activity. He did not know the Lord Jesus personally, and it seems that this may be the reason why St Luke in the Acts never gives him the title 'Apostle' which he reserves to the Twelve. Paul makes good his claim to this title since he received his call from Jesus himself when the latter appeared to him on the Damascus road (see no. 24). In the following pages we shall relate the outstanding events of his life.

Barnabas, of Cypriot origin, is presented in the Acts as a person of primary importance next to the Twelve, first in Jerusalem and then in Antioch. His special merit was to have introduced Paul to the apostolate, in which he was also his companion for a time. When he left Paul, tradition has it that he continued his apostolate in Cyprus and that he suffered martyrdom there in the city of Salamis.

31

Gish (the ancient Giscala), the home of Paul's parents.

THE LIFE OF ST PAUL

His double name Saul-Paul is derived from the contemporary custom of coupling with the Jewis name another belonging to the Graeco-Roman milieu.

Paul was born at Tarsus between 5 and 10 A.D. and possessed Roman citizenship. At home he received a very strict Jewish upbringing, but life in Tarsus opened his mind to wider horizons. At Jerusalem he attended the rabbinical school of the Pharisee Gamaliel, and was so faithful a disciple that he won the confidence of the Jewish authorities, who eventually authorized him to suppress the new Christian sect. There is no record of his having met Jesus. The Acts of the Apostles tell us about Paul from his conversion until his captivity in Rome, dwelling much on his three apostolic journeys and the voyage which took him, after a terrible shipwreck, to the capital of the Empire; the book ends its story with Paul a prisoner in Rome. He was freed, perhaps by an act of Clemency on the part of the Emperor Nero, and seems then to have visited Spain. But later he was arrested for the second time, at Troas, and was again taken to Rome, where he suffered martyrdom in about 67. Tradition indicates the place called 'Aquae Salviae', where the Basilica of the Tre Fontane now stands, as the place where he was beheaded.

Rome. The Church of the Tre Fontane, built on the site of St Paul's martyrdom.

RACES AND RELIGIONS

Israelites, that is descendants of Israel, more often called Jacob, is the name by which those belonging to the people of God called themselves. Their distinguishing marks were: — descent from Abraham (through Isaac and Jacob), circumcision, and obedience to the religious Law given by Moses.

Hebrews is the name by which the Israelites were called by other peoples and which they themselves used in their relations with others.

Hebrews, as opposed to Hellenists, indicated the Hebrew population which, having remained in Palestine, spoke Hebrew or, more usually, Palestinian Aramaic.

Jews originally meant the Hebrews who lived in Judea; so in the Gospel the Jews are sometimes distinguished from the Galileans.

Jews is normally the synonym for Israelites, because after the fall of Samaria in 721 B.C. the only Israelites who survived were those of the kingdom of Judah, and mainly of the tribe of Judah. In this more general sense the term 'Jew' is contrasted with Proselytes (who were not Hebrews by race), Samaritans and Gentiles.

Hellenists was the name given to those Israelites who were born in the Diaspora, i.e. the Hebrew communities scattered in the cities of the Graeco-Roman world. They spoke Greek (hence their name) even if they returned to live in the land of their fathers and had their own synagogues in Jerusalem, where the Bible was read in Greek. Hellenists who became Christians (like St Paul) played the principal part in bringing pagans to the Gospel.

Proselytes were pagans converted to the Hebrew religion; they were not of Hebrew origin (i.e. descended from Abraham) but accepted circumcision, and so were on an equal footing with the Israelites. Sympathizers with Hebrew monotheism who did not take the decisive step of accepting circumcision were called 'Godfearers' or 'Worshippers' of God (Acts 10,2-22; 13,16-26; 13,43-50; 17,4-17).

Samaritans, i.e. inhabitants of the region of Samaria, were said to be the descendants of Israelites of the kingdom of Israel who, after the fall of Samaria in 721 B.C. and the subsequent deportation, had mingled with the foreign populations brought in by the Assyrians. They were circumcized and honoured the Pentateuch as Divine Law but the Jews considered them to be foreigners (by reason of their mixed descent) and heretics.

Gentiles, that is belonging to the Nations (*gentes*; Greek *ethne*; Hebrew *goyim*), were all the non-Israelites and were considered unclean. We often translate this word as 'pagans' but it is to be noted that pagans converted to Christianity, without becoming proselytes first, were considered to be in the category of 'Gentiles' (Rom. 11,13; 15,27; 16,4; Gal. 2,12-14; Ephes. 3,1).

The Christians in the primitive Church called each other **Brethren** and **Saints** (Acts 1,15; 9,30; 10,23; 11,29 ff.; 9,13-32; etc.). The term 'Christian', first used in Antioch (Acts 11,28), was not adopted by the Christians themselves, but by others (Acts 26,28) perhaps somewhat sarcastically (1 Pet. 4,17).

Miniature in a Gospel-book of the twelfth century, portraying the evangelist St Luke in the act of writing under divine inspiration (Milan, Ambrosian Library).

III · THE BOOKS

THE ACTS OF THE APOSTLES

The book called the Acts of the Apostles is a natural sequel to the third Gospel. It does not set out to give us a biography of Peter and Paul so much as the history of the Early Church as, under the impulse of the Holy Spirit, it gradually expanded from Jerusalem into the whole of the then known world.

Its author was St Luke who wrote the third Gospel. He was a convert from paganism, coming from the Hellenistic environment of Antioch, and became a faithful fellow-worker with St Paul.

In writing both the Gospel and the Acts of the Apostles he had, as he himself affirms, recourse to authentic sources or to facts and experiences of which he had been an eye-witness. He also collected direct evidence from others, first from the Apostles and Elders who had remained in Jerusalem, and later from the testimony and accounts given by St Paul and his companions. Luke himself, as has already been said, was St Paul's companion on some of his journeys, and for this reason he uses the first person plural in some parts of the book (the 'we-sections', see nos. 45-46, 65-69, 101 and 112-115).

Time of writing

The abrupt ending of the book with St Paul's captivity in Rome in the year 63 or 64, and without any reference to the outcome of the trial, leads us to suppose that it was finished shortly afterwards.

Place of writing

It was, most probably, written on various occasions and finished in Rome during St Paul's first captivity.

Page of the Muratorian Codex, of the eighth century but reproducing a text of the second.

THE LETTERS OF THE APOSTLES

Page of the Vatican Codex (fourth century) in parchment in book form. This reproduction is of the beginning of the Acts of the Apostles.

Milan, Ambrosian Library. The Muratorian Codex (second century) open at the page where it is stated that St Luke is the author of the Acts.

St Paul wrote fourteen Letters to the first churches which he himself had founded and he wrote them for particular reasons: they were generally answers to queries of a spiritual or practical nature. The letters to the Romans and to the Hebrews, whose contents are specifically doctrinal, are exceptions to this rule. The style is that which was customary at the time; at the beginning were the author's name followed by that of the recipients to whom was addressed a greeting, followed by a thanksgiving to God. At the end St Paul was wont to send a special greeting addressed to some of the more distinguished people involved. Then, since the Letters were written from dictation, by a scribe, St Paul added a message in his own hand. This ending is characteristic of the Letter to the Galatians and shows that St Paul, accustomed to manual work, wrote in very large script.

The letters of the other Apostles followed very much the same pattern, though each writer expresses his own personal characteristic in matter and style.

See the introductions to the individual letters in the text.

MATERIALS USED FOR THE NEW TESTAMENT WRITINGS

Parchment was very suitable for writing but it was very expensive. It consisted of strips of tanned goat- or lamb-skin, joined together, which, when rolled up, formed the 'volume' or 'scroll'. Later, scribes preferred to trim the parchment in double sheets and sew them in the form of a 'codex', like a modern book. Codices of the fourth century contain the whole Bible.

Papyrus of the 2nd century B.C. kept in the Ambrosian Library at Milan.

Papyrus was cheaper but less easy to use. It was made of thin sheets of papyrus bark pressed one upon the other with the veining perpendicular. Many papyri found in Egypt, where the dry climate is favourable to their preservation, contain fragments, and even very considerable extracts, from the New Testament.

Detail of the illustration above. The fibres of the papyrus stalk can be seen arranged perpendicularly in strips.

Generally the Apostles used cheaper material and employed a 'scribe' who, sitting on the ground, held the scroll or sheet with his left hand propped on his knee, while with his right he wrote with a pointed reed called a 'calamus'.

The time spent in writing was clearly very considerable.

IV - THE EXPANSION OF CHRISTIANITY

THE THREE STAGES OF EXPANSION

The narrative of the Acts presents us with the history of the early Church and the proclamation of the universality of salvation. The diffusion of the new faith took place under the inspiration of the Holy Spirit, and had at its focal point the Figure of Christ and the fact of his resurrection.

First stage - *Jewish-Christian period, about 30-40 A.D.*

Attempt to break with traditional Jewish religion.

At Pentecost: proclamation of the new teaching to the Jews and proselytes coming from all the countries of the then known world and gathered together in Jerusalem for the Jewish Festival.

Spread of Christianity in the surrounding regions (Judea and Samaria).

Beginning and progress of missionary work among the pagans. Mission of Peter at Caesarea, affirming the breakdown of the barrier between pagans and Jews in the face of the Christian appeal.

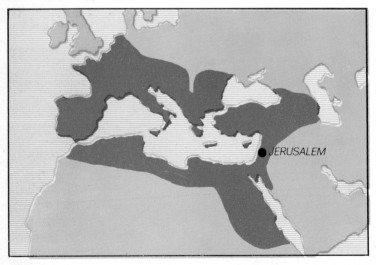

The area of the first stage of the expansion of Christianity (30-40 A.D.) was Palestine, with Jerusalem as the centre of action.

Second stage - *Pagan-Christian period (about 40-60 A.D.).*

After the persecution of the new religion in Jerusalem, Antioch took its place, becoming the seat of St Peter and the new centre for the spread of Christianity.
In the second part of the book of the Acts Paul becomes the central figure. It was from Antioch that he set out on all his journeys, mainly with the object of the conversion of the pagans. Peter moved to Rome about 55-60 and Paul arrived there in the spring of 61.

Third stage - *Gradual advance of Christianity towards Rome and among the pagans in the Empire, from 60 A.D. onwards.*

In this third stage the Gospel was offered chiefly to the pagans on completely equal terms with the Jews.

The Jewish-Christian community in Jerusalem, opposed by official Judaism and tied to a conservatism of long tradition, lost importance in the work of evangelization.

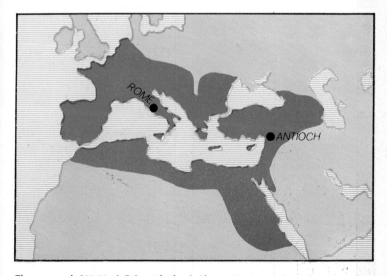

The second (40-60 A.D.) and third (from 60 onwards) stages had as their respective centres of activity Antioch and Rome.

CHRONOLOGY OF THE ACTS

YEAR A.D.	ROMAN EMPEROR	PROCURATOR OR KING IN PALESTINE	YEAR A.D.	EVENTS
14	TIBERIUS CAESAR			
		PILATE	26	Pentecost
			36	
37		MARCELLUS OR MARULLUS	36	36 Martyrdom of St Stephen Conversion of St Paul
				St Paul in Arabia
37	CALIGULA			39 St Paul at Jerusalem
41		KING HEROD AGRIPPA I	41 41	
41	CLAUDIUS			42 Martyrdom of St James the Great.
		CUSPIUS FADUS	44 44	
				45 First journey of St Paul
		TIBERIUS JULIUS ALEXANDER	46 46	
		VENTIDIUS CUMANUS	48 48	48
				49 Council of Jesusalem

YEAR A.D.	ROMAN EMPEROR	PROCURATOR OR KING IN PALESTINE	YEAR A.D.	EVENTS
			50	Paul's second journey (Letter of James?) First draft of Matthew's Gospel
			52	
		ANTONIUS FELIX	52	
54			53	Paul's third voyage Galatians 1 & 2 Corinthians Romans
			58	
54	NERO		58	Paul's arrest and captivity at Caesarea Mark's Gospel
			60	
		PORCIUS FESTUS	60	Paul's journey to Rome as a prisoner. St James' Letter
			61	Paul's first captivity in Rome Philippians Colossians Philemon Ephesians
			62	
		LUCIUS ALBINUS	62	62 Martyrdom of James the Less Luke's Gospel
			63	Acts 1 Peter
			63	Paul's journey to Spain
	Burning of Rome		64	
		GESSIUS FLORUS	64	Paul's stay in Italy Hebrews
			64	Paul's journey in the East 1 Timothy Titus
			66	

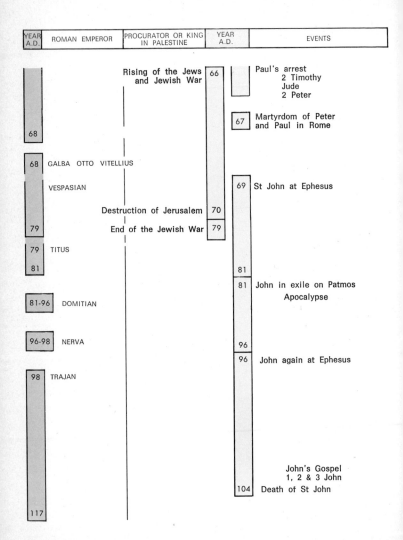

YEAR A.D.	ROMAN EMPEROR	PROCURATOR OR KING IN PALESTINE	YEAR A.D.	EVENTS
		Rising of the Jews and Jewish War	66	Paul's arrest 2 Timothy Jude 2 Peter
			67	Martyrdom of Peter and Paul in Rome
68				
68	GALBA OTTO VITELLIUS			
	VESPASIAN		69	St John at Ephesus
		Destruction of Jerusalem	70	
79		End of the Jewish War	79	
79	TITUS			
81			81	
			81	John in exile on Patmos Apocalypse
81-96	DOMITIAN			
96-98	NERVA		96	
			96	John again at Ephesus
98	TRAJAN			
				John's Gospel 1, 2 & 3 John
			104	Death of St John
117				

First Period

THE CHURCH OF JERUSALEM
FROM PENTECOST
TILL THE PERSECUTION
UNDER AGRIPPA I
(30-44 A. D.)

The city of Jerusalem seen from the south-west. On the left, the slopes of the western hill on which stands the Cenacle; in the centre, the site of the ancient City of David; on the right, the Mount of Olives. Jesus went down from these slopes to climb the Mount of Olives for his Ascension.

I. The birth of the Church

1   Prologue
        (Acts 1, 1-2)

[1] In the first book, (1) O Theophilus, I have dealt with all that Jesus began to do and teach, [2] until the day when he was taken up, after he had given commandment through the Holy Spirit to the apostles whom he had chosen.

(1) St Luke, following the custom of the day, addresses himself to an imaginary reader to tell him the story of the spread of the Christian message. He presents this book as a sequel to his Gospel.

2   The ascension of Jesus
        (Acts 1, 3-14)

[3] To them he presented himself alive after his passion by many proofs, appearing to them during forty days, and speaking of the kingdom of God. [4] And while staying with them he charged them not to depart from Jerusalem, but to wait for the promise of the Father, which, he said, "you heard from me, [5] for John baptized with water, but before many days you shall be baptized with the Holy Spirit."
[6] So when they had come together, they asked him, "Lord, will you at this time restore the kingdom to Israel?" [7] He said to them, "It is not for you to know times or seasons which the Father has fixed by his own authority. [8] But you shall receive power when the Holy Spirit has come upon you; and you shall be my witnesses in Jerusalem and in all Judea and Samaria and to the end of the earth."

The Mount of Olives from the Mosque of Omar on the site of the
ancient Temple.
**'Then they returned from the Mount called Olivet which is near
Jerusalem, a sabbath day's journey away'** (Acts 1, 12).

⁹ And when he had said this, as they were looking on, he was lifted up, and a cloud took him out of their sight. ¹⁰ And while they were gazing into heaven as he went, behold, two men stood by them in white robes, ¹¹ and said, "Men of Galilee, why do you stand looking into heaven? This Jesus, who was taken up from you into heaven, will come in the same way as you saw him go into heaven."

¹² Then they returned to Jerusalem from the mount called Olivet, which is near Jerusalem, a sabbath day's journey (1) away; ¹³ and when they had entered, they went up to the upper room, where they were staying, Peter and John and James and Andrew, Philip and Thomas, Bartholomew and Matthew, James the son Alphaeus and Simon the Zealot and Judas the son of James. ¹⁴ All these with one accord devoted themselves to prayer, together with the women and Mary the mother of Jesus, and with his brethren.

(1) This indicates the length of the journey which a Jew might make on a feast-day (the sabbath) without violating the precept of rest on the feast-day. It corresponds to a little less than a kilometre.

The history of the Apostles, which begins with the commission specially entrusted to them by Jesus on his last appearance, is the theme of the book of the Acts and the justification of the whole Christian movement. In it are contained or foreshadowed certain principles which remain fixed in the development of the early Church. Jesus commanded his apostles to be his witnesses because they had seen him. Their witness, however, must not be founded only on the human fact of having seen, but they must wait in the city for the baptism of the Holy Spirit which was to clothe them with power. Thus Pentecost was proclaimed as the starting-point. The Holy Spirit is shown to be the interior expansive force of the new community. In the book of the Acts he appears as the only true protagonist not only for the first Pentecost but also for all the manifestations of Christian activity; it is to him that the early

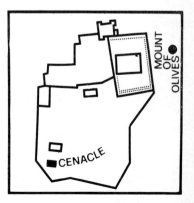

The Shrine of the Ascension, built on the highest point of the Mount of Olives, held to be the site of the Ascension. This little octagonal building is the last remains of a great medieval Crusader church, built on the ruins of a fourth century basilica.

In the shrine of the Ascension is shown an area of exposed rock upon which tradition says Jesus stepped before ascending to heaven.

Church constantly refers and he who truly guides it.

The Apostles were appointed as witnesses and such a function was to remain for ever an essential element in the description of an apostle. This very characteristic, of being a witness, causes St Luke in the book of the Acts to give the title of Apostle to none but the Twelve, not even to St Paul.

Finally, the universal proclamation of the Gospel was foretold. The Lord predicted the stages by which Christianity would spread.

In fact, the Gospel, in the course of the Acts was first proclaimed to orthodox Jewry in Jerusalem and Judea; the second stage was in Samaria where jews who were considered heretical lived (see Old Testament, no. 142); finally it was announced to everybody, beyond the narrow confines of religious and legalistic Judaism. This line of approach, enjoined by Jesus, is that which appears constantly to have been followed by the Apostles (see St Paul's method in the Jewish communities of the Diaspora).

3   Matthias is elected to the number of the Apostles (Acts 1, 15-26)

[15] In those days Peter stood up among the brethren (the company of persons was in all about a hundred and twenty),

Akeldama, the 'field of blood', in the Valley of Gehenna. The Orthodox monastery is built on the traditional site of Judas' suicide (Acts 1,17-19).

and said, [16] "Brethren, the scripture had to be fulfilled, which the Holy Spirit spoke beforehand by the mouth of David, concerning Judas who was guide to those who arrested Jesus. [17] For he was numbered among us, and was allotted his share in this ministry. [18] (Now this man bought a field with the reward of his wickedness; and falling headlong he burst open in the middle and all his bowels gushed out. [19] And it became known to all the inhabitants of Jerusalem, so that the field was called in their language Akeldama, that is, Field of Blood.) [20] For it is written in the Book of Psalms, (1)

'Let his habitation become desolate,
and let there be no one to live in it'; and
'His office let another take.'

[21] So one of the men who have accompanied us during all the time that the Lord Jesus went in and out among us, [22] beginning from the baptism of John until the day when he was taken up from us—one of these men must become with us a witness to his resurrection." [23] And they put forward two, Joseph called Barsabbas, who was surnamed Justus, and Matthias. [24] And they prayed and said, "Lord, who knowest the hearts of all men, show which one of these two thou hast chosen [25] to take the place in this ministry and apostleship from which Judas turned aside, to go to his own place." [26] And they cast lots for them, and the lot fell on Matthias; and he was enrolled with the eleven apostles.

(1) See Psalms 69,26 and 109,8.

The reality and significance of the Church was slowly revealed and it is here shown as truly founded on the Twelve Witnesses of Jesus. Peter appears among them as head of the 'college'. The essential qualification emphasized here is that of having witnessed; the Apostle must have personally seen Jesus' acts and heard his words, to be a true witness of him. The special mention of Jesus' resurrection was due to the fact that by this miracle Jesus himself was declared God's Envoy: to be a witness of his resurrection was therefore to be a witness of the truth of his mission.

The idea of the Church's being founded on the Twelve is not further developed in the Acts, in fact St Luke ends by losing sight of the others and confining himself to Peter and John in the first part and to St Paul afterwards. The newly-elected Matthias is not mentioned again in the book. The

Jerusalem. The Basilica of the Dormition (i.e. the Death) of Mary, on the site of the ancient Basilica of Sion erected alongside the Cenacle building. Tradition assigns the death of Mary to this place, whereas her Assumption is remembered in her tomb in the valley of the Kedron.

reason for this is the purpose which inspired St Luke in writing these 'Acts of the Apostles'. That purpose was certainly neither to provide us with a biography of the Apostles nor with a history of the whole of the early Church, but to show us how the Christian witness continued until it reached the centre of the then known world, Rome (see Introduction, p. 14).

4   Pentecost
(Acts 2, 1-13)

[1] When the day of Pentecost (1) had come, they were all together in one place. [2] And suddenly a sound came from heaven like the rush of a mighty wind, and it filled all the house where they were sitting. [3] And there appeared to them tongues as of fire, distributed and resting on each one of them. [4] And they were all filled with the Holy Spirit and began to speak in other tongues, as the Spirit gave them utterance.

[5] Now there were dwelling in Jerusalem Jews, devout men from every nation under heaven. [6] And at this sound the multitude came together, and they were bewildered, because each one heard them speaking in his own language. [7] And they were amazed and wondered, saying, "Are not all these who are speaking Galileans? [8] And how is it that we hear, each of us in his own native language? [9] Parthians and Medes and Elamites and residents of Mesopotamia, Judea and Cappadocia, Pontus and Asia, [10] Phrygia and Pamphylia, Egypt and the parts of Libya belonging to Cyrene, and visitors from Rome, both Jews and proselytes, [11] Cretans and Arabians, we hear them telling in our own tongues the mighty works of God." [12] And all were amazed and perplexed, saying to one another, "What does this mean?" [13] But others mocking said, "They are filled with new wine."

(1) Pentecost means 'fiftieth day' (after Easter). During this feast the first loaves of bread made with corn of the new harvest are offered to God.

The miracle of Pentecost is the foundation of the new community.

It fulfils what Jesus foretold at his Ascension and becomes the

The interior of the Cenacle after its restoration in the fourteenth century. Some parts of the walls of the outer building are undoubtedly of the Roman period, that is of Jesus' time. With this place are associated the memories of the Last Supper and of Pentecost.

starting point of the Christian Church.

The descent of the Holy Spirit is presented by St Luke as the actual birth of the Church which, after this event, can never be considered a purely human institution. The Apostles become the tools of the Holy Spirit and act under his guidance. He is the new element which enters the earliest community as its principle of life and as such he will remain throughout the development of the book of the Acts. St Luke will continue to show us the Church as directly inspired by the Holy Spirit in the interior life of the community (see the episode of Ananias and Sapphira, no. 12), in the choice of the direction in which it is to expand (see the episode of Cornelius, no. 30, in which the Holy Spirit really seems to anticipate the Church)

and above all, in the determination of the line of conduct to be followed in the face of the difficulties which are to arise from time to time (see the Council of Jerusalem, no. 42).

In the episode of Pentecost there was further affirmation, and in a manner which was solemn even in its literary form, of the universal scope of the Christian message. St Luke expresses this with a list of peoples awaiting its announcement as they attended the festival. The list is drawn up in a vaguely geographical order from Asia Minor to the Mediterranean, with reference to the languages which the people spoke. It is to be noted that the foreigners present were all Jews of the Diaspora or at least proselytes: we are still, that is to say, in the area of orthodox Judaism.

Jerusalem. Small courtyard of the Cenacle. The room in which the Last Supper and the Event of Pentecost took place is on the first floor.

5   **Peter's speech**
     (Acts 2, 14-41)

[14] But Peter, standing with the eleven, lifted up his voice and addressed them, "Men of Judea and all who dwell in Jerusalem, let this be known to you, and give ear to my words. [15] For these men are not drunk, as you suppose, since it is only the third hour (1) of the day; [16] but this is what was spoken by the prophet Joel:

[17] 'And in the last days it shall be, God declares,
    that I will pour out my Spirit upon all flesh,
    and your sons and your daughters shall prophesy,
    and your young men shall see visions, and our old men shall
    dream dreams;

[18] yea, and on my menservants and my maidservants in those
    days
    I will pour out my Spirit; and they shall prophesy.

[19] And I will show wonders in the heaven above
    and signs on the earth beneath,
    blood, and fire, and vapour of smoke;

[20] the sun shall be turned into darkness
    and the moon into blood,
    before the day of the Lord comes,
    the great and manifest day.

[21] And it shall be that whoever calls on the name of the Lord
    shall be saved.' (2)

[22] "Men of Israel, hear these words: Jesus of Nazareth, a man attested to you by God with mighty works and wonders and signs which God did through him in your midst, as you yourselves know— [23] this Jesus, delivered up according to the definite plan and foreknowledge of God, you crucified and killed by the hands of lawless men. [24] But God raised him up, having loosed the pangs of death, because it was not possible for him to be held by it. [25] For David says concerning him,

'I saw the Lord always before me,
    for he is at my right hand that I may not be shaken;

[26] therefore my heart was glad, and my tongue rejoiced;
    moreover my flesh will dwell in hope.

²⁷ For thou wilt not abandon my soul to Hades,
nor let thy Holy One see corruption.

²⁸ Thou hast made known to me the ways of life;
thou wilt make me full of gladness with thy presence.' (3)

²⁹ "Brethren, I may say to you confidently of the patriarch David that he both died and was buried, and his tomb is with us to this day. ³⁰ Being therefore a prophet, and knowing that God had sworn with an oath to him that he would set one of his descendants upon his throne, ³¹ he foresaw and spoke of the resurrection of the Christ, that he was not abandoned to Hades, nor did his flesh see corruption. ³² This Jesus God raised up, and of that we all are witnesses. ³³ Being therefore exalted at the right hand of God, and having received from the Father the promise of the Holy Spirit, he has poured out this which you see and hear. ³⁴ For David did not ascend into the heavens; but he himself says,

'The Lord said to my Lord, Sit at my right hand,
³⁵ till I make thy enemies a stool for thy feet.' (4)

³⁶ Let all the house of Israel therefore know assuredly that God has made him both Lord and Christ, this Jesus whom you crucified."

³⁷ Now when they heard this they were cut to the heart, and said to Peter and the rest of the apostles, "Brethren, what shall we do?" ³⁸ And Peter said to them, "Repent, and be baptized every one of you in the name of Jesus Christ for the forgiveness of your sins; and you shall receive the gift of the Holy Spirit. ³⁹ For the promise is to you and to your children and to all that are far off, every one whom the Lord our God calls to him." ⁴⁰ And he testified with many other words and exhorted them, saying, "Save yourselves from this crooked generation." ⁴¹ So those who received his word were baptized, and there were added that day about three thousand souls.

(1) The 'third' hour of the morning corresponds to nine o'clock.
(2) See Joel 3,1-5. (3) Psalm 15,8-11. (4) Psalm 109,1.

The speeches recorded for us by St Luke all follow an almost uniform plan. They represent the public proclamation of the Christ-

ian message, and show the plan of the primitive teaching. The basis of the proclamation to the Jews is clearly the Old Testament seen in its Messianic perspective. The events of the life of Christ and the Church are looked at in the light of texts of the Old Testament which are quoted to show the sense in which God means them to be understood in the actual situation. This demonstrates clearly that individual events are included in the great Event of the history of salvation, interpreted in the light of Holy Scripture. Now at last the Messianic Age has been reached and the whole of the Old Covenant has been superseded. Jesus of Nazareth is the Messiah in whom all the prophecies are fulfilled. Jesus, whom the Sanhedrin has condemned to death, is risen and in him is realized the Divine plan of universal salvation. We must now accept his message and be baptized in his name in order to be saved.

6   The first Christian community
(Acts 2, 42-47)

[42] And they devoted themselves to the apostles' teaching and fellowship, to the breaking of bread and the prayers.
[43] And fear came upon every soul; and many wonders and signs were done through the apostles. [44] And all who believed were together and had all things in common; [45] and they sold their possessions and goods and distributed them to all, as any had need. (1) [46] And day by day, attending the temple together and breaking bread in their homes, they partook of food with glad and generous hearts, [47] praising God and having favour with all the people. And the Lord added to their number day by day those who were being saved.

(1) Their free and voluntary sharing of goods was a consequence of their faith in and love for the Lord, and of their hope for the eternal blessings of the Kingdom of God.

II. The first persecutions and the martyrdom of St Stephen

Effects of the first persecution

As we have seen the new Christian community lived in the setting of orthodox Judaism, and was judged by the religious authorities as one of its many sects (see page 115, the first Church in Jerusalem). Even in the last chapter of the Acts the Jews continue to call the new community a 'sect' (see no. 107).

The strongest reaction came from the priestly aristocracy, the sect of the Sadducees, which had earlier been responsible for the condemnation of Jesus and therefore felt itself directly accused by the Apostles' preaching. Furthermore the Sadducees denied the possibility of resurrection (see the 'Gospel of Jesus', pp. 23 & 272), so the defenders of Jewish orthodoxy intervened, in the first instance with threats, then with arrests and punishments.

Their reaction had two effects on the new community. First of all, it gave it an opportunity of explaining its own teaching more thoroughly and of pointing out more and more clearly its difference from Judaism. This clarification specially affected the mind of official Judaism which, from a vague opinion about the new movement, came, from Peter's speeches and the interrogations of those arrested, to have a more exact knowledge of the significance of what the new community affirmed.

The second effect of the persecution was to drive the first believers to leave Jerusalem and so to carry Jesus' message to other people also, first in Judea and then in Samaria.

7 The cure of a cripple
(Acts 3, 1-10)

[1] Now Peter and John were going up to the temple at the hour of prayer, the ninth hour. (1) [2] And a man lame from birth

The site of the 'Beautiful Gate' in the Temple Area in Jerusalem. In the background, the Mosque of Omar, seen from the East. The arches, built by the Moslems, mark the highest part of the sacred area.

was being carried, whom they laid daily at that gate of the temple which is called Beautiful to ask alms of those who entered the temple. ³ Seeing Peter and John about to go into the temple, he asked for alms. ⁴ And Peter directed his gaze at him, with John, and said, "Look at us." ⁵ And he fixed his attention upon them, expecting to receive something from them. ⁶ But Peter said, "I have no silver and gold, but I give you what I have; in the name of Jesus Christ of Nazareth, walk." ⁷ And he took him by the right hand and raised him up; and immediately his feet and ankles were made strong. ⁸ And leaping up he stood and walked and entered the temple with them, walking and leaping and praising God. ⁹ And all the people saw him walking and praising God, ¹⁰ and recognized him as the one who sat for alms at the Beautiful Gate of the temple; and they were filled with wonder and amazement at what had happened to him.

(1) At the 'ninth' hour (three o'clock in the afternoon) the evening sacrifice was offered in the Temple; this was followed by the offering of incense during the prayer of the people and by the great priestly blessing. The 'Beautiful' Gate gave access from the east to the first Temple Court properly so called (the Court of the Women). It was thus named because of its ornamentation in gold, silver and bronze.

8 Peter's speech in the Temple
(Acts 3, 11-26)

¹¹ While he clung to Peter and John, all the people ran together to them in the portico called Solomon's, astounded. ¹² And when Peter saw it he addressed the people, "Men of Israel, why do you wonder at this, or why do you stare at us, as though by our own power or piety we had made him walk? ¹³ The God of Abraham and of Isaac and of Jacob, the God of our fathers, glorified his servant Jesus, whom you delivered up and denied in the presence of Pilate, when he had decided to release him. ¹⁴ But you denied the Holy and Righteous One, and asked for a murderer to be granted to you, ¹⁵ and killed the Author of life,

The eastern side of the great court around the Temple. Here gathered the crowd which Peter addressed after the cure of the cripple. On the left is the place where stood the eastern gate of the Temple, called today the 'Golden Gate'.

whom God raised from the dead. To this we are witnesses. [16] And his name, by faith in his name, has made this man strong whom you see and know; and the faith which is through Jesus has given the man this perfect health in the presence of you all.

[17] "And now, brethren, I know that you acted in ignorance, as did also your rulers. [18] But what God foretold by the mouth of all the prophets, that his Christ should suffer, he thus fulfilled. [19] Repent therefore, and turn again, that your sins may be blotted out, that times of refreshing may come from the presence of the Lord, [20] and that he may send the Christ appointed for you, Jesus, [21] whom heaven must receive until the time for establishing all that God spoke by the mouth of his holy prophets from of old. [22] Moses said, 'The Lord God will raise up for you a prophet from your brethren as he raised me up. You shall listen to him in whatever he tells you. [23] And it shall be that every soul that does not listen to that prophet shall be destroyed from the people.' (1) [24] And all the prophets who have spoken, from Samuel and those who came afterwards, also proclaimed these days. [25] You are the sons of the prophets and of the covenant which God gave to your fathers, saying to Abraham, 'And in your posterity shall all the families of the earth be blessed.' (2) [26] God having raised up his servant, sent him to you first, to bless you in turning every one of you from your wickedness."

(1) Deuteronomy 18,18-19. (2) Genesis 22,18.

9 Peter and John before the Sanhedrim
(Acts 4, 1-22)

[1] And as they were speaking to the people, the priests and the captain of the temple and the Sadducees (1) came upon them, [2] annoyed because they were teaching the people and proclaiming in Jesus the resurrection from the dead. [3] And they arrested them and put them in custody until the morrow, for it was already evening. [4] But many of those who heard the word believed; and the number of the men came to about five thousand.

Jerusalem. The Roman stairway from the lower city, climbing the western hill on which stood the Cenacle and the house of Caiaphas. Jesus and the Apostles often went up these steps.

⁵ On the morrow their rulers and elders and scribes were gathered together in Jerusalem, ⁶ with Annas the high priest and Caiaphas and John and Alexander, and all who were of the high-priestly family. ⁷ And when they had set them in the midst, they inquired, "By what power or by what name did you do this?" ⁸ Then Peter, filled with the Holy Spirit, said to them, "Rulers of the people and elders, ⁹ if we are being examined today concerning a good deed done to a cripple, by what means this man has been healed, ¹⁰ be it known to you all, and to all the people of Israel, that by the name of Jesus Christ of Nazareth, whom you crucified, whom God raised from the dead, by him this man is standing before you well. ¹¹ This is the stone which was rejected by you builders, (2) but which has become the head of the corner. ¹² And there is salvation in no one else, for there is no other name under heaven given among men by which we must be saved."

¹³ Now when they saw the boldness of Peter and John, and perceived that they were uneducated, common men, they wondered; and they recognized that they had been with Jesus. ¹⁴ But seeing the man that had been healed standing beside them, they had nothing to say in opposition. ¹⁵ But when they had commanded them to go aside out of the council, they conferred with one another, ¹⁶ saying, "What shall we do with these men? For that a notable sign has been performed through them is manifest to all the inhabitants of Jerusalem, and we cannot deny it. ¹⁷ But in order that it may spread no further among the people, let us warn them to speak no more to any one in this name." ¹⁸ So they called them and charged them not to speak or teach at all in the name of Jesus. ¹⁹ But Peter and John answered them, "Whether it is right in the sight of God to listen to you rather than to God, you must judge; ²⁰ for we cannot but speak of what we have seen and heard." ²¹ And when they had further threatened them, they let them go, finding no way to punish them, because of the people; for all men praised God for what had happened. ²² For the man on whom this sign of healing was performed was more than forty years old.

(1) The Sadducees formed a genuine political party composed mainly of aristocrats and priests. They did not admit any oral traditions, and of the written law kept only the Pentateuch, which, in their opinion, permitted them even to deny the resurrection of the dead.

(2) Psalm 117,2.

10 The prayer of the persecuted community
(Acts 4, 23-31)

²³ When they were released they went to their friends and reported what the chief priests and the elders had said to them. ²⁴ And when they heard it, they lifted their voices together to God and said, "Sovereign Lord, who didst make the heaven and the earth and the sea and everything in them, ²⁵ who by the mouth of our father David, thy servant, didst say by the Holy Spirit,

'Why did the Gentiles rage,
and the peoples imagine vain things?
²⁶ The kings of the earth set themselves in array,
and the rulers were gathered together,
against the Lord and against his Anointed' (1)

²⁷ for truly in this city there were gathered together against thy holy servant Jesus, whom thou didst anoint, both Herod and Pontius Pilate, with the Gentiles and the peoples of Israel, ²⁸ to do whatever thy hand and thy plan had predestined to take place. ²⁹ And now, Lord, look upon their threats, and grant to thy servants to speak thy word with all boldness, ³⁰ while thou stretchest out thy hand to heal, and signs and wonders are performed through the name of thy holy servant Jesus." ³¹ And when they had prayed, the place in which they were gathered together was shaken; and they were all filled with the Holy Spirit and spoke the word of God with boldness.

(1) Psalm 2,1-2.

11 Brotherly love of the first Christians
(Acts 4, 32-37)

³² Now the company of those who believed were of one heart and soul, and no one said that any of the things which he possessed was his own, but they had everything in common. ³³ And

with great power the apostles gave their testimony to the resurrection of the Lord Jesus, and great grace was upon them all. ³⁴ There was not a needy person among them, for as many as were possessors of lands or houses sold them, and brought the proceeds of what was sold ³⁵ and laid it at the apostles' feet; and distribution was made to each as any had need. ³⁶ Thus Joseph who was surnamed by the apostles Barnabas (which means, Son of encouragement), a Levite, a native of Cyprus, ³⁷ sold a field which belonged to him, and brought the money and laid it at the apostles' feet.

12 The deceit of Ananias and Sapphira
(Acts 5, 1-11)

¹ But a man named Ananias with his wife Sapphira sold a piece of property, ² and with his wife's knowledge he kept back some of the proceeds, and brought only a part and laid it at the apostles' feet. ³ But Peter said, "Ananias, why has Satan filled your heart to lie to the Holy Spirit and to keep back part of the proceeds of the land? ⁴ While it remained unsold, did it not remain your own? And after it was sold, was it not at your disposal? How is it that you have contrived this deed in your heart? You have not lied to men but to God." ⁵ When Ananias heard these words, he fell down and died. And great fear came upon all who heard of it. ⁶ The young men rose and wrapped him up and carried him out and buried him.

⁷ After an interval of about three hours his wife came in, not knowing what had happened. ⁸ And Peter said to her, "Tell me whether you sold the land for so much." And she said, "Yes, for so much." ⁹ But Peter said to her, "How is it that you have agreed together to tempt the Spirit of the Lord? Hark, the feet of those that have buried your husband are at the door, and they will carry you out." ¹⁰ Immediately she fell down at his feet and died. When the young men came in they found her dead, and they carried her out and buried her beside her

The eastern gate of the Temple Area (the Golden Gate) seen from outside. This gate, now walled up, gave access to 'Solomon's Porch' where the first Christians assembled for prayer (Acts 5,12).

husband. [11] And great fear came upon the whole church, and upon all who heard of these things.

13 Growth of the Christian community
(Acts 5, 12-16)

[12] Now many signs and wonders were done among the people by the hands of the apostles. And they were all together in Solomon's Portico. (1) [13] None of the rest dared join them, but the people held them in high honour. [14] And more than ever believers were added to the Lord, multitudes both of men and women, [15] so that they even carried out the sick into the streets, and laid them on beds and pallets, that as Peter came by at least his shadow might fall on some of them. [16] The people also gathered from the towns around Jerusalem, bringing the sick and those afflicted with unclean spirits, and they were all healed.

(1) The porch called 'Solomon's' adorned the eastern side of the great esplanade of the Temple. It overlooked the valley of the Kedron.

Interior of the so-called 'Golden Gate'. Some architectural features may go back to Jesus' time.

The south side of the Temple Area was occupied by a lofty portico with three aisles, called 'Herod's Basilica'. The Mosque of Omar in the background in this photograph is built on a part of the site of the ancient portico whose size can be judged from the surviving capitols.

14 The Apostles are arrested and brought before the Sanhedrim
(Acts 5, 17-33)

[17] But the high priest rose up and all who were with him, that is, the party of the Sadducees, and filled with jealousy [18] they arrested the apostles and put them in the common prison. [19] But at night an angel of the Lord opened the prison doors and brought them out and said, [20] "Go and stand in the temple and speak to the people all the words of this Life." [21] And when they heard this, they entered the temple at daybreak and taught.

Now the high priest came and those who were with him and called together the council and all the senate of Israel, and sent to the prison to have them brought. [22] But when the officers came, they did not find them in the prison, and they returned and reported, [23] "We found the prison securely locked and the sentries standing at the doors, but when we opened it we found no one inside." [24] Now when the captain of the temple and the chief prests heard these words, they were much perplexed about them, wondering what this would come to. [25] And some one came and told them, "The men whom you put in prison are standing in the temple and teaching the people." [26] Then the captain with the officers went and brought them, but without violence, for they were afraid of being stoned by the people.

[27] And when they had brought them, they set them before the council. And the high priest questioned them, [28] saying, "We strictly charged you not to teach in this name, yet here you have filled Jerusalem with your teaching and you intend to bring this man's blood upon us." [29] But Peter and the apostles answered, "We must obey God rather than men. [30] The God of our fathers raised Jesus whom you killed by hanging him on a tree. [31] God exalted him at his right hand as Leader and Saviour, to give repentance to Israel and forgiveness of sins. [32] And we are witnesses to these things, and so is the Holy Spirit whom

Beth Shearim. The tombs of famous rabbis, among them the descendants of that Gamaliel who is spoken of in the text of the Acts (5, 34), have been excavated from the rock in this district of Galilee.

God has given to those who obey him." [33] When they heard this they were enraged and wanted to kill them.

15 Intervention by Gamaliel
(Acts 5, 34-42)

[34] But a Pharisee in the council named Gamaliel, (1) a teacher of the law, held in honour by all the people, stood up and ordered the men to be put outside for a while. [35] And he said to them, "Men of Israel, take care what you do with these men. [36] For before these days Theudas arose, giving himself out to be somebody, and a number of men, about four hundred, joined him; but he was slain and all who followed him were dispersed and came to nothing. [37] After him Judas the Galilean arose in the days of the census and drew away some of the people after him; he also perished, and all who followed him were scattered. [38] So in the present case I tell you, keep away from these men and let them alone; for if this plan or this undertaking is of men, it will fail; [39] but if it is of God, you will not be able to overthrow them. You might even be found opposing God!"

[40] So they took his advice, and when they had called in the apostles, they beat them and charged them not to speak in the name of Jesus, and let them go. [41] Then they left the presence of the council, rejoicing that they were counted worthy to suffer dishonour for the name. [42] And every day in the temple and at home they did not cease teaching and preaching Jesus as the Christ.

(1) Gamaliel was St Paul's teacher and also a person of influence in the Sanhedrim, where he represented a moderate tendency in the interpretation of the Mosaic Law and the Jewish traditions.

The two persons to whom he refers are: — the former, a certain Theudas (a false Messiah of this name is mentioned by the historian Josephus Flavius) who, having proclaimed himself Messiah, aroused the people against the Romans; the latter, one Judas, was a native of Galilee who rebelled against the Romans on the occasion of the census of the years 6-7 A.D. His movement had a big following, lasted longer and was more difficult to suppress. Both preached armed rebellion in the name of an earthly Messianic kingdom, in accordance with popular expectations.

16 Election of the seven deacons
(Acts 6, 1-7)

¹ Now in these days when the disciples were increasing in number, the Hellenists (1) murmured against the Hebrews because their widows were neglected in the daily distribution. ² And the twelve summoned the body of the disciples and said, "It is not right that we should give up preaching the word of God to serve tables. ³ Therefore, brethren, pick out from among you seven men of good repute, full of the Spirit and of wisdom, whom we may appoint to this duty. ⁴ But we will devote ourselves to prayer and to the ministry of the word." ⁵ And what they said pleased the whole multitude, and they chose Stephen, a man full of faith and of the Holy Spirit, and Philip, and Prochorus, and Nicanor, and Timon, and Parmenas, and Nicolaus, a proselyte of Antioch. ⁶ These they set before the apostles, and they prayed and laid their hands upon them.

⁷ And the word of God increased; and the number of the disciples multiplied greatly in Jerusalem, and a great many of the priests were obedient to the faith.

(1) Concerning the Hellenists, see Introduction, page 20. When they returned to their fatherland they were treated rather like foreigners, to the extent that even in the Christian community they were overlooked in the daily distribution to the poor of food given by the free and voluntary offerings of other members of the same community.

The Church at this point in its history, still gathered around the Twelve in Jerusalem as it was, had already opened its doors to the Hellenists. These, living in the Diaspora (see Introduction, pages 20 and 24), had eventually absorbed something of the atmosphere of Hellenistic culture and had therefore a more open vision of reality than the Jews who were traditionally more conservative. Among the things for which the Hellenists were blamed was their tendency to exceed the bounds of narrow nationalism. The very names of the chosen seven are all Greek.

The Office to which they were elected was the 'diakonia', that is the serving of the poor in the community. Because of this fact Christian tradition has ascribed the rise of the institution of the Diaconate to that time.

The episode, in St Luke's story, serves to introduce Stephen, whose persecution is presented as the cause of the diffusion of Christianity, first, among the heretical Jews in Samaria (see no. 21) and secondly, as far as to Antioch. It is on this occasion that Paul, the hero of the second part of the book, makes his first appearance.

17 Stephen on trial before the Sanhedrim
(Acts 6, 8-15)

⁸ And Stephen, full of grace and power, did great wonders and signs among the people. ⁹ Then some of those who belonged to the synagogue of the Freedmen (as it was called), and of the Cyrenians, and of the Alexandrians, and of those from Cilicia and Asia, arose and disputed with Stephen. ¹⁰ But they could not withstand the wisdom and the Spirit with which he spoke. ¹¹ Then they secretly instigated men, who said, "We have heard him speak blasphemous words against Moses and God." ¹² And they stirred up the people and the elders and the scribes, and they came upon him and seized him, and brought him before the council, ¹³ and set up false witnesses who said, "This man never ceases to speak words against this holy place and the law; ¹⁴ for we have heard him say that this Jesus of Nazareth will destroy this place, and will change the customs which Moses delivered to us." ¹⁵ And gazing at him, all who sat in the council saw that his face was like the face of an angel.

18 Stephen's speech
(Acts 7, 1-53)

¹ And the high priest said, "Is this so?" ² And Stephen said: "Brethren and fathers, hear me. The God of glory appeared to our father Abraham, when he was in Mesopotamia, before he lived in Haran, ³ and said to him, 'Depart from your land and from your kindred and go into the land which I will show you.' (1) ⁴ Then he departed from the land of the Chaldeans, and lived in Haran. And after his father died, God removed him from there into this land in which you are now living; ⁵ yet he gave him no inheritance in it, not even a foot's length, but promised to give it to him in possession and to his posterity after him, though he had no child. ⁶ And God spoke to this

Desert of Sinai: Wadi Gharandel, probably the thermal spring of Elim, one of the halting-places of the Israelites after the exodus from Egypt under Moses' leadership. Stephen's speech recalls these places.

effect, that his posterity would be aliens in a land belonging to others, who would enslave them and ill-treat them (2) four hundred years. ⁷ 'But I will judge the nation which they serve,' said God, 'and after that they shall come out and worship me in this place.' ⁸ And he gave him the covenant of circumcision. And so Abraham became the father of Isaac, and circumcised him on the eighth day; (3) and Isaac became the father of Jacob, and Jacob of the twelve patriarchs.

⁹ "And the patriarchs, jealous of Joseph, sold him into Egypt; but God was with him, ¹⁰ and rescued him out of all his afflictions, and gave him favour and wisdom before Pharaoh, king of Egypt, who made him governor over Egypt and over all his household. ¹¹ Now there came a famine throughout all Egypt and Canaan, and great affliction, and our fathers could find no food. ¹² But when Jacob heard that there was grain in Egypt, he sent forth our fathers the first time. ¹³ And at the second visit Joseph made himself known to his brothers, and Joseph's family became known to Pharaoh. ¹⁴ And Joseph sent and called to him Jacob his father and all his kindred, seventy-five souls; ¹⁵ and Jacob went down into Egypt. And he died, himself and our fathers, ¹⁶ and they were carried back to Shechem and laid in the tomb that Abraham had bought for a sum of silver from the sons of Hamor in Shechem.

¹⁷ "But as the time of the promise drew near, which God had granted to Abraham, the people grew and multiplied in Egypt ¹⁸ till there arose over Egypt another king who had not known Joseph. ¹⁹ He dealt craftily with our race and forced our fathers to expose their infants, that they might not be kept alive. ²⁰ At this time Moses was born, and was beautiful before God. And he was brought up for three months in his father's house; ²¹ and when he was exposed, Pharaoh's daughter adopted him and brought him up as her own son. ²² And Moses was instructed in all the wisdom of the Egyptians, and he was mighty in his words and deeds.

²³ "When he was forty years old, it came into his heart to visit his brethren, the sons of Israel. ²⁴ And seeing one of them being wronged, he defended the oppressed man and avenged him by striking the Egyptian. ²⁵ He supposed that his brethren understood that God was giving them deliverance by his hand, but they did not understand. ²⁶ And on the following day he appeared to them as they were quarrelling and would have reconciled them, saying, 'Men, you are brethren, why do you wrong each other?' ²⁷ But the man who was wronging his neighbour thrust him aside, saying, 'Who made you a ruler and a judge over us? ²⁸ Do you want to kill me as you killed the Egyptian yesterday?' (4)

The mountain mass of Sinai from the summit of Gebel Musa (i.e. Moses' Mountain). On these heights God revealed himself to his people and spoke with Moses.
'He received living oracles to give to us' (Acts 7,38).

²⁹ At this retort Moses fled, and became an exile in the land of Midian, where he became the father of two sons. ³⁰ Now when forty years had passed, an angel appeared to him in the wilderness of Mount Sinai, in a flame of fire in a bush. (5) ³¹ When Moses saw it he wondered at the sight; and as he drew near to look, the voice of the Lord came, ³² 'I am the God of your fathers, the God of Abraham and of Isaac and of Jacob.' And Moses trembled and did not dare to look. ³³ And the Lord said to him, 'Take off the shoes from your feet, for the place where you are standing is holy ground. ³⁴ I have surely seen the ill-treatment of my people that are in Egypt and heard their groaning, and I have come down to deliver them. And now come, I will send you to Egypt.'

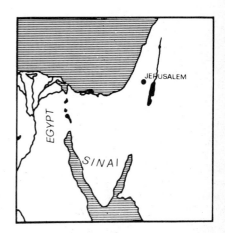

The places mentioned by St Stephen in his speech: Egypt, Sinai and Jerusalem.

³⁵ This Moses whom they refused, saying, 'Who made you a ruler and a judge?' God sent as both ruler and deliverer by the hand of the angel that appeared to him in the bush. ³⁶ He led them out, having performed wonders and signs in Egypt and at the Red Sea, and in the wilderness for forty years. ³⁷ This is the Moses who said to the Israelites, 'God will raise up for you a prophet from your brethren as he raised me up.' ³⁸ This is he who was in the congregation in the wilderness with the angel who spoke to him at Mount Sinai, and with our fathers; and he received living oracles to give to us. ³⁹ Our fathers refused

Jerusalem: the Temple Area. In the centre is visible the Mosque of Omar (or 'Dome of the Rock') on the site where Solomon's Temple formerly stood.

'David asked leave to find a habitation for the God of Jacob. But it was Solomon who built a house for him. Yet the Most High does not dwell in houses made with hands' (Acts 7,46-48).

to obey him, but thrust him aside, and in their hearts they turned to Egypt, ⁴⁰ saying to Aaron, 'Make for us gods to go before us; as for this Moses who led us out from the land of Egypt, we do not know what has become of him.' ⁴¹ And they made a calf in those days, and offered a sacrifice to the idol and rejoiced in the works of their hands. ⁴² But God turned and gave them over to worship the host of heaven, as it is written in the book of the prophets:

> 'Did you offer to me slain beasts and sacrifices,
> forty years in the wilderness, O house of Israel?
> ⁴³ And you took up the tent of Moloch, and the star of the god Rephan,
> the figures which you made to worship;
> and I will remove you beyond Babylon.' (6)

⁴⁴ Our fathers had the tent of witness in the wilderness, even as he who spoke to Moses directed him to make it, according to the pattern that he had seen. ⁴⁵ Our fathers in turn brought it in with Joshua when they dispossessed the nations which God thrust out before our fathers. So it was until the days of David, ⁴⁶ who found favour in the sight of God and asked leave to find a habitation for the God of Jacob. ⁴⁷ But it was Solomon who built a house for him. ⁴⁸ Yet the Most High does not dwell in houses made with hands; as the prophet says:

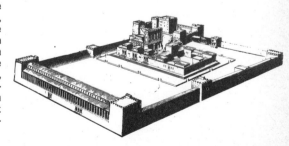

Herod's Temple in Jerusalem, built on the site of Solomon's. On the left (south side) is the Royal Portico, still called Herod's Basilica; on the right (east side) stands Solomon's Porch.

Jerusalem. In the Valley of the Kedron (or of Josaphat) outside the eastern wall, is the traditional site of the martyrdom of St Stephen. The Orthodox church, on the right, preserves his memory.

'They rushed together upon him; then they cast him out of the city and stoned him' (Acts 7,57).

⁴⁹ 'Heaven is my throne,
   and earth my footstool.
   What house will you build for me, says the Lord,
   or what is the place of my rest?
⁵⁰ Did not my hand make all these things?' (7)
⁵¹ You stiff-necked people, uncircumcised in heart and ears, you always resist the Holy Spirit. As you fathers did, so do you. ⁵² Which of the prophets did not our fathers persecute? And they killed those who announced beforehand the coming of the Righteous One, whom you have now betrayed and murdered, ⁵³ you who received the law as delivered by angels and did not keep it."

(1) Gen. 12,1 ff. (2) Gen. 14,13 ff. (3) Gen. 17; for the history of the patriarch see Gen. 21-25. (4) Exod. 2,14. (5) Exod. 3. (6) see Amos 5,25-27. Moloch is the name of a god whose worship was widespread, specially in the region of Phoenicia: it was to him that even human sacrifices were offered. (7) Isaiah 66,1 ff.

19 The martyrdom of Stephen
(Acts 7, 54-60)

⁵⁴ Now when they heard these things they were enraged, and they ground their teeth against him. ⁵⁵ But he, full of the Holy Spirit, gazed into heaven and saw the glory of God, and Jesus standing at the right hand of God; ⁵⁶ and he said, "Behold, I see the heavens opened, and the Son of man standing at the right hand of God." ⁵⁷ But they cried out with a loud voice and stopped their ears and rushed together upon him. ⁵⁸ Then they cast him out of the city and stoned him; (1) and the witnesses laid down their garments at the feet of a young man named Saul. ⁵⁹ And as they were stoning Stephen, he prayed, "Lord Jesus, receive my spirit." ⁶⁰ And he knelt down and cried with a loud voice, "Lord, do not hold this sin against them." And when he had said this, he fell asleep.

(1) The Law of Moses (see Deut. 17,7) decreed that blasphemers should be stoned in the presence of witnesses, who had to fling the first stones.

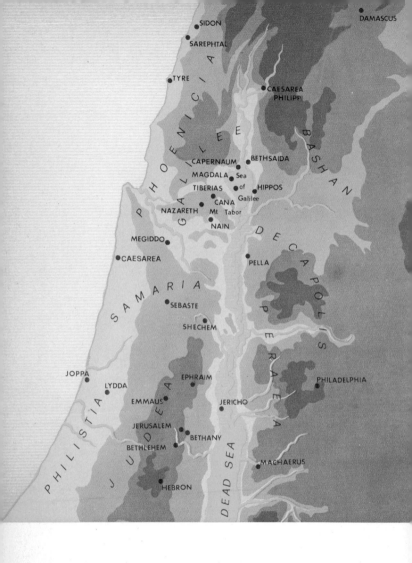

Palestine in the time of the Apostles. Samaria and Judea, the sphere of action of Peter and Philip, can be seen in the lower half of the map.

III. The missions of Philip and of Peter in Judea and in Samaria

Peter's and Philip's missions

The persecutions of which the Church in Jerusalem was the object drove the first disciples away from the city. They bore witness to the recent events in the cities and other places to which they went.

The first journey about which St Luke tells us is that of Philip to Samaria (see no. 21). The persecutions were not, however, the only reason which sent the Gospel to other places: there was also its own interior power: it was the Holy Spirit who directed Philip to the south of Jerusalem where he baptized an Ethiopian (see no. 23).

From the account of Saul's conversion we learn that there was a Christian community at Damascus. That community must

have been of noteworthy importance for the Jerusalem authorities to have welcomed Saul's request and sent him as their envoy to arrest Christians and 'bring them bound' to Jerusalem (see no. 24). Peter himself carried his message to the Mediterranean coast at Joppa and Lydda (see no. 27).

The early Church in this period continued to revolve round Jerusalem where lived the 'Twelve', or at least the most authoritative of the Apostles. Saul himself (Paul) after his conversion felt it necessary to come to Jerusalem.

From the Holy City, Christianity took practical steps to proclaim, under the inspiration of the Holy Spirit, its universalist principle which was later to be justified doctrinally by Peter's vision at Caesarea (see no. 29).

20 Persecution of the Church at Jerusalem
(Acts 8, 1-3)

[1] And Saul was consenting to his death.

And on that day a great persecution arose against the church in Jerusalem; and they were all scattered throughout the region of Judea and Samaria, except the apostles. [2] Devout men buried

Stephen, and made great lamentation over him. ³ But Saul laid waste the church, and entering house after house, he dragged off men and women and committed them to prison.

21 Philip's missionary activity in Samaria
(Acts 8, 4-8)

⁴ Now those who were scattered went about preaching the word. ⁵ Philip went down to a city of Samaria, and proclaimed to them the Christ. ⁶ And the multitudes with one accord gave heed to what was said by Philip, when they heard him and saw the signs which he did. ⁷ For unclean spirits came out of many who were possessed, crying with a loud voice; and many who were paralyzed or lame were healed. ⁸ So there was much joy in that city.

The ruins of a caravanserai in the valley of Lebona (today Lubban), on the boundary between Judea and Samaria.

22   Simon Magus
(Acts 8, 9-25)

⁹ But there was a man named Simon who had previously practised magic in the city and amazed the nation of Samaria, saying that he himself was somebody great. ¹⁰ They all gave heed to him, from the least to the greatest, saying, "This man is that power of God which is called Great." ¹¹ And they gave heed to him, because for a long time he had amazed them with his magic. ¹² But when they believed Philip as he preached good news about the kingdom of God and the name of Jesus Christ, they were baptized, both men and women. ¹³ Even Simon himself believed, and after being baptized he continued with Philip. And seeing signs and great miracles performed, he was amazed.

¹⁴ Now when the apostles at Jerusalem heard that Samaria had received the word of God, they sent to them Peter and John, ¹⁵ who came down and prayed for them that they might receive the Holy Spirit; ¹⁶ for it had not yet fallen on any of them, but they had only been baptized in the name of the Lord Jesus. ¹⁷ Then they laid their hands on them and they received the Holy Spirit. ¹⁸ Now when Simon saw that the Spirit was given through the laying on of the apostles' hands, he offered them money, ¹⁹ saying, "Give me also this power, that any one on whom I lay my hands may receive the Holy Spirit." ²⁰ But Peter said to him, "Your silver perish with you, because you thought you could obtain the gift of God with money! ²¹ You have neither part nor lot in this matter, for your heart is not right before God. ²² Repent therefore of this wickedness of yours, and pray to the Lord that, if possible, the intent of your heart may be forgiven you. ²³ For I see that you are in the gall of bitterness and in the bond of iniquity." ²⁴ And Simon answered, "Pray for me to the Lord, that nothing of what you have said may come upon me."

²⁵ Now when they had testified and spoken the word of the Lord, they returned to Jerusalem, preaching the gospel to many villages of the Samaritans.

(1) The word 'simony' which means the buying and selling of holy things, is derived from Simon Magus' act in wishing to buy the Holy Spirit with money.

Ain Dirwe, south of Bethlehem, is called 'Philip's Fountain' and is the traditional site of the Ethiopian's baptism.
'**And he commanded the chariot to stop and they both went down into the water, and Philip baptized him**' (Acts 8,38).

23 The baptism of the Ethiopian
(Acts 8, 26-40)

[26] But an angel of the Lord said to Philip, "Rise and go toward the south to the road that goes down from Jerusalem to Gaza." This is a desert road. [27] And he rose and went. And behold, an Ethiopian, a eunuch (1), a minister of Candace the queen of the Ethiopians, in charge of all her treasure, had come to Jerusalem to worship [28] and was returning; seated in his chariot, he was reading the prophet Isaiah. [29] And the Spirit said to Philip, "Go up and join this chariot." [30] So Philip ran to him, and heard him reading Isaiah the prophet, and asked, "Do you understand what you are reading?" [31] And he said, "How can I, unless some one guides me?" And he invited Philip to come up and sit with him. [32] Now the passage of the scripture which he was reading was this:

"As a sheep led to the slaughter
or a lamb before its shearer is dumb,
so he opens not his mouth.
[33] In his humiliation justice was denied him.
Who can describe his generation?
For his life is taken up from the earth." (2)

[34] And the eunuch said to Philip, "About whom, pray, does the prophet say this, about himself or about some one else?" [35] Then Philip opened his mouth, and beginning with this scripture he told him the good news of Jesus. [36] And as they went along the road they came to some water, and the eunuch said, "See, here is water! What is to prevent my being baptized?" [[37]] [38] And he commanded the chariot to stop, and they both went down into the water, Philip and the eunuch, and he baptized him. [39] And when they came up out of the water, the Spirit of the Lord caught up Philip; and the eunuch saw him no more, and went on his way rejoicing. [40] But Philip was found at Azotus, and passing on he preached the gospel to all the towns till he came to Caesarea.

(1) 'Eunuch' had the general meaning of minister of the queen. 'Candace' was the generic title of the Queen of Ethiopia as 'Pharaoh' was that of the kings of Egypt.
(2) Isaiah 53,7 ff.
[[37]] 'Philip answered "If you believe with all your heart it is possible!". The eunuch then said: "I believe that Jesus is the Son of God"'.
This verse does not appear in the best codices.

Damascus. The ancient wall of the city, which recalls the flight of St Paul.

24 The conversion of Saul
(Acts 9, 1-19)

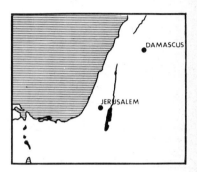

The region between Jerusalem and Damascus. Paul's conversion took place near the latter city.

¹ But Saul, still breathing threats and murder against the disciples of the Lord, went to the high priest ² and asked him for letters to the synagogues at Damascus, so that if he found any belonging to the Way, men or women, he might bring them bound to Jerusalem. ³ Now as he journeyed he approached Damascus, and suddenly a light from heaven flashed about him. ⁴ And he fell to the ground and heard a voice saying to him, "Saul, Saul, why do you persecute me?" ⁵ And he said, "Who are you, Lord?" And he said, "I am Jesus, whom you are persecuting; ⁶ but rise and enter the city, and you will be told what you are to do." ⁷ The men who were travelling with him stood speechless, hearing the voice but seeing no one. ⁸ Saul arose from the ground; and when his eyes were opened, he could see nothing; so they led him by the hand and brought him into Damascus. ⁹ And for three days he was without sight, and neither ate nor drank.

¹⁰ Now there was a disciple at Damascus named Ananias. The Lord said to him in a vision, "Ananias." And he said, "Here I am, Lord." ¹¹ And the Lord said to him, "Rise and go to the street called Straight, and inquire in the house of Judas for a man of Tarsus named Saul; for behold, he is praying, ¹² and he has seen a man named Ananias come in and lay his hands on him so that he might regain his sight." ¹³ But Ananias answered, "Lord, I have heard from many about this man, how much evil he has done

A section of the walls of Damascus. The window of a dwelling built on the walls can be seen.
'His disciples took him by night and let him down over the wall, lowering him in a basket' (Acts 9,25).

to thy saints at Jerusalem; [14] and here he has authority from the chief priests to bind all who call upon thy name." [15] But the Lord said to him, "Go, for he is a chosen instrument of mine to carry my name before the Gentiles and kings and the sons of Israel; [16] for I will show him how much he must suffer for the sake of my name." [17] So Ananias departed and entered the house. And laying his hands on him he said, "Brother Saul, the Lord Jesus who appeared to you on the road by which you came, has sent me that you may regain your sight and be filled with the Holy Spirit." [18] And immediately something like scales fell from his eyes and he regained his sight. Then he rose and was baptized, [19] and took food and was strengthened.

The centre of the new community is still Jerusalem. The incident is consonant with the development of the idea that the persecution in Jerusalem was the occasion for the conversion of the Gentiles (i.e. the pagans). The narrative of Saul's conversion at this point in the story has a special significance— the introduction of the most important agent in the conversion of the pagans, the principal hero of the second part of the book and the most ardent propagandist of the universality of the Church. St Luke sets enormous store by St Paul's conversion which is related no fewer than three times in the book of the Acts (see nos. 103 & 110).

The whole episode stresses Christ's direct and continual intervention; the fundamental experience which made the 'Twelve' into 'Apostles' was the vision of the risen Christ who sent them into the world. Paul always declared himself to be an apostle, and always emphasized the fact that he also was a witness of the risen Christ who sent him on his evangelizing mission.

25 Saul's preaching at Damascus
(Acts 9, 19-25)

For several days he was with the disciples at Damascus. [20] And in the synagogues immediately he proclaimed Jesus, saying, "He is the Son of God." [21] And all who heard him were amazed, and said, "Is not this the man who made havoc in Jerusalem of those who called on this name? And he has come here for this purpose, to bring them bound before the chief priests." [22] But

Tarsus, birthplace of St Paul. Remains of Roman baths.
'The Hellenists were seeking to kill Saul. And when the brethren knew it they brought him down to Caesarea and sent him off to Tarsus' (Acts 9,30).

Saul increased all the more in strength, and confounded the Jews who lived in Damascus by proving that Jesus was the Christ. ²³ When many days had passed, the Jews plotted to kill him, ²⁴ but their plot became known to Saul. They were watching the gates day and night, to kill him; ²⁵ but his disciples took him by night and let him down over the wall, lowering him in a basket.

The region of Tarsus, Damascus and Jerusalem where the events connected with Paul's first apostolic activities took place.

26 Saul's visit to Jerusalem
(Acts 9, 26-30)

²⁶ And when he had come to Jerusalem (1) he attempted to join the disciples; and they were all afraid of him, for they did not believe that he was a disciple. ²⁷ But Barnabas took him, and brought him to the apostles, and declared to them how on the road he had seen the Lord, who spoke to him, and how at Damascus he had preached boldly in the name of Jesus. ²⁸ So he went in and out among them at Jerusalem, ²⁹ preaching boldly in the name of the Lord. And he spoke and disputed against the Hellenists; but they were seeking to kill him. ³⁰ And when the brethren knew it, they brought him down to Caesarea, and sent him off to Tarsus.

(1) St Paul himself (in the Letter to the Galatians, see no. 86) specifies that he spent three years in the Arabian Desert before presenting himself at Jerusalem. St Luke omits this detail which is not directly concerned with his story.

Joppa, today Jaffa, a suburb of Tel Aviv. The church of St Peter which commemorates the apostle's stay in this city.

27 Peter's missionary activity at Lydda and Joppa
(Acts 9, 31-43)

The cities of Joppa and Lydda where St Peter, by God's will, opened the gates of Christianity to the pagans.

³¹ So the church throughout all Judea and Galilee and Samaria had peace and was built up; and walking in the fear of the Lord and in the comfort of the Holy Spirit it was multiplied. ³² Now as Peter went here and there among them all, he came down also to the saints that lived at Lydda. ³³ There he found a man named Aeneas, who had been bedridden for eight years and was paralyzed. ³⁴ And Peter said to him, "Aeneas, Jesus Christ heals you; rise and make your bed." And immediately he rose. ³⁵ And all the residents of Lydda and Sharon saw him, and they turned to the Lord.

³⁶ Now there was at Joppa a disciple named Tabitha, which means Dorcas or Gazelle. She was full of good works and acts of charity. ³⁷ In those days she fell sick and died; and when they had washed her, they laid her in an upper room. ³⁸ Since Lydda was near Joppa. the disciples, hearing that Peter was there, sent two men to him entreating him, "Please come to us without delay." ³⁹ So Peter rose and went with them. And when he had come, they took him to the upper room. All the widows stood beside him weeping, and showing coats and garments which Dorcas made while she was with them. ⁴⁰ But Peter put them all outside and knelt down and prayed; then turning to the body he said, "Tabitha, rise." And she opened her eyes, and

Joppa, today Jaffa; near the minaret on the right is shown the site of the house of Simon the Tanner where St Peter saw his vision (see Acts 10,9-16).

when she saw Peter she sat up. ⁴¹ And he gave her his hand
and lifted her up. Then calling the saints and widows he presented
her alive. ⁴² And it became known throughout all Joppa, and many
believed in the Lord. ⁴³ And he stayed in Joppa for many days
with one Simon, a tanner.

28 The calling of Cornelius the Centurion
(Acts 10, 1-8)

¹ At Caesarea there was a man named Cornelius (1), a centurion
of what was known as the Italian Cohort, ² a devout man who
feared God with all his household, gave alms liberally to the
people, and prayed constantly to God. ³ About the ninth hour
of the day he saw clearly in a vision an angel of God coming
in and saying to him, "Cornelius." ⁴ And he stared at him in
terror, and said, "What is it, Lord?" And he said to him, "Your
prayers and your alms have ascended as a memorial before God.
⁵ And now send men to Joppa, and bring one Simon who is
called Peter; ⁶ he is lodging with Simon, a tanner, whose house
is by the seaside." ⁷ When the angel who spoke to him had
departed, he called two of his servants and a devout soldier
from among those that waited on him, ⁸ and having related
everything to them, he sent them to Joppa.

(1) Cornelius was a centurion of the Roman army and sympathetic
towards the Jewish religion. The Roman procurator resided at Caesarea
with his garrison.

29 Interlude: Peter's vision
(Acts 10, 9-16)

⁹ The next day, as they were on their journey and coming
near the city, Peter went up on the housetop to pray, about
the sixth hour. ¹⁰ And he became hungry and desired something

Joppa, the modern Jaffa. A characteristic alley in the old sea-side city.

to eat; but while they were preparing it, he fell into a trance [11] and saw the heaven opened, and something descending, like a great sheet, let down by four corners upon the earth. [12] In it were all kinds of animals and reptiles and birds of the air. [13] And there came a voice to him, "Rise, Peter; kill and eat." [14] But Peter said, "No, Lord; for I have never eaten anything that is common or unclean." (1) [15] And the voice came to him again a second time, "What God has cleansed, you must not call common." [16] This happened three times, and the thing was taken up at once to heaven.

(1) The hour mentioned corresponds to noon. The Mosaic Law (see Leviticus 11,1 ff.) considered certain kinds of animals 'unclean' and forbade their use for food. Some were animals which neighbouring peoples worshipped as symbols of the deity. The uncircumcized, and Gentiles as a whole, i.e. all non-Jews, were similarly considered 'unclean'.

30 Peter baptizes Cornelius
(Acts 10, 17-48)

[17] Now while Peter was inwardly perplexed as to what the vision which he had seen might mean, behold, the men that were sent by Cornelius, having made inquiry for Simon's house, stood before the gate [18] and called out to ask whether Simon who was called Peter was lodging there. [19] And while Peter was pondering the vision, the Spirit said to him, "Behold, three men are looking for you. [20] Rise and go down, and accompany them without hesitation; for I have sent them." [21] And Peter went down to the men and said, "I am the one you are looking for; what is the reason for your coming?" [22] And they said, "Cornelius, a centurion, an upright and God-fearing man, who is well spoken of by the whole Jewish nation, was directed by a holy angel to send for you to come to his house, and to hear what you have to say." [23] So he called them in to be his guests.

The next day he rose and went off with them, and some of the brethren from Joppa accompanied him. [24] And on the following

Caesarea in Palestine, the administrative capital of Judea, where the procurator resided with his cohorts. Cornelius, the first pagan to be converted, belonged to this Roman garrison.

day they entered Caesarea. Cornelius was expecting them and had called together his kinsmen and close friends. ²⁵ When Peter entered, Cornelius met him and fell down at his feet and worshipped him. ²⁶ But Peter lifted him up, saying, "Stand up; I too am a man." ²⁷ And as he talked with him, he went in and found many persons gathered; ²⁸ and he said to them, "You yourselves know how unlawful it is for a Jew to associate with or to visit any one of another nation; but God has shown me that I should not call any man common or unclean. ²⁹ So when I was sent for, I came without objection. I ask then why you sent for me."

³⁰ And Cornelius said, "Four days ago, about this hour, I was keeping the ninth hour of prayer in my house; and behold, a man stood before me in bright apparel, ³¹ saying, 'Cornelius, your prayer has been heard and your alms have been remembered before God. ³² Send therefore to Joppa and ask for Simon who is called Peter; he is lodging in the house of Simon, a tanner, by the seaside.' ³³ So I sent to you at once, and you have been kind enough to come. Now therefore we are all here present in the sight of God, to hear all that you have been commanded by the Lord."

³⁴ And Peter opened his mouth and said: "Truly I perceive that God shows no partiality, ³⁵ but in every nation any one who fears him and does what is right is acceptable to him. ³⁶ You know the word which he sent to Israel, preaching good news of peace by Jesus Christ (he is Lord of all), ³⁷ the word which was proclaimed throughout all Judea, beginning from Galilee after the baptism which John preached: ³⁸ how God anointed Jesus of Nazareth with the Holy Spirit and with power; how he went about doing good and healing all that were oppressed by the devil, for God was with him. ³⁹ And we are witnesses to all that he did both in the country of the Jews and in Jerusalem. They put him to death by hanging him on a tree; ⁴⁰ but God raised him on the third day and made him manifest; ⁴¹ not to all the people but to us who were chosen by God as witnesses, who ate and drank with him after he rose from the dead. ⁴² And he commanded us to preach to the people, and to testify that he is the one ordained by God to be judge of the living and the dead. ⁴³ To him all the prophets bear witness that every one who believes in him receives forgiveness of sins through his name."

Caesarea in Palestine. Remains of a Roman temple, probably that of Augustus. It was in this city that Cornelius became a Christian.
'And Peter... said: "Truly I perceive that God shows no partiality, but in every nation anyone who fears him and does what is right is acceptable to him" ' (Acts 10,34-35).

⁴⁴ While Peter was still saying this, the Holy Spirit fell on all who heard the word. ⁴⁵ And the believers from among the circumcised who came with Peter were amazed, because the gift of the Holy Spirit had been poured out even on the Gentiles. ⁴⁶ For they heard them speaking in tongues and extolling God. Then Peter declared, ⁴⁷ "Can any one forbid water for baptizing these people who have received the Holy Spirit just as we have?" ⁴⁸ And he commanded them to be baptized in the name of Jesus Christ. Then they asked him to remain for some days.

The conversion of the centurion Cornelius is to be considered an event of fundamental importance in the early Church, and a key point in the structure of the book of the Acts, for it marks the official beginning and justification of preaching to the pagans.

The expansive power of the new faith in the Messiah, Christ, under the influence of the Holy Spirit forced the first Christians to go beyond the limits of official Jewish orthodoxy and to acquire a more universal outlook. Even before this episode other people had been received into the new community from paganism, and a difficult problem concerning them had to be faced: to become a Christian, was it necessary first to become a Jew (i.e. to receive circumcision), or, on the other hand, did faith in Christ wholly take the place of the old rite? Peter's vision, narrated no less than twice (nos. 29 & e 31) and referred to a third time (no. 42) was to provide a first doctrinal justification for what was already done in practice. Christianity was realizing more and more that it went beyond the old covenant based on circumcision. In fact Messianic salvation and the Holy Spirit could be received on the basis of faith in Christ alone (see nos. 30 & 31). This was one of the most important decisions of the first community led by Peter under the guidance of the Holy Spirit. From the doctrinal point of view this was the first step towards the awareness of the universality of Christian salvation. In the Council of Jerusalem that truth was to receive its full acknowledgement. Its total practical application was to take place finally at Antioch in the argument between Peter and Paul (no. 88), and was thereafter to be the basis of all Paul's missionary work.

31   At Jerusalem Peter justifies Cornelius' baptism
(Acts 11, 1-18)

¹ Now the apostles and the brethren who were in Judea heard that the Gentiles also had received the word of God.

Antioch in Syria, the eastern metropolis of the Roman Empire, where for the first time believers in Jesus Christ were called 'Christians'.

[2] So when Peter went up to Jerusalem, the circumcision party criticized him, [3] saying, "Why did you go to uncircumcised men and eat with them?" [4] But Peter began and explained to them in order: [5] "I was in the city of Joppa praying; and in a trance I saw a vision, something descending, like a great sheet, let down from heaven by four corners; and it came down to me. [6] Looking at it closely I observed animals and beasts of prey and reptiles and birds of the air. [7] And I heard a voice saying to me, 'Rise, Peter; kill and eat.' [8] But I said, 'No, Lord; for nothing common or unclean has ever entered my mouth.' [9] But the voice answered a second time from heaven, 'What God has cleansed you must not call common.' [10] This happened three times, and all was drawn up again into heaven. [11] At that very moment three men arrived at the house in which we were, sent to me from Caesarea. [12] And the Spirit told me to go with them, making no distinction. These six brethren also accompanied me, and we entered the man's house. [13] And he told us how he had seen the angel standing in his house and saying, "Send to Joppa and bring Simon called Peter; [14] he will declare to you a message by which you will be saved, you and all your household.' [15] As I began to speak, the Holy Spirit fell on them just as on us at the beginning. [16] And I remembered the word of the Lord, how he said, 'John baptized with water, but you shall be baptized with the Holy Spirit.' [17] If then God gave the same gift to them as he gave to us when we believed in the Lord Jesus Christ, who was I that I could withstand God?" [18] When they heard this they were silenced. And they glorified God, saying, "Then to the Gentiles also God has granted repentance unto life."

32 The beginning of the Church in Antioch, and help for the Church in Jerusalem
(Acts 11, 19-30)

[19] Now those who were scattered because of the persecution that arose over Stephen travelled as far as Phoenicia and Cyprus

Antioch in Syria. Not only St Paul but also St Peter lived there for some time. This ancient church, hollowed from the living rock, commemorates him.

and Antioch, speaking the word to none except Jews. [20] But there were some of them, men of Cyprus and Cyrene, who on coming to Antioch spoke to the Greeks also, preaching the Lord Jesus. [21] And the hand of the Lord was with them, and a great number that believed turned to the Lord. [22] News of this came to the ears of the church in Jerusalem, and they sent Barnabas to Antioch. [23] When he came and saw the grace of God, he was glad; and he exhorted them all to remain faithful to the Lord with steadfast purpose; [24] for he was a good man, full of the Holy Spirit and of faith. And a large company was added to the Lord. [25] So Barnabas went to Tarsus to look for Saul; [26] and when he had found him, he brought him to Antioch. For a whole year they met with the church, and taught a large company of people; and in Antioch the disciples were for the first time called Christians.

[27] Now in these days prophets came down from Jerusalem to Antioch. [28] And one of them named Agabus stood up and foretold by the Spirit that there would be a great famine over all the world; and this took place in the days of Claudius. [29] And the disciples determined, every one according to his ability, to send relief to the brethren who lived in Judea; [30] and they did so, sending it to the elders by the hand of Barnabas and Saul.

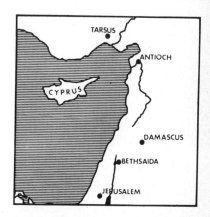

Antioch in Syria, the city where for the first time the disciples of Jesus were called 'Christians'.

Jerusalem. The Armenian church of St James the Great on the traditional site of his martyrdom.
'Herod killed James, the brother of John, with the sword' (Acts 12,2).

IV. The persecution under Agrippa I

33 **The martyrdom of James, and Peter's release**
(Acts 12, 1-19)

[1] About that time Herod the king (1) laid violent hands upon some who belonged to the church. [2] He killed James the brother of John with the sword; [3] and when he saw that it pleased the Jews, he proceeded to arrest Peter also. This was during the days of Unleavened Bread. [4] And when he had seized him, he put him in prison, and delivered him to four squads of soldiers to guard him, intending after the Passover to bring him out to the people. [5] So Peter was kept in prison; but earnest prayer for him was made to God by the church.

[6] The very night when Herod was about to bring him out, Peter was sleeping between two soldiers, bound with two chains, and sentries before the door were guarding the prison; [7] and behold, an angel of the Lord appeared, and a light shone in the cell; and he struck Peter on the side and woke him, saying, "Get up quickly." And the chains fell off his hands. [8] And the angel said to him, "Dress yourself and put on your sandals." And he did so. And he said to him, "Wrap your mantle around you and follow me." [9] And he went out and followed him; he did not know that what was done by the angel was real, but thought he was seeing a vision. [10] When they had passed the first and the second guard, they came to the iron gate leading into the city. It opened to them of its own accord, and they went out and passed on through one street; and immediately the angel

left him. [11] And Peter came to himself, and said, "Now I am sure that the Lord has sent his angel and rescued me from the hand of Herod and from all that the Jewish people were expecting."

[12] When he realized this, he went to the house of Mary, the mother of John whose other name was Mark, where many were gathered together and were praying. [13] And when he knocked at the door of the gateway, a maid named Rhoda came to answer. [14] Recognizing Peter's voice, in her joy she did not open the gate but ran in and told that Peter was standing at the gate. [15] They said to her, "You are mad." But she insisted that it was so. They said, "It is his angel!" [16] But Peter continued knocking; and when they opened, they saw him and were amazed. [17] But motioning to them with his hand to be silent, he described to them how the Lord had brought him out of the prison. And he said, "Tell this to James and to the brethren." Then he departed and went to another place.

[18] Now when day came, there was no small stir among the soldiers over what had become of Peter. [19] And when Herod had sought for him and could not find him, he examined the sentries and ordered that they should be put to death. Then he went down from Judea to Caesarea, and remained there.

(1) King Herod, more properly called Agrippa I, was the grandson of Herod the Great who had planned to kill the Infant Jesus. In the year 37 he was appointed king of the region to the north of Galilee by decree of the Emperor Caligula. In 41 Claudius made him king of Galilee and Judea also: he was the last 'King of the Jews'. For his persecution see, on page 115, 'The early Church in Jerusalem'.

34 The death of Herod Agrippa
(Acts 12, 20-23)

[20] Now Herod was angry with the people of Tyre and Sidon; and they came to him in a body, and having persuaded Bastus, the king's chamberlain, they asked for peace, because their country depended on the king's country for food. [21] On an appointed day Herod put on his royal robes, took his seat upon the throne, and made an oration to them. [22] And the people shouted, "The voice of a god, and not of man!" [23] Immediately an angel of the Lord smote him, because he did not give God the glory; and he was eaten by worms and died.

35 Barnabas and Saul again at Antioch
(Acts 12, 24-25)

²⁴ But the word of God grew and multiplied.
²⁵ And Barnabas and Saul returned from Jerusalem when they had fulfilled their mission, bringing with them John whose other name was Mark.

CONCLUSION OF THE FIRST PART

The early Church in Jerusalem

The Church was born in Jerusalem, in the bosom of the official Jewish religion of which, in God's plan, it represents the natural historical development. Jerusalem was always thought of in Jewish history as the only and ideal centre of religion. In it was the only temple in which God wished his presence to be honoured in a special way. In the 'Holy City' the supreme religious authorities felt themselves the trustees of perfect orthodoxy. Their just pre-occupation with keeping intact the purity of God's revelation had caused the official religiosity of the period immediately before Jesus to evolve into a rigid and largely legalistic conservatism. The different sects were distinguished by particular interpretations of the Law and, although they differed among themselves, they rediscovered their unity in the unique thread of their ancient tradition. Against such a background the new community was considered by the Jewish authority.

St Luke shows us the earliest community still deeply involved in the Jewish religion. It takes part in the liturgical life of the Temple, having as its own particular external distinctions the sharing of possessions and the 'breaking of the bread', a term used to describe the Eucharistic rite, then celebrated in private houses. It seems to have been organized around the 'Twelve', witnesses of the resurrection of Christ and guided by the power of the Holy Spirit.

Jerusalem is thus seen as the centre of Christianity whence the mission to the pagans is being slowly prepared. The transition happens gradually; the first step is towards Jews and Hellenists who are orthodox and circumcized, the second is towards the Samaritans, circumcized but unorthodox, who join the new Church without attaching themselves to official Judaism.

The first group of converted Hellenists is very active and is the cause of great friction with the religious authorities (see Stephen, no. 17). It provokes a certain uneasiness even among the converted Jews of Jewish speech. Jerusalem has always been a centre of conservatism whether Jewish or Christian. The Jews would have resigned themselves to accepting the Christian movement as a sect of Judaism but they could not accept the universalism, first of the Hellenists and then of St Paul. In that they saw the destruction of Judaism itself. The first reaction therefore comes from the religious authority which tries to absorb the new sect, keeping it as least outwardly within the bounds of orthodoxy. Thus a sort of compromise is reached between the new Church and Judaism, a compromise which undergoes various vicissitudes, and later results in the apostles and the most active exponents of Christianity leaving the city for other centres.

The second reaction came some time afterwards from political Judaism in the person of Agrippa I who, in addition to being a Jew, had also the title of King. To ingratiate himself with the Sanhedrim and the Jews, he posed as the defender of orthodox Judaism and, above all, he persecuted the Twelve, who were obnoxious to the Jewish leaders for having welcomed even pagans into the new sect. The persecution ended with his death, but meanwhile had provoked the final flight of the Church from Jerusalem. Peter left the city and we find him later at Antioch, capital of the Middle East and third city of the Empire. At Jerusalem remained James, the Lord's cousin, revered even by the Jews for his repect for the Law. The Holy City thus slipped into the background and had no further important part to play in the history of Christianity.

PAUL'S MISSION TO THE PAGANS - FROM THE ESTABLISHMENT OF THE CHURCH AT ANTIOCH TILL THE BEGINNING OF THE PERSECUTION OF NERO

(44-64 A. D.)

St Paul's first missionary journey. Setting out from Antioch in Syria and embarking at Seleucia, he called at Salamis and Paphos on the island of Cyprus. Then he disembarked at Attalia and went to Antioch in Pisidia, whence he visited Iconium, Derbe and Lystra. He returned from Antioch through Perga and embarked for Syria at Attalia.

I. St Paul's first two missionary journeys

FIRST JOURNEY

The rapid expansion of Christianity among the pagans at Antioch and the special revelation which he had personally received, brought home to Paul the vastness of the field of labour presented by the pagan world. In this, his first missionary activity of wide range, Paul was not satisfied with limiting his efforts to pagans who lived in the area of Jewish influence, but went directly to seek them out. The wonderful results which he achieved among them again brought to a head the problem of the way in which they were to be received into the new Christian community (see No. 41). That problem was to be finally resolved by the Council of Jerusalem which, in the plan of the Acts, represents the conclusion of Paul's first missionary journey (see No. 42).

36 Paul and Barnabas receive their commission
(Acts 13, 1-3)

¹ Now in the church at Antioch there were prophets and teachers, Barnabas, Symeon who was called Niger, Lucius of Cyrene, Manaen a member of the court of Herod the tetrarch, and Saul. ² While they were worshipping the Lord and fasting, the Holy Spirit said, "Set apart for me Barnabas and Saul for the work to which I have called them." ³ Then after fasting and praying they laid their hands on them and sent them off.

37 Cyprus
(Acts 13, 4-12)

⁴ So, being sent out by the Holy Spirit, they went down to Seleucia; and from there they sailed to Cyprus. ⁵ When they

Attalia, now Antalya, the port of Perga where St Paul disembarked on his way from Cyprus and whence he set sail to return to Antioch in Pisidia at the end of his first missionary journey (see Acts 14,25).

arrived at Salamis, they proclaimed the word of God in the synagogues of the Jews. And they had John to assist them. [6] When they had gone through the whole island as far as Paphos, they came upon a certain magician, a Jewish false prophet, named Bar-Jesus. [7] He was with the proconsul, Sergius Paulus, a man of intelligence, who summoned Barnabas and Saul and sought to hear the word of God. [8] But Elymas the magician (for that is the meaning of his name) withstood them, seeking to turn away the proconsul from the faith. [9] But Saul, who is also called Paul, filled with the Holy Spirit, looked intently at him [10] and said, "You son of the devil, you enemy of all righteousness, full of all deceit and villainy, will you not stop making crooked the straight paths of the Lord? [11] And now, behold, the hand of the Lord is upon you, and you shall be blind and unable to see the sun for a time." Immediately mist and darkness fell upon him and he went about seeking people to lead him by the hand. [12] Then the proconsul believed, when he saw what had occurred, for he was astonished at the teaching of the Lord

38 Antioch in Pisidia
(Acts 13, 13-52)

[13] Now Paul and his company set sail from Paphos, and came to Perga in Pamphylia. And John left them and returned to Jerusalem; [14] but they passed on from Perga and came to Antioch of Pisidia. And on the sabbath day they went into the synagogue and sat down. [15] After the reading of the law and the prophets, the rulers of the synagogue sent to them, saying, "Brethren, if you have any word of exhortation for the people, say it." [16] So Paul stood up, and motioning with his hand said:

"Men of Israel, and you that fear God, listen. [17] The God of this people Israel chose our fathers and made the people great during their stay in the land of Egypt, and with uplifted arm he led them out of it. (1) [18] And for about forty years he bore with them in the wilderness. [19] And when he had destroyed seven nations in the land of Canaan, he gave them their land as an inheritance, (2) for about four hundred and fifty years. [20] And after that he gave them judges until Samuel the prophet.

Antioch in Pisidia, evangelized by St Paul on his first missionary journey. Remains of the Roman aqueduct.

²¹ Then they asked for a king; and God gave them Saul the son of Kish, a man of the tribe of Benjamin, for forty years. ²² And when he had removed him, he raised up David to be their king; of whom he testified and said, 'I have found in David the son of Jesse a man after my heart, who will do all my will.' (3) ²³ Of this man's posterity God has brought to Israel a Saviour, Jesus, as he promised. ²⁴ Before his coming John had preached a baptism of repentance to all the people of Israel. ²⁵ And as John was finishing his course, he said, 'What do you suppose that I am? I am not he. No, but after me one is coming, the sandals of whose feet I am not worthy to untie.'

²⁶ "Brethren, sons of the family of Abraham, and those among you that fear God, to us has been sent the message of this salvation. ²⁷ For those who live in Jerusalem and their rulers, because they did not recognize him nor understand the utterances of the prophets which are read every sabbath, fulfilled these by condemning him. ²⁸ Though they could charge him with nothing deserving death, yet they asked Pilate to have him killed. ²⁹ And when they had fulfilled all that was written of him, they took him down from the tree, and laid him in a tomb. ³⁰ But God raised him from the dead; ³¹ and for many days he appeared to those who came up with him from Galilee to Jerusalem, who are now his witnesses to the people. ³² And we bring you the good news that what God promised to the fathers, ³³ this he has fulfilled to us their children by raising Jesus; as also it is written in the second psalm,

'Thou art my Son,
today I have begotten thee.' (4)

³⁴ And as for the fact that he raised him from the dead, no more to return to corruption, he spoke in this way,

'I will give you the holy and sure blessing of David.' (5)

³⁵ Therefore he says also in another psalm,

'Thou wilt not let thy Holy One see corruption.' (6)

³⁶ For David, after he had served the counsel of God in his own generation, fell asleep, and was laid with his fathers, and saw corruption; ³⁷ but he whom God raised up saw no corruption. ³⁸ Let it be known to you therefore, brethren, that through this man forgiveness of sins is proclaimed to you, ³⁹ and by him every one that believes is freed from everything from which you could not be freed by the law of Moses. ⁴⁰ Beware, therefore, lest there come upon you what is said in the prophets:

Site of the ancient city of Lystra in Lycaonia, near the present day
Hakinsaray. It was the home of Timothy, St Paul's disciple and
collaborator (see Acts 16, 1-3).

[41] 'Behold, you scoffers, and wonder, and perish;
  for I do a deed in your days,
  a deed you will never believe, if one declares it to you.' " (7)
[42] As they went out, the people begged that these things might be told them the next sabbath. [43] And when the meeting of the synagogue broke up, many Jews and devout converts to Judaism followed Paul and Barnabas, who spoke to them and urged them to continue in the grace of God.

[44] The next sabbath almost the whole city gathered together to hear the word of God. [45] But when the Jews saw the multitudes, they were filled with jealousy, and contradicted what was spoken by Paul, and reviled him. [46] And Paul and Barnabas spoke out boldly, saying, "It was necessary that the word of God should be spoken first to you. Since you thrust it from you, and judge yourselves unworthy of eternal life, behold, we turn to the Gentiles. [47] For so the Lord has commanded us, saying,
  'I have set you to be a light for the Gentiles,
  that you may bring salvation to the uttermost parts of
  the earth.' " (8)
[48] And when the Gentiles heard this, they were glad and glorified the word of God; and as many as were ordained to eternal life believed. [49] And the word of the Lord spread throughout all the region. [50] But the Jews incited the devout women of high standing and the leading men of the city, and stirred up persecution against Paul and Barnabas, and drove them out of their district. [51] But they shook off the dust from their feet against them, and went to Iconium. [52] And the disciples were filled with joy and with the Holy Spirit.

(1) Exodus 6,6. (2) Deuteronomy 7,1. (3) 1 Samuel 13,14. (4) Psalm 2,7. (5) Isaiah 55,3. (6) Psalm 16,10. (7) Habbakuk 1,5. (8) Isaiah 49,6.

39   Iconium, Lystra and Derbe
(Acts 14, 1-20)

[1] Now at Iconium they entered together into the Jewish synagogue, and so spoke that a great company believed, both of Jews and of Greeks. [2] But the unbelieving Jews stirred up the Gentiles and poisoned their minds against the brethren. [3] So

Another view of Lystra in Lycaonia where St Paul and Barnabas were mistaken for Zeus and Hermes.
'**Barnabas they called Zeus and Paul, because he was the chief speaker, they called Hermes**' (Acts 14,12).

they remained for a long time, speaking boldly for the Lord, who bore witness to the word of his grace, granting signs and wonders to be done by their hands. ⁴ But the people of the city were divided; some sided with the Jews, and some with the apostles. ⁵ When an attempt was made by both Gentiles and Jews, with their rulers, to molest them and to stone them, ⁶ they learned of it and fled to Lystra and Derbe, cities of Lycaonia, and to the surrounding country; ⁷ and there they preached the gospel.

⁸ Now at Lystra there was a man sitting, who could not use his feet; he was a cripple from birth, who had never walked. ⁹ He listened to Paul speaking: and Paul, looking intently at him and seeing that he had faith to be made well, ¹⁰ said in a loud voice, "Stand upright on your feet." And he sprang up and walked. ¹¹ And when the crowds saw what Paul had done, they lifted up their voices, saying in Lycaonian, "The gods have come down to us in the likeness of men!" ¹² Barnabas they called Zeus, and Paul, because he was the chief speaker, they called Hermes. ¹³ And the priest of Zeus, whose temple was in front of the city, brought oxen and garlands to the gates and wanted to offer sacrifice with the people. ¹⁴ But when the apostles Barnabas and Paul heard of it, they tore their garments and rushed out among the multitude, crying, ¹⁵ "Men, why are you doing this? We also

R o m a n bas-relief picturing the sacrifice of a bull.

Site of the ancient Derbe visited by St Paul on his first missionary journey.

are men, of like nature with you, and bring you good news, that you should turn from these vain things to a living God who made the heaven and the earth and the sea and all that is in them. [16] In past generations he allowed all the nations to walk in their own ways; [17] yet he did not leave himself without witness, for he did good and gave you from heaven rains and fruitful seasons, satisfying your hearts with food and gladness." (1) [18] With these words they scarcely restrained the people from offering sacrifice to them.

[19] But Jews came there from Antioch and Iconium; and having persuaded the people, they stoned Paul and dragged him out of the city, supposing that he was dead. [20] But when the disciples gathered about him, he rose up and entered the city; and on the next day he went on with Barnabas to Derbe.

(1) From this speech of St Paul we can gather the sort of arguments he used with the pagans. The central problems of popular philosophy at that time were God and the revelation of the divine in the world. Starting from this current idea, the Apostle announced the historical revelation of God in Jesus Christ.

40 Return to Antioch
(Acts 14, 21-28)

[21] When they had preached the gospel to that city and had made many disciples, they returned to Lystra and to Iconium and to Antioch, [22] strengthening the souls of the disciples, exhorting them to continue in the faith, and saying that through many tribulations we must enter the kingdom of God. [23] And when they had appointed elders for them in every church, with prayer and fasting, they committed them to the Lord in whom they believed.

[24] Then they passed through Pisidia, and came to Pamphylia. [25] And when they had spoken the word in Perga, they went down to Attalia; [26] and from there they sailed to Antioch, where they had been commended to the grace of God for the work which they had fulfilled. [27] And when they arrived, they gathered the

Seleucia in Pieria (present day Magharagik), the ancient port of Antioch in Syria. There St Paul embarked for his first missionary journey.

church together and declared all that God had done with them, and how he had opened a door of faith to the Gentiles. ²⁸ And they remained no little time with the disciples.

41   Difficulties raised by Judaizing Christians
(Acts 15, 1-5)

¹ But some men came down from Judea and were teaching the brethren, "Unless you are circumcised according to the custom of Moses, you cannot be saved." ² And when Paul and Barnabas had no small dissension and debate with them, Paul and Barnabas and some of the others were appointed to go up to Jerusalem to the apostles and the elders about this question. ³ So, being sent on their way by the church, they passed through both Phoenicia and Samaria, reporting the conversion of the Gentiles, and they gave great joy to all the brethren. ⁴ When they came to Jerusalem, they were welcomed by the church and the apostles and the elders, and they declared all that God had done with them. ⁵ But some believers who belonged to the party of the Pharisees rose up, and said, "It is necessary to circumcise them, and to charge them to keep the law of Moses."

The district between Antioch and Jerusalem, traversed by Paul and Barnabas on their way to join the Apostles in the latter city.

42 The Council of Jerusalem
(Acts 15, 6-21)

⁶ The apostles and the elders were gathered together to consider this matter. ⁷ And after there had been much debate, Peter rose and said to them, "Brethren, you know that in the early days God made choice among you, that by my mouth the Gentiles should hear the word of the gospel and believe. ⁸ And God who knows the heart bore witness to them, giving them the Holy Spirit just as he did to us; ⁹ and he made no distinction between us and them, but cleansed their hearts by faith. ¹⁰ Now therefore why do you make trial of God by putting a yoke upon the neck of the disciples which neither our fathers nor we have been able to bear? ¹¹ But we believe that we shall be saved through the grace of the Lord Jesus, just as they will."

¹² And all the assembly kept silence; and they listened to Barnabas and Paul as they related what signs and wonders God had done through them among the Gentiles. ¹³ After they finished speaking, James replied, "Brethren, listen to me. ¹⁴ Symeon has related how God first visited the Gentiles, to take out of them a people for his name. ¹⁵ And with this the words of the prophets agree, as it is written,

¹⁶ 'After this I will return,
and I will rebuild the dwelling of David, which has fallen;
I will rebuild its ruins,
and I will set it up,
¹⁷ that the rest of men may seek the Lord,
and all the Gentiles who are called by my name,
¹⁸ says the Lord, who has made these things known from of old.' (1)
¹⁹ Therefore my judgment is that we should not trouble those of the Gentiles who turn to God, ²⁰ but should write to them to abstain from the pollutions of idols and from unchastity and from what is strangled and from blood. ²¹ For from early generations Moses has had in every city those who preach him, for he is read every sabbath in the synagogues."

(1) See Amos 9,11-12. James's proposal followed the same line of principle as that of Peter and Paul. The suggestions he made were simply to facilitate the solution of the problem on practical grounds. (See also the practical attitude of Paul in No. 45 and No. 101). The

mention of strangled animals and of blood refers to the ban on blood in the Mosaic Law, motivated by the idea that blood was the seal and symbol of life and therefore holy, reserved to God.

Concerning the problem of the way of accepting pagans into the new community, that is to say, whether it was necessary to pass through Judaism or not, the Council of Jerusalem did no more than give official confirmation of an already accepted fact.

The question had been put by some converted Jews who still thought of the new community as a sect of official Judaism.

The doctrinal preparation for this decision was Peter's vision at Joppa (see No. 29). The historical preparation was Paul's conversion (see No. 24) and the movement of the centre of the

propagation of Christianity from Jerusalem to Antioch. The apostolic decree broke the ties of Christianity with Judaism in an official and definitive form and acknowledged its universal messianic significance.

The problem was to be raised again on other occasions but only from the point of view of questions of a practical nature (see also No. 45 and No. 101).

In the plan of the book of the Acts, the Council of Jerusalem sanctions Paul's apostolate on his first journey and then allows him to act in complete independence and freedom on the two following journeys.

43 The Apostolic Decree
(Acts 15, 22-35)

²² Then it seemed good to the apostles and the elders, with the whole church, to choose men from among them and send them to Antioch with Paul and Barnabas. They sent Judas called Barsabbas, and Silas, leading men among the brethren, ²³ with the following letter: "The brethren, both the apostles and the elders, to the brethren who are of the Gentiles in Antioch and Syria and Cilicia, greeting. ²⁴ Since we have heard that some persons from us have troubled you with words, unsettling your minds, although we gave them no instructions, ²⁵ it has seemed good to us in assembly to choose men and send them to you with our beloved Barnabas and Paul, ²⁶ men who have risked their lives for the sake of our Lord Jesus Christ. ²⁷ We have therefore sent Judas and Silas, who themselves will tell you the same things by word of mouth. ²⁸ For it has seemed good to the Holy Spirit and to us (1) to lay upon you no greater burden than these necessary things: ²⁹ that you abstain from

Paul's second Apostolic Journey: leaving Antioch, accompanied by Silas, he went through Tarsus and the 'Gates of Cilicia', and reached Derbe and Lystra whence he took with him the faithful Timothy. He then visited Iconium and Antioch in Pisidia and reached Troas where Luke joined the party. Thence he went to Europe, disembarking at Neapolis in Macedonia whence, following the 'Via Egnatia' he evangelized Philippi, Amphipolis, Apollonia and Thessalonica. Thence he had to flee to Beroea and then to Athens and to go to Corinth where he spent a year and a half as guest of Aquila and Priscilla. Then having called at Ephesus, Caesarea and Jerusalem, he returned to Antioch.

what has been sacrificed to idols and from blood and from what is strangled and from unchastity. If you keep yourselves from these, you will do well. Farewell."

[30] So when they were sent off, they went down to Antioch; and having gathered the congregation together, they delivered the letter. [31] And when they read it, they rejoiced at the exhortation. [32] And Judas and Silas, who were themselves prophets, exhorted the brethren with many words and strengthened them. [33] And after they had spent some time, they were sent off in peace by the brethren to those who had sent them. [[34]] [35] But Paul and Barnabas remained in Antioch, teaching and preaching the word of the Lord, with many others also.

(1) The phrase '... It has seemed good to the Holy Spirit and to us...' became from that time the classical expression of Ecumenical Councils when expressing the definition of a dogma *de fide*.
[[34]] This verse is omitted in the best codices.

SECOND JOURNEY

Paul's second journey begins in the light of the Council of Jerusalem which, with its decision by the college of Apostles, has cleared up doctrinally all the uncertainties about the conversion of pagans.

This journey presents two special features. First, under the direct guidance of the Holy Spirit which St Luke explicitly emphasizes (see No. 45) Christianity enters Europe. Secondly, Paul mindful of Christ's command that the Gospel must be taken 'to the

ends of the earth', feels the need to remain in close contact with his first churches, 'to strengthen' the first communities already founded. For the same reason Paul began to write his first Letters — from Corinth to the Thessalonians (see No. 54) — during this journey.

This is one of the busiest periods of his missionary life. It was just at this time that the most important Christian communities were formed.

44 Paul's second mission
(Acts 15, 36-40)

[36] And after some days Paul said to Barnabas, "Come, let us return and visit the brethren in every city where we proclaimed

Turkey, the Gates of Cilicia. This gorge in the Taurus mountain range, a few kilometres from Tarsus, was the only practicable pass leading to the Anatolian Plateau. St Paul passed this way several times on his missionary journeys.

the word of the Lord, and see how they are." ³⁷ And Barnabas wanted to take with them John called Mark. ³⁸ But Paul thought best not to take with them one who had withdrawn from them in Pamphylia, and had not gone with them to the work. ³⁹ And there arose a sharp contention, so that they separated from each other; Barnabas took Mark with him and sailed away to Cyprus, ⁴⁰ but Paul chose Silas and departed, being commended by the brethren to the grace of the Lord.

45   Visit to the Churches of Asia Minor
(Acts 15, 41 - 16, 1-10)

15, ⁴¹ And he went through Syria and Cilicia, strengthening the churches.

16, ¹ And he came also to Derbe and to Lystra. A disciple was there, named Timothy, the son of a Jewish woman who was a believer; but his father was a Greek. ² He was well spoken of by the brethren at Lystra and Iconium. ³ Paul wanted Timothy to accompany him; and he took him and circumcised him because of the Jews that were in those places, for they all knew that his father was a Greek. ⁴ As they went on their way through the cities, they delivered to them for observance the decisions which had been reached by the apostles and elders who were at Jerusalem. ⁵ So the churches were strengthened in the faith, and they increased in numbers daily.

⁶ And they went through the region of Phrygia and Galatia, having been forbidden by the Holy Spirit to speak the word in Asia. ⁷ And when they had come opposite Mysia, they attempted to go into Bithynia, but the Spirit of Jesus did not allow them; ⁸ so, passing by Mysia, they went down to Troas. ⁹ And a vision appeared to Paul in the night: a man of Macedonia was standing beseeching him and saying, "Come over to Macedonia and help us." ¹⁰ And when he had seen the vision, immediately we sought to go on into Macedonia, concluding that God had called us to preach the gospel to them. (1)

(1) From v. 10 to v. 17 of the following number is a passage called a 'we-section'. It does in fact change without warning from the third person to 'we'. This gives rise to the opinion that in these events the author, St Luke, was himself present (see Introduction on page 31). This passage is also important because it marks the passage of Christianity from Asia into Europe.

Neapolis, today Kavalla, was the principal port of Macedonia. St Paul landed here during his second missionary journey on his way to the neighbouring city of Philippi. In the foreground in the photograph we can see the ancient Roman 'Via Egnatia', the first European road which St Paul used.

46
Paul's arrival in Europe: Philippi
(Acts 16, 11-40)

¹¹ Setting sail therefore from Troas we made a direct voyage to Samothrace, and the following day to Neapolis, ¹² and from there to Philippi, which is the leading city of the district of Macedonia, and a Roman colony. We remained in this city some days; ¹³ and on the sabbath day we went outside the gate to the riverside, where we supposed there was a place of prayer; and we sat down and spoke to the women who had come together. ¹⁴ One who heard us was a woman named Lydia, from the city of Thyatira, a seller of purple goods, who was a worshipper of God. The Lord opened her heart to give heed to what was said by Paul. ¹⁵ And when she was baptized, with her household, she besought us, saying, "If you have judged me to be faithful to the Lord, come to my house and stay." And she prevailed upon us.

¹⁶ As we were going to the place of prayer, we were met by a slave girl who had a spirit of divination and brought her owners much gain by soothsaying. ¹⁷ She followed Paul and us, crying, "These men are servants of the Most High God, who proclaim to you the way of salvation." ¹⁸ And this she did for many days. But Paul was annoyed, and turned and said to the spirit, "I charge you in the name of Jesus Christ to come out of her." And it came out that very hour.

¹⁹ But when her owners saw that their hope of gain was gone, they seized Paul and Silas and dragged them into the market place before the rulers; ²⁰ and when they had brought them to the magistrates they said, "These men are Jews and they are disturbing our city. ²¹ They advocate customs which it is not lawful for us Romans to accept or practise." ²² The crowd joined in attacking them; and the magistrates tore the garments off them and gave orders to beat them with rods. ²³ And when they had inflicted many blows upon them, they threw them into prison, charging the jailer to keep them safely. ²⁴ Having received this charge, he put them into the inner prison and fastened their feet in the stocks.

²⁵ But about midnight Paul and Silas were praying and singing hymns to God, and the prisoners were listening to them, ²⁶ and suddenly there was a great earthquake, so that the foundations of the prison were shaken; and immediately all the doors were opened and every one's fetters were unfastened. ²⁷ When the jailer woke and saw that the prison doors were open, he drew his sword and was about to kill himself, supposing that the prisoners had escaped. ²⁸ But Paul cried with a loud

The so-called 'Prison of St Paul' among the ruins of the ancient city of Philippi. In this prison, partly hollowed out of the rock, the Apostle Paul was imprisoned with Silas, after disturbances had broken out in the city (see Acts 16,23).

voice, "Do not harm yourself, for we are all here." ²⁹ And he called for lights and rushed in, and trembling with fear he fell down before Paul and Silas, ³⁰ and brought them out and said, "Men, what must I do to be saved?" ³¹ And they said, "Believe in the Lord Jesus, and you will be saved, you and your household." ³² And they spoke the word of the Lord to him and to all that were in his house. ³³ And he took them the same hour of the night, and washed their wounds, and he was baptized at once, with all his family. ³⁴ Then he brought them up into his house, and set food before them; and he rejoiced with all his household that he had believed in God.

³⁵ But when it was day, the magistrates sent the police, saying, "Let those men go." ³⁶ And the jailer reported the words to Paul, saying, "The magistrates have sent to let you go; now therefore come out and go in peace." ³⁷ But Paul said to them, "They have beaten us publicly, uncondemned, men who are Roman citizens, (1) and have thrown us into prison; and do they now cast us out secretly? No! let them come themselves and take us out." ³⁸ The police reported these words to the magistrates, and they were afraid when they heard that they were Roman citizens; ³⁹ so they came and apologized to them. And they took them out and asked them to leave the city. ⁴⁰ So they went out of the prison, and visited Lydia; and when they had seen the brethren, they exhorted them and departed.

(1) The Roman citizen enjoyed a privileged position as compared with the other subjects of the empire with regard to the penal law. The Lex Portia of 248 B.C. had absolutely forbidden the beating with rods of a Roman citizen before a formal death sentence. That law was later on brought up to date in favour of the Roman citizen. In Paul's day it gave him the further right to appeal to the Imperial Tribunal during any stage of a lawsuit, and so to withdraw himself from any local tribunal (see also Nos. 104-109).

47 **Paul at Thessalonica**
(Acts 17, 1-9)

¹ Now when they had passed through Amphipolis and Apollonia, they came to Thessalonica, where there was a synagogue of the

Beroea, now Veria, situated on a plateau at the foot of the range of Olympus. Here St Paul came after being sent away from Thessalonica because of a demonstration staged against him by the Jews (see Acts 17,5-10).

Jews. ² And Paul went in, as was his custom, and for three weeks he argued with them from the scriptures, ³ explaining and proving that it was necessary for the Christ to suffer and to rise from the dead, and saying, "This Jesus, whom I proclaim to you, is the Christ." ⁴ And some of them were persuaded, and joined Paul and Silas; as did a great many of the devout Greeks and not a few of the leading women. ⁵ But the Jews were jealous, and taking some wicked fellows of the rabble, they gathered a crowd, set the city in an uproar, and attacked the house of Jason, seeking to bring them out to the people. ⁶ And when they could not find them, they dragged Jason and some of the brethren before the city authorities, crying, "These men who have turned the world upside down have come here also, ⁷ and Jason has received them; and they are all acting against the decrees of Caesar, saying that there is another king, Jesus." ⁸ And the people and the city authorities were disturbed when they heard this. ⁹ And when they had taken security from Jason and the rest, they let them go.

48 Beroea
(Acts 17, 10-15)

¹⁰ The brethren immediately sent Paul and Sılas away by night to Beroea; and when they arrived they went into the Jewish synagogue. ¹¹ Now these Jews were more noble than those in Thessalonica, for they received the word with all eagerness, examining the scriptures daily to see if these things were so. ¹² Many of them therefore believed, with not a few Greek women of high standing as well as men. ¹³ But when the Jews of Thessalonica learned that the word of God was proclaimed by Paul at Beroea also, they came there too, stirring up and inciting the crowds. ¹⁴ Then the brethren immediately sent Paul off on his way to the sea, but Silas and Timothy remained there. ¹⁵ Those who conducted Paul brought him as far as Athens; and receiving a command for Silas and Timothy to come to him as soon as possible, they departed.

Athens. In the foreground can be seen the 'Agora' or City Square. At the back (on the left) is the Acropolis, the citadel where the chief temples to the gods were. In front of the Acropolis there is the Areopagus (see also the following photograph).

49 Paul reaches Athens
(Acts 17, 16-21)

[16] Now while Paul was waiting for them at Athens, his spirit was provoked within him as he saw that the city was full of idols. [17] So he argued in the synagogue with the Jews and the devout persons, and in the market place every day with those who chanced to be there. [18] Some also of the Epicurean and Stoic philosophers met him. And some said, "What would this babbler say?" Others said, "He seems to be a preacher of foreign divinities"—because he preached Jesus and the resurrection. [19] And they took hold of him and brought him to the Areopagus, saying, "May we know what this new teaching is which you present? [20] For you bring some strange things to our ears; we wish to know therefore what these things mean." [21] Now all the Athenians and the foreigners who lived there spent their time in nothing except telling or hearing something new.

Athens. From the height of the Acropolis can be seen, lower down on the left, the Agora overlooked on the left by the bare rock of the Areopagus.

Athens. From the top of the Areopagus the majestic view of the Acropolis. On this rock St Paul made his speech to the learned men of Athens. From this spot he must have turned towards the temples of the Acropolis while he was saying 'God does not live in shrines made by man' (Acts 17,24).

50 The Speech on the Areopagus
(Acts 17, 22-34)

²² So Paul, standing in the middle of the Areopagus, said: "Men of Athens, I perceive that in every way you are very religious. ²³ For as I passed along, and observed the objects of your worship, I found also an altar with this inscription, 'To an unknown god.' What therefore you worship as unknown, this I proclaim to you. ²⁴ The God who made the world and everything in it, being Lord of heaven and earth, does not live in shrines made by man, ²⁵ nor is he served by human hands, as though he needed anything, since he himself gives to all men life and breath and everything. ²⁶ And he made from one every nation of men to live on all the face of the earth, having determined allotted periods and the boundaries of their habitation, ²⁷ that they should seek God, in the hope that they might feel after him and find him. Yet he is not far from each one of us, ²⁸ for

'In him we live and move and have our being;'
as even some of your poets have said,
'For we are indeed his offspring.' (1)

²⁹ Being then God's offspring, we ought not to think that the Deity is like gold, or silver, or stone, a representation by the art and imagination of man. ³⁰ The times of ignorance God overlooked, but now he commands all men everywhere to repent, ³¹ because he has fixed a day on which he will judge the world in righteousness by a man whom he has appointed, and of this he has given assurance to all men by raising him from the dead."

³² Now when they heard of the resurrection of the dead, some mocked; but others said, "We will hear you again about this." ³³ So Paul went out from among them. ³⁴ But some men joined him and believed, among them Dionysius the Areopagite and a woman named Damaris and others with them.

(1) The quotation is from the Greek poet Aratos (Phenomena 5). In Chreon's Hymn to Zeus also there is a similar expression, which incidentally was quite usual in popular poetry.

In the time of the Apostle Paul Corinth was one of the most beautiful cities and among the most important commercial and artistic centres in Greece; the Temple of Aphrodite was well known to all. Here St Paul founded the first large Gentile-Christian community which was also the liveliest and most unruly of those he founded.

51 Paul at Corinth
(Acts 18, 1-11)

¹ After this he left Athens and went to Corinth. ² And he found a Jew named Aquila, a native of Pontus, lately come from Italy with his wife Priscilla, because Claudius had commanded all the Jews to leave Rome. (1) And he went to see them; ³ and because he was of the same trade he stayed with them, and they worked, for by trade they were tentmakers. ⁴ And he argued in the synagogue every sabbath, and persuaded Jews and Greeks.

⁵ When Silas and Timothy arrived from Macedonia, Paul was occupied with preaching, testifying to the Jews that the Christ was Jesus. ⁶ And when they opposed and reviled him, he shook out his garments and said to them, "Your blood be upon your heads! I am innocent. From now on I will go to the Gentiles." ⁷ And he left there and went to the house of a man named

A cross carved on an architectural fragment found on the Acropolis at Athens, surviving from some Christian Church built in the early centuries.

149

Titius Justus, a worshipper of God; his house was next door to the synagogue. [8] Crispus, the ruler of the synagogue, believed in the Lord, together with all his household; and many of the Corinthians hearing Paul believed and were baptized. [9] And the Lord said to Paul one night in a vision, "Do not be afraid, but speak and do not be silent; [10] for I am with you, and no man shall attack you to harm you; for I have many people in this city." [11] And he stayed a year and six months, teaching the word of God among them.

(1) In his life of the Emperor Claudius the Roman historian Suetonius writes in Chapter 25: 'He drove the Jews from Rome because they were continually rioting at the behest of Crestus' (he means Christ). This happened between 48 and 50 A.D.

52 The Proconsul refuses to judge Paul
(Acts 18, 12-17)

[12] But when Gallio (1) was proconsul of Achaia, the Jews made a united attack upon Paul and brought him before the tribunal, [13] saying, "This man is persuading men to worship God contrary to the law." [14] But when Paul was about to open his mouth, Gallio said to the Jews, "If it were a matter of wrongdoing or vicious crime, I should have reason to bear with you, O Jews; [15] but since it is a matter of questions about words and names and your own law, see to it yourselves; I refuse to be a judge of these things." [16] And he drove them from the tribunal. [17] And they all seized Sosthenes, the ruler of the synagogue, and beat him in front of the tribunal. But Gallio paid no attention to this.

(1) Gallio, proconsul of Achaia in the years 51-52, was the brother of the Roman philosopher Seneca.

53 Return to Antioch
(Acts 18, 18-22)

¹⁸ After this Paul stayed many days longer and then took leave of the brethren and sailed for Syria, and with him Priscilla and Aquila. At Cenchreae he cut his hair, for he had a vow. (1) ¹⁹ And they came to Ephesus, and he left them there; but he himself went into the synagogue and argued with the Jews. ²⁰ When they asked him to stay for a longer period, he declined; ²¹ but on taking leave of them he said, "I will return to you if God wills," and he set sail from Ephesus.

²² When he had landed at Caesarea, he went up and greeted the church, and then went down to Antioch.

(1) We know neither when nor why Paul had taken the vow which is referred to. The vow was that of a Nazirite (see Numbers 6,1-21) which involved abstention from alcoholic drinks and from cutting the hair for the whole of its duration.

In the Agora (or business forum) of ancient Corinth the remains of the 'Bema' (or rostrum) on which the proconsul Gallio heard the charges preferred by the Jews against St Paul who was dragged before him.

THE TEXT OF THE ACTS IS RESUMED AT NO. 61

The city of Thessalonica, where the Christians received the oldest of the New Testament writings, St Paul's first Letter addressed to them from Corinth in the year 52 A.D.

II. St Paul's Letters written during the second missionary journey

From St Paul's First Letter to the Thessalonians

The district of Thessalonica, capital of Macedonia.

The first Letter to the Christians in Thessalonica is probably the first New Testament writing. The Gospel was still being preached verbally without anyone having thought of writing it in literary form, when St Paul, for a particular reason, started to communicate by letter with the Christians he had converted, who needed his intervention in disputes which had arisen since he saw them. The system of completing his preaching by means of letters proved effective and St Paul made use of it till the end of his life. When St Paul wrote this, which was his first Letter, he was at Corinth at the beginning of the evangelization of that great city (see No. 51) towards the end of the year 51 or the beginning of 52.

Thessalonica, which in more modern times is called Saloniki, was already in ancient times a commercial city, because of its position on the sea and the Via Egnatia which from Durazzo, almost opposite Brindisi, crossing Macedonia reached the Bosphorus, thus connecting Italy with the East. Thessalonica was the seat of the proconsul of the Roman Province of Macedonia. St Paul had evangelized it for some months during his second missionary journey towards the end of the year 50 (see No. 47). As he had to leave this Christian community in haste, several things remained to be confirmed or clarified. St Paul was concerned about them and, when he received from Timothy news which he was hoping for, he wrote to the Thessalonians exhorting them to

Thessalonica (today Saloniki) seen from the ancient Turkish fortifications. It was one of the most important ports of Macedonia. The city, evangelized by St Paul, contained one of the most flourishing Christian communities of Apostolic times.

persevere, and completing his teaching on the second coming of Christ and on the resurrection of the dead. His disciples and *fellow-workers Silvanus (or Silas, see No. 44) and the young Timothy (see No. 45) were associated with St Paul in the Letter.*

The beginning of the first Letter to the Thessalonians in the Vatican Codex (4th century).

54   Introduction
(1, 1-10)

¹ Paul, Silvanus, and Timothy,
To the church of the Thessalonians in God the Father and the Lord Jesus Christ:
Grace to you and peace.
² We give thanks to God always for you all, constantly mentioning you in our prayers, ³ remembering before our God and Father your work of faith and labour of love and steadfastness of hope in our Lord Jesus Christ. ⁴ For we know, brethren beloved by God, that he has chosen you; ⁵ for our gospel came to you not only in word, but also in power and in the Holy Spirit and with full conviction. You know what kind of men we proved to be among you for your sake. ⁶ And you became imitators of us and of the Lord, for you received the word in much affliction, with joy inspired by the Holy Spirit; ⁷ so that you became an example to all the believers in Macedonia and

Apollonia in Macedonia. Here is what remains of the Roman road near the site of Apollonia, through which St Paul passed on his way from Philippi to Thessalonica (Acts 17,1).

in Achaia. ⁸ For not only has the word of the Lord sounded forth from you in Macedonia and Achaia, but your faith in God has gone forth everywhere, so that we need not say anything. ⁹ For they themselves report concerning us what a welcome we had among you, and how you turned to God from idols, to serve a living and true God, ¹⁰ and to wait for his Son from heaven, whom he raised from the dead, Jesus, who delivers us from the wrath to come.

55 Paul wishes to see the Thessalonians again (2, 17-20)

¹⁷ But since we were bereft of you, brethren, for a short time, in person not in heart, we endeavoured the more eagerly and with great desire to see you face to face; ¹⁸ because we wanted to come to you—I, Paul, again and again—but Satan hindered us. ¹⁹ For what is our hope or joy or crown of boasting before our Lord Jesus at his coming? Is it not you? ²⁰ For you are our glory and joy.

The Apostle continues his letter by referring to the circumstances of his preaching at Thessalonica: 'We worked night and day that we might not burden any of you', and to the sufferings which the young Christian community has had to endure at the hands of certain Jews, jealous of the results which Paul had achieved in conversions of the pagans. Then, in the lines quoted here, he expresses the most lively desire to return to these faithful converts of his. Two things are noticeable: the use of the first person plural ('we' instead of 'I') which was often adopted by ancient writers as a sign of humility and modesty, and in the second place, the reference to the second coming of Jesus which is the keynote of all — the Christian hope. The fruits of good works alone will avail at that moment. Then for Paul also the conversion and holy life of the faithful of Thessalonica will be his 'joy' and 'glory'.

Athens. The Areopagus. The steep stairway of fifteen steps, partly cut out of the rock, which climbs the Areopagus. While St Paul remained alone at Athens (see 1 Thess. 3,1) some Athenian philosophers (see Acts 17, 18 ff) invited him on to the Areopagus so as better to explain his teaching to them.

56 Timothy's Mission
(3, 1-13)

¹ Therefore when we could bear it no longer, we were willing to be left behind at Athens alone, ² and we sent Timothy, our brother and God's servant in the gospel of Christ, to establish you in your faith and to exhort you, ³ that no one be moved by these afflictions. You yourselves know that this is to be our lot. ⁴ For when we were with you, we told you beforehand that we were to suffer affliction; just as it has come to pass, and as you know. ⁵ For this reason, when I could bear it no longer, I sent that I might know your faith, for fear that somehow the tempter had tempted you and that our labour would be in vain.

⁶ But now that Timothy has come to us from you, and has brought us the good news of your faith and love and reported that you always remember us kindly and long to see us, as we long to see you—⁷ for this reason, brethren, in all our distress and affliction we have been comforted about you through your faith; ⁸ for now we live, if you stand fast in the Lord. ⁹ For what thanksgiving can we render to God for you, for all the joy which we feel for your sake before our God, ¹⁰ praying earnestly night and day that we may see you face to face and supply what is lacking in your faith?

¹¹ Now may our God and Father himself, and our Lord Jesus, direct our way to you; ¹² and may the Lord make you increase and abound in love to one another and to all men, as we do to you, ¹³ so that he may establish your hearts unblamable in holiness before our God and Father, at the coming of our Lord Jesus with all his saints.

St Paul had arrived at Athens from Macedonia after the enforced interruption of evangelization at Thessalonica and later at Beroea (see No. 48); from Athens he betook himself to Corinth whence he sent this letter. The loneliness of Athens must have weighed heavily on his heart. The apostle found himself in the midst of an environment completely foreign to his mentality; even his ingenious attempt to meet the Athenians by adapting himself to the religious language of Greek philosophers, had been fruitless (see No. 50).

We note how again in this section of the letter he returns to the thought of the second coming of Christ as the source of hope and perseverance.

In the part that follows (here omitted) the Apostle exhorts the new converts to practise purity in their lives, to grow in brotherly love and to live worthily by their own labour. So the love of work is presented by the Apostle as a Christian virtue (see No. 60).

57 The lot of departed Christians (4, 13-18)

[13] But we would not have you ignorant, brethren, concerning those who are asleep, that you may not grieve as others do who have no hope. [14] For since we believe that Jesus died and rose again, even so, through Jesus, God will bring with him those who have fallen asleep. [15] For this we declare to you by the word of the Lord, that we who are alive, who are left until the coming of the Lord, shall not precede those who have fallen asleep. [16] For the Lord himself will descend from heaven with a cry of command, with the archangel's call, and with the sound of the trumpet of God. And the dead in Christ will rise first; [17] then we who are alive, who are left, shall be caught up together with them in the clouds to meet the Lord in the air; and so we shall always be with the Lord. [18] Therefore comfort one another with these words.

This is the most important passage of the Letter, in which St Paul finishes his teaching on the 'Parousia'. This Greek word, which means 'Presence' or 'Arrival' in state of the Sovereign, had become the popular term to mean the second coming of Christ in glory. Note that Holy Scripture makes use of the word 'coming' and 'come', and never of 'return'. Christ 'will come' or 'comes'; he will not 'return' for he has never 'gone away' but is always invisibly present in his Church. For this reason St Paul also uses the expression 'manifestation' or appearance in glory; Christ, risen, has entered into glory, that is, into the inaccessible world of God which, although invisible to our senses, is not 'far away'. To this invisible world we ourselves belong by baptism and divine grace which unites us to Jesus, but it does not yet appear what we are. When Christ 'comes' then will be manifested his glorious presence and at the same time our sharing in his glory (see the Letter to the Colossians No. 122). In that same moment the resurrection of the dead will also take place.

St Paul had told the Thessalonians repeatedly of our life in expectation of the 'Parousia', but these new Christians had not understood everything and were concerned about the fate of their dear ones who had died in the meantime. 'What will become of them?' they asked, 'when the Lord comes (i.e. Jesus in glory), shall we meet him before our dead and without them?'.

St Paul replies by dissipating their ignorance and consoling us with the Christian hope. Our dead are 'in Christ', and by virtue of Christ's redemption will arise to be with the risen Christ when he 'comes'. Thus those who are alive at the time of the coming of Christ 'will not arrive first' or 'will not precede' those who are already dead, for the general resurrection will immediately precede the final reunion of all, living and risen, with Christ in glory.

The mention of the rising of the elect to meet Christ 'in the clouds, in the air' implies that the dead will arise in an entirely new state and even that the living will be radically transformed in their material form. On this point St Paul will insist at greater length when writing to the Christians at Corinth (see No. 80).

The Thessalonian Christians hoped still to be alive at the time of the 'Parousia'. St Paul does not take away this hope from them, for in truth no one can know whether the 'day of the Lord' will arrive soon or late (see No. 58 which follows). However the imminence of the Parousia will be ruled out in the second Letter to the Thessalonians (see No. 59).

58 The Day of the Lord will come unexpectedly (5, 1-6)

[1] But as to the times and the seasons, brethren, you have no need to have anything written to you. [2] For you yourselves know well that the day of the Lord will come like a thief in the night. [3] When people say. "There is peace and security," then sudden destruction will come upon them as travail comes upon a woman with child, and there will be no escape. [4] But you are not in darkness, brethren, for that day to surprise you like a thief.

[5] For you are all sons of light and sons of the day; we are not of the night or of darkness. [6] So then let us not sleep, as others do, but let us keep awake and be sober.

The 'day of the Lord' is the last intervention of God in human history which will then be at its end. Then God will display the glory of Christ as universal judge. 'Lord' in this phrase, expresses the divinity and kingship of Christ glorified.

The 'day of the Lord' therefore coincides with the second coming of Christ, with the resurrection of the dead, the universal judgment and the beginning of the reign of God with the elect, unopposed and without end. St Paul had already instructed the faithful of Thessalonica on this matter, which was fundamental to the apostolic preaching, and went back to the words of Christ himself. Now, one of the characteristics of this 'day' is the impossibility of knowing its date beforehand. Jesus refused to reveal this secret (Mt. 24, 36) and desired his disciples and the Church always to be vigilant, adorned with good works and spiritually ready to go to meet Christ when he comes. This is exactly the teaching which St Paul wishes to give in this passage from his Letter. The expression 'sons of the light and sons of the day' refers to Christians who, enlightened by Christ's revelation, know where they are going and how they ought to behave, while the wiles of Satan are compared to the night, a time of confusion, bewilderment and licentiousness.

We may notice that ignorance about the Parousia, so heavily stressed in this passage, ought to have saved the Thessalonians from all worry about its date: but it was not so: they considered themselves authorized to retain 'belief in' the imminent coming of Jesus, to such an extent that they lived in anxious expectation and neglected the duties of everyday life. Because of this St Paul had to intervene with a second Letter (see Introduction, No. 59).

From St Paul's Second Letter to the Thessalonians

Beginning of 2 Thessalonians in the Vatican Codex (4th century)

Some months after the first Letter St Paul was still at Athens when he heard that serious trouble had broken out in the young Church of Thessalonica: certain excited souls had begun to spread alarm among the faithful as though, from some revelation of the Holy Spirit (see No. 78) or from some other sure sign, it followed that now they were to expect the Parousia or coming of Christ as Judge from one day to the next. St Paul then intervened with a second Letter, in which, after an introduction of thanksgiving to God for the faithful life of the Thessalonians, he went on to an exposition of its chief subject: the Parousia cannot be so imminent.

The Apostle does not deny the fact that its time is unknown and cannot be known, but he points out that before the Parousia certain things must happen that have not happened, and cannot take place in a short time. The order of events may be clearly summarized thus:

(1) At the present time the hidden power of evil (the mystery of iniquity) is working against the forces of salvation in action in the Church and in the world. But there exists an obstacle (person or institution) which prevents the manifestation of this hostile power.

(2) The moment will come when this obstacle will be 'eliminated' and then the 'man of iniquity' will be manifested.

(3) This person (or institution) will have his own 'parousia' which will imitate the Parousia of Christ, with miracles true or false but ostentatious, which will seduce those who have hearts prepared to betray their own faith in Christ.

(4) Thus there will arise a great 'apostasy' (defection): Christians who are indifferent or wavering will abandon the faith in large numbers and will follow the teacher (or teachers) of error.

(5) The man of iniquity whom, with St John, we may call Anti-

Thessalonica, now Saloniki. The road which runs along the outside of the old Turkish walls. St Paul always remained deeply attached to this as 'his own' Christian community.

'But we were gentle among you, like a mother taking care of her children. So... we were ready to share with you not only the gospel of God, but also our own selves, because you had become very dear to us' (1 Thess. 2, 7-8).

christ (see No. 164). will show himself also as Anti-God; he will fight not only against Christ's faithful, but also against every idea of God, putting himself in God's place. The forces of Satan and the power of the world which is at his disposal would give him the victory, if Christ did not intervene in person.

(6) Then, when all seems lost for Christ's faithful, the 'Parousia' will take place and Antichrist will be overthrown in a flash of lightning.

Two things remain obscure in this prophetic vision: who is Antichrist? And what is the obstacle which prevents his manifestation?

(a) Antichrist is the human instrument used by Satan to make his plan of perdition triumph. He may be a single person, or a group of persons or an institu-

tion. In fact Jesus prophesied that in the last times 'false prophets and false Christs' would arise (Mt. 24,11-24), and on the other hand St Paul writes that the 'mystery of iniquity' is already in action in his day though in a hidden manner.

(b) The obstacle must be known to the Thessalonians, for St Paul had spoken of it previously. For us the problem is insoluble. Perhaps it is the preaching and witness of the Apostles and their successors to whom Christ has given the task of guarding and proclaiming the word of salvation. Perhaps it is the evangelization itself which at a certain point will come to an end, according to Jesus' saying: 'This gospel of the kingdom will be preached throughout the whole world, as a testimony to all nations; and then the end will come'. (Mt. 24,14).

59 The coming of the Lord is not imminent
(2, 1-12)

¹ Now concerning the coming of our Lord Jesus Christ and our assembling to meet him, we beg you, brethren, ² not to be quickly shaken in mind or excited, either by spirit or by word, or by letter purporting to be from us, to the effect that the day of the Lord has come. ³ Let no one deceive you in any way; for that day will not come, unless the rebellion comes first, and the man of lawlessness is revealed, the son of perdition, ⁴ who opposes and exalts himself against every so-called god or object of worship, so that he takes his seat in the temple of God, proclaiming himself to be God. ⁵ Do you not remember that when I was still with you I told you this? ⁶ And you know

what is restraining him now so that he may be revealed in his time. [7] For the mystery of lawlessness is already at work; only he who now restrains it will do so until he is out of the way. [8] And then the lawless one will be revealed, and the Lord Jesus will slay him with the breath of his mouth and destroy him by his appearing and his coming. [9] The coming of the lawless one by the activity of Satan will be with all power and with pretended signs and wonders, [10] and with all wicked deception for those who are to perish, because they refused to love the truth and so be saved. [11] Therefore God sends upon them a strong delusion, to make them believe what is false, [12] so that all may be condemned who did not believe the truth but had pleasure in unrighteousness.

60 The warning to the disorderly (3, 6-18)

[6] Now we command you, brethren, in the name of our Lord Jesus Christ, that you keep away from any brother who is living in idleness and not in accord with the tradition that you received from us. [7] For you yourselves know how you ought to imitate us; we were not idle when we were with you, [8] we did not eat any one's bread without paying, but with toil and labour we worked night and day, that we might not burden any of you. [9] It was not because we have not that right, but to give you in our conduct an example to imitate. [10] For even when we were with you, we gave you this command: If any one will not work, let him not eat. [11] For we hear that some of you are living in idleness, mere busybodies, not doing any work. [12] Now such persons we command and exhort in the Lord Jesus Christ to do their work in quietness and to earn their own living. [13] Brethren, do not be weary in welldoing.

[14] If any one refuses to obey what we say in this letter, note that man, and have nothing to do with him, that he may be ashamed. [15] Do not look on him as an enemy, but warn him as a brother.

[16] Now may the Lord of peace himself give you peace at all times in all ways. The Lord be with you all.

[17] I, Paul, write this greeting with my own hand. This is the mark in every letter of mine; it is the way I write. [18] The grace of our Lord Jesus Christ be with you all.

St Paul continues his letter by congratulating the faithful who show all the signs of being numbered among the elect, called to share in the glory of Christ. But he has to reprove some of them who with the excuse of the immediate expectation of the coming of Jesus, neglect their duties and are no longer working. In paganism work was not honoured; slaves were saddled with it. The new converts must instead understand, from the example of St Paul himself, that true dignity means to earn one's living with one's own hands.

The Letter ends with a greeting written personally by St Paul (the rest was dictated to a scribe) to avoid the propagation of false letters, as had in fact happened at Thessalonica.

Thessalonica: Pagan funeral altar of the Roman period. 'We would not have you ignorant, concerning those who are asleep, that you may not grieve as others do, who have no hope' (1 Thess. 4,13).

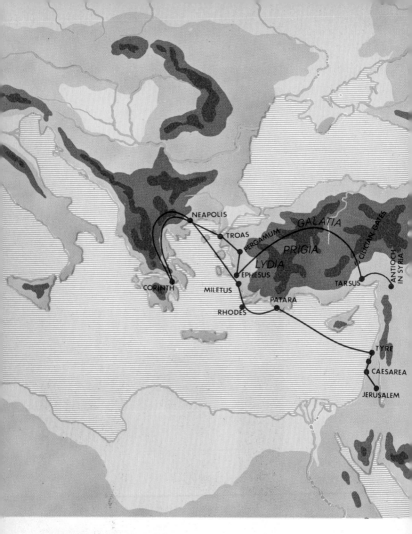

Paul's third apostolic journey: from Antioch he revisited Galatia, Phrygia and Lydia, and reached Ephesus, where he stayed for two years. Thence via Pergamum and Troas he retraced the second journey as far as Corinth and back. Then, touching the islands of Chios and Samos, he went ashore at Miletus. Thence, touching Rhodes and Patara, he landed at Tyre and from there made his way by land to Ptolemais, Caesarea and Jerusalem.

III. St Paul's third missionary journey

Paul's third missionary journey is noteworthy for his long stay at Ephesus. The city was one of the most flourishing of the Roman Empire in the East, and the centre of much commercial activity between East and West. Its population was estimated at about 300,000. The city became a centre from which Christianity spread to the neighbouring cities;

new communities had been founded by his disciples, e.g. Colossae, Laodicea, Hierapolis, and Paul had not yet visited them.

The absence of any personal reference in the Letter called 'To the Ephesians' (see Introduction, No. 124) has led some scholars to suppose that it may have been a circular Letter to all the communities centred in Ephesus.

61 Departure and visit to the churches of Galatia
(Acts 18, 23)

[23] After spending some time there he departed and went from place to place through the region of Galatia and Phrygia, strengthening all the disciples.

62 Apollos at Ephesus and Corinth
(Acts 18, 24-28)

[24] Now a Jew named Apollos, (1) a native of Alexandria, came to Ephesus. He was an eloquent man, well versed in the scriptures. [25] He had been instructed in the way of the Lord; and being fervent in spirit, he spoke and taught accurately the

In the Taurus Range. After the narrow gorge of the 'Cilician Gates' the valley climbs, opening out in fascinating views. This valley has been from remote times the easiest way of reaching the Anatolian Plateau from Syria and the Mediterranean coasts.

things concerning Jesus, though knew only the baptism of John.
²⁶ He began to speak boldly in the synagogue; but when Priscilla
and Aquila heard him, they took him and expounded to him
the way of God more accurately. ²⁷ And when he wished to cross
to Achaia, the brethren encouraged him, and wrote to the
disciples to receive him. When he arrived, he greatly helped those
who through grace had believed, ²⁸ for he powerfully confuted
the Jews in public, showing by the scriptures that the Christ
was Jesus.

(1) The appearance of Apollos, a Hellenistic Jew, tells us of the
beginning of the Christian Church at Alexandria in Egypt and shows us
how the echo of the preaching of John the Baptist and Jesus reached
as far as the most important centres of the Diaspora. His teaching,
evidently, knew nothing of the developments of that preaching after
Pentecost.

63 Paul at Ephesus
(Acts 19, 1-22)

¹ While Apollos was at Corinth, Paul passed through the upper
country and came to Ephesus. There he found some disciples.
² And he said to them, "Did you receive the Holy Spirit when
you believed?" And they said, "No, we have never even heard
that there is a Holy Spirit." ³ And he said, "Into what then were
you baptized?" They said, "Into John's baptism." ⁴ And Paul
said, "John baptized with the baptism of repentance, telling the
people to believe in the one who was to come after him, that
is, Jesus." ⁵ On hearing this, they were baptized in the name
of the Lord Jesus. ⁶ And when Paul had laid his hands upon
them, the Holy Spirit came on them; and they spoke with
tongues and prophesied. ⁷ There were about twelve of them
in all.
⁸ And he entered the synagogue and for three months spoke
boldly, arguing and pleading about the kingdom of God; ⁹ but
when some were stubborn and disbelieved, speaking evil of the
Way before the congregation, he withdrew from them, taking
the disciples with him, and argued daily in the hall of Tyrannus.

Ephesus. The central street of the ancient city paved with huge slabs of marble. Along this street St Paul often walked during his long sojourn at Ephesus.

[10] This continued for two years, so that all the residents of Asia heard the word of the Lord, both Jews and Greeks. [11] And God did extraordinary miracles by the hands of Paul, [12] so that handkerchiefs or aprons were carried away from his body to the sick, and diseases left them and the evil spirits came out of them. [13] Then some of the itinerant Jewish exorcists undertook to pronounce the name of the Lord Jesus over those who had evil spirits, saying, "I adjure you by the Jesus whom Paul preaches." [14] Seven sons of a Jewish high priest (1) named Sceva were doing this. [15] But the evil spirit answered them, "Jesus I know, and Paul I know; but who are you?" [16] And the man in whom the evil spirit was leaped on them, mastered all of them, and overpowered them, so that they fled out of that house naked and wounded. [17] And this became known to all residents of Ephesus, both Jews and Greeks; and fear fell upon them all; and the name of the Lord Jesus was extolled. [18] Many also of those who were now believers came, confessing and divulging their practices. [19] And a number of those who practised magic arts brought their books together and burned them in the sight of all; and they counted the value of them and found it came to fifty thousand pieces of silver. [20] So the word of the Lord grew and prevailed mightily.

[21] Now after these events Paul resolved in the Spirit to pass through Macedonia and Achaia and go to Jerusalem, saying, "After I have been there, I must also see Rome." [22] And having sent into Macedonia two of his helpers, Timothy and Erastus, he himself stayed in Asia for a while.

(1) The description 'High Priest' merely shows that this man belonged to a family from which had come some High Priests.

64   **The riot of the silversmiths of Ephesus**
        (Acts 19, 23-41)

[23] About that time there arose no little stir concerning the Way. (1) [24] For a man named Demetrius, a silversmith, who made silver shrines of Artemis, brought no little business to

Ephesus. The place in which stood the Temple of Artemis (see Introduction, page 23) whom 'all Asia and the world worship' (Acts 19,27). On the site of the Temple, then considered one of the seven 'wonders of the world', there remain no more than a few insignificant relics in the midst of a swamp.

the craftsmen. [25] These he gathered together, with the workmen of like occupation, and said, "Men, you know that from this business we have our wealth. [26] And you see and hear that not only at Ephesus but almost throughout all Asia this Paul has persuaded and turned away a considerable company of people, saying that gods made with hands are not gods. [27] And there is danger not only that this trade of ours may come into disrepute but also that the temple of the great goddess Artemis may count for nothing, and that she may even be deposed from her magnificence, she whom all Asia and the world worship."

[28] When they heard this they were enraged, and cried out, "Great is Artemis of the Ephesians!" [29] So the city was filled with the confusion; and they rushed together into the theatre, dragging with them Gaius and Aristarchus, Macedonians who were Paul's companions in travel. [30] Paul wished to go in among the crowd, but the disciples would not let him; [31] some of the Asiarchs also, who were friends of his, sent to him and begged him not to venture into the theatre. [32] Now some cried one thing, some another; for the assembly was in confusion, and most of them did not know why they had come together. [33] Some of the crowd prompted Alexander, whom the Jews had put forward. And Alexander motioned with his hand, wishing to make a defence to the people. [34] But when they recognized that he was a Jew, for about two hours they all with one voice cried out, "Great is Artemis of the Ephesians!" [35] And when the town clerk had quieted the crowd, he said, "Men of Ephesus, what man is there who does not know that the city of the Ephesians is temple keeper of the great Artemis, and of the sacred stone that fell from the sky? [36] Seeing then that these things cannot be contradicted, you ought to be quiet and do nothing rash. [37] For you have brought these men here who are neither sacrilegious nor blasphemers of our goddess. [38] If therefore Demetrius and the craftsmen with him have a complaint against any one, the courts are open, and there are proconsuls; let them bring charges against one another. [39] But if you seek anything further, it shall be settled in the regular assembly. [40] For we are in danger of being charged with rioting today,

The peaceful countryside of Macedonia in the neighbourhood of Amphipolis. This region was traversed many times by St Paul during his missionary journeys.

there being no cause that we can give to justify this commotion."
⁴¹ And when he had said this, he dismissed the assembly.

(1) 'The Way' was one of the names which came to be used to mean the new doctrine, i.e. the Way of the Lord. See also Nos. 103 and 107. For notes about the Ephesian Artemis see Introduction, p. 23.

65   A short stay in Greece
(Acts 20, 1-6)

¹ After the uproar ceased, Paul sent for the disciples and having exhorted them took leave of them and departed for Macedonia. ² When he had gone through these parts and had given them much encouragement, he came to Greece. ³ There he spent three months, and when a plot was made against him by the Jews as he was about to set sail for Syria, he determined to return through Macedonia. ⁴ Sopater of Beroea, the son of Pyrrhus, accompanied him; and of the Thessalonians, Aristarchus and Secundus; and Gaius of Derbe, and Timothy; and the Asians, Tychicus and Trophimus. ⁵ These went on and were waiting for us at Troas, (1) ⁶ but we sailed away from Philippi after the days of Unleavened Bread, and in five days we came to them at Troas, where we stayed for seven days.

(1) Here begins the second 'we-section' which goes on to No. 69 and starts again at No. 101 (see notes to Nos. 45 and 112, and Introduction p. 37).

66   The Return Journey: Troas
(Acts 20, 7-12)

⁷ On the first day of the week, when we were gathered together to break bread, Paul talked with them, intending to depart on the morrow; and he prolonged his speech until midnight. ⁸ There were many lights in the upper chamber where we were gathered. ⁹ And a young man named Eutychus was sitting

From the ruins of the ancient city of Troy.
The plain slopes down towards the sea in the direction of the site
of the small town of Troas mentioned by St Luke in Acts 20,6-12.

in the window. He sank into a deep sleep as Paul talked still longer; and being overcome by sleep, he fell down from the third storey and was taken up dead. [10] But Paul went down and bent over him, and embracing him said, "Do not be alarmed, for his life is in him." [11] And when Paul had gone up and had broken bread and eaten, he conversed with them a long while, until daybreak, and so departed. [12] And they took the lad away alive, and were not a little comforted.

67 Troas to Miletus
(Acts 20, 13-16)

[13] But going ahead to the ship, we set sail for Assos, intending to take Paul aboard there; for so he had arranged, intending himself to go by land. [14] And when he met us at Assos, we took him on board and came to Mitylene. [15] And sailing from there we came the following day opposite Chios; the next day we touched at Samos; and the day after that we came to Miletus. [16] For Paul had decided to sail past Ephesus, so that he might not have to spend time in Asia; for he was hastening to be at Jerusalem, if possible, on the day of Pentecost.

68 The farewell to the Elders of Ephesus
(Acts 20, 17-38)

[17] And from Miletus he sent to Ephesus and called to him the elders of the church. [18] And when they came to him he said to them:

"You yourselves know how I lived among you all the time from the first day that I set foot in Asia, [19] serving the Lord with all humility and with tears and with trials which befell

The remains of the Roman theatre at Miletus which must have been one of the largest Roman buildings in Asia Minor. On the horizon can be seen the harbour where St Paul gathered together the heads of the Church of Ephesus for his last farewell (Acts 20,17).

At Ephesus. Among the ruins of St John's Church it is possible to make out pictures of St Peter and St Paul in a very old fresco which is still well preserved.

me through the plots of the Jews; ²⁰ how I did not shrink from declaring to you anything that was profitable, and teaching you in public and from house to house, ²¹ testifying both to Jews and to Greeks of repentance to God and of faith in our Lord Jesus Christ. ²² And now, behold, I am going to Jerusalem, bound in the Spirit, not knowing what shall befall me there; ²³ except that the Holy Spirit testifies to me in every city that imprisonment and afflictions await me. ²⁴ But I do not account my life of any value nor as precious to myself, if only I may accomplish my course and the ministry which I received from the Lord Jesus, to testify to the gospel of the grace of God. ²⁵ And now, behold, I know that all you among whom I have gone about preaching the kingdom will see my face no more. ²⁶ Therefore I testify to you this day that I am innocent of the blood of all of you, ²⁷ for I did, not shrink from declaring to you the whole counsel of God. ²⁸ Take heed to yourselves and to all the flock, in which the Holy Spirit has made you guardians, to feed the church of the Lord which he obtained with his own blood. ²⁹ I know that after my departure fierce wolves will come in among you, not sparing the flock; ³⁰ and from among your own selves will arise men speaking perverse things, to draw away the disciples after them. ³¹ Therefore be alert, remembering that for three years I did not cease night or day to admonish every

Ruins of Miletus which in the first century was one of the most flourishing cities of the Roman Empire in Asia Minor. St Paul paused there on his return from the third missionary journey (Acts 20,15-38).

one with tears. [32] And now I commend you to God and to the word of his grace, which is able to build you up and to give you the inheritance among all those who are sanctified. [33] I coveted no one's silver or gold or apparel. [34] You yourselves know that these hands ministered to my necessities, and to those who were with me. [35] In all things I have shown you that by so toiling one must help the weak, remembering the words of the Lord Jesus, how he said, 'It is more blessed to give than to receive.'"

[36] And when he had spoken thus, he knelt down and prayed with them all. [37] And they all wept and embraced Paul and kissed him, [38] sorrowing most of all because of the word he had spoken, that they should see his face no more. And they brought him to the ship.

69 From Miletus to Tyre and Caesarea
(Acts 21, 1-14)

[1] And when we had departed from them and set sail, we came by a straight course to Cos, and the next day to Rhodes, and from there to Patara. [2] And having found a ship crossing to Phoenicia, we went aboard, and set sail. [3] When we had come in sight of Cyprus, leaving it on the left we sailed to Syria, and landed at Tyre; for there the ship was to unload its cargo. [4] And having sought out the disciples, we stayed there for seven days. Through the Spirit they told Paul not to go on to Jerusalem. [5] And when our days there were ended, we departed and went on our journey; and they all, with wives and children, brought us on our way till we were outside the city; and kneeling down on the beach we prayed and bade one another farewell. [6] Then we went on board the ship, and they returned home. [7] When we had finished the voyage from Tyre, we arrived at Ptolemais; and we greeted the brethren and stayed with them for one day. [8] On the morrow we departed and came to Caesarea; and we entered the house of Philip the evangelist, who was one of the seven, and stayed with him. [9] And he had four unmarried daughters, who prophesied. [10] While we were staying for some days, a prophet named Agabus came down from Judea. [11] And coming to us he took Paul's girdle and bound his own feet

and hands, and said, "Thus says the Holy Spirit, 'So shall the Jews at Jerusalem bind the man who owns this girdle and deliver him into the hands of the Gentiles.'" (1) [12] When we heard this, we and the people there begged him not to go up to Jerusalem. [13] Then Paul answered, "What are you doing, weeping and breaking my heart? For I am ready not only to be imprisoned but even to die at Jerusalem for the name of the Lord Jesus." [14] And when he would not be persuaded, we ceased and said, "The will of the Lord be done."

(1) The action taken by the prophet Agabus was symbolic in the manner of the prophets of the Old Testament. See similar analogous actions in Isaiah 20 and Jeremiah 19 and 27,2-10. It was a mode of expression dear to orientals, in which words were accompanied by an exterior action expressing the same message in visible form.

> THE TEXT OF THE ACTS IS RESUMED IN NO. 101

IV. St Paul's Letters written during the third missionary journey

From St Paul's First Letter to the Corinthians

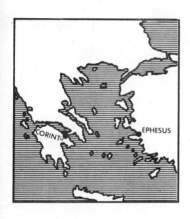

The region of Corinth and Ephesus.

The first Letter to the Church in Corinth was written during St Paul's long residence in Ephesus (see No. 63) between the years 55 and 57.

Corinth, a commercial and cosmopolitan city and the seat of the proconsul of Achaia, had been evangelized by St Paul in the course of the second missionary journey during his stay of at least 18 months beginning to-wards the end of the year 50 (see No. 51). The community at Corinth was zealous and generous, in fact extraordinary gifts of the Holy Spirit appeared among them (see No. 78), but they showed themselves somewhat unruly and liable to split up into factions or parties, according to each person's sympathy with particular preachers of the Gospel. One of these was Paul himself, another was Cephas (or better Kephas), i.e. the apostle Peter, another was Apollos who came to Corinth for a short time (see No. 62) and aroused enthusiasm by his biblical learning and Greek eloquence.

There were also other disorders of a moral and disciplinary nature. Because of all this St Paul, not being able to return immediately to Corinth, wrote this first letter. It is of great doctrinal importance and falls into two principal sections. In the first part the Apostle condemns the disorders in the Corinthian Christian community, i.e. the division into religious parties, the exaggerated esteem of style in preaching (which is divine and not human wisdom), a case of public scandal, going before pagan tribunals with suits between Christians, and lastly the fact that many were falling back into the vice of fornication.

A street in the Agora of Ephesus. From the City of Ephesus St Paul wrote his Letters to the Christians of Corinth where he had proclaimed the word of God for about a year and a half.

In the second part St Paul gives the answers to various questions posed by the Corinthians, about marriage.and virginity, about the use of meats offered to idols, *about order in liturgical assemblies, about the use of charisms and about the resurrection of the dead. We record here the outstanding points, still pertinent in the Church today.*

The beginning of the 1st Letter to the Corinthians in the Vatican Codex (4th century).

70 Introduction
(1, 1-17)

¹ Paul, called by the will of God to be an apostle of Christ Jesus, and our brother Sosthenes,

² To the church of God which is at Corinth, to those sanctified in Christ Jesus, called to be saints together with all those who in every place call on the name of our Lord Jesus Christ, both their Lord and ours:

³ Grace to you and peace from God our Father and the Lord Jesus Christ.

⁴ I give thanks to God always for you because of the grace of God which was given you in Christ Jesus, ⁵ that in every way you were enriched in him with all speech and all knowledge —⁶ even as the testimony to Christ was confirmed among you—

Corinth, site of the ancient western harbour. A feature of Corinth was its particular geographical position which made it a city of two harbours. As the canal did not yet exist, many goods were unloaded in one harbour and carried across to the other, so as to avoid the long voyage round the Peloponnese.

⁷ so that you are not lacking in any spiritual gift, as you wait for the revealing of our Lord Jesus Christ; ⁸ who will sustain you to the end, guiltless in the day of our Lord Jesus Christ. ⁹ God is faithful, by whom you were called into the fellowship of his Son, Jesus Christ our Lord.

¹⁰ I appeal to you, brethren, by the name of our Lord Jesus Christ, that all of you agree and that there be no dissensions among you, but that you be united in the same mind and the same judgment. ¹¹ For it has been reported to me by Chloe's people that there is quarrelling among you, my brethren. ¹² What I mean is that each one of you says, "I belong to Paul," or "I belong to Apollos," or "I belong to Cephas," or "I belong to Christ." ¹³ Is Christ divided? Was Paul crucified for you? Or were you baptized in the name of Paul? ¹⁴ I am thankful that I baptized none of you except Crispus and Gaius; ¹⁵ lest any one should say that you were baptized in my name. ¹⁶ (I did baptize also the household of Stephanas. Beyond that, I do not know whether I baptized any one else.) ¹⁷ For Christ did not send me to baptize but to preach the gospel, and not with eloquent wisdom, lest the cross of Christ be emptied of its power.

71   Divisions and discords among the Christians in Corinth
(3, 1-23)

¹ But I, brethren, could not address you as spiritual men, but as men of the flesh, as babes in Christ. ² I fed you with milk, not solid food; for you were not ready for it; and even yet you are not ready, ³ for you are still of the flesh. For while there is jealousy and strife among you, are you not of the flesh, and behaving like ordinary men? ⁴ For when one says, "I belong to Paul," and another, "I belong to Apollos," are you not merely men?

⁵ What then is Apollos? What is Paul? Servants through whom you believed, as the Lord assigned to each. ⁶ I planted, Apollos

Anatolian Plateau. Characteristic scene of threshing by old traditional methods. St Paul often saw scenes like this, and the hard toil of peasants who worked on a miserly soil of this sort must have inspired him with the saying: '**Neither he who plants nor he who waters is anything, but God gave the growth**' (1 Cor. 3,7).

watered, but God gave the growth. [7] So neither he who plants nor he who waters is anything, but only God who gives the growth. [8] He who plants and he who waters are equal, and each shall receive his wages according to his labour. [9] For we are God's fellow workers; you are God's field, God's building.

[10] According to the commission of God given to me, like a skilled master builder I laid a foundation, and another man is building upon it. Let each man take care how he builds upon it. [11] For no other foundation can any one lay than that which is laid, which is Jesus Christ. [12] Now if any one builds on the foundation with gold, silver, precious stones, wood, hay stubble— [13] each man's work will become manifest; for the Day will disclose it, because it will be revealed with fire, and the fire will test what sort of work each one has done. [14] If the work which any man has built on the foundation survives, he will receive a reward. [15] If any man's work is burned up, he will suffer loss, though he himself will be saved, but only as through fire.

[16] Do you not know that you are God's temple and that God's Spirit dwells in you? [17] If any one destroys God's temple, God will destroy him. For God's temple is holy, and that temple you are.

[18] Let no one deceive himself. If any one among you thinks that he is wise in this age, let him become a fool that he may become wise. [19] For the wisdom of this world is folly with God. For it is written, "He catches the wise in their craftiness," [20] and again, "The Lord knows that the thoughts of the wise are futile." [21] So let no one boast of men. For all things are yours; [22] whether Paul or Apollos or Cephas or the world or life or death or the present or the future, all are yours; [23] and you are Christ's; and Christ is God's.

'Carnal' as opposed to 'spiritual' in St Paul's language, indicates those who reason with a human mentality, instead of being inspired by the logic of the faith.

The Corinthian Christians were 'carnal' because they judged the 'wisdom' of the preachers by their external qualities. Apollos,

a person otherwise worthy and straightforward enough, must have charmed some with his eloquence and use of philosophical ideas while others, of Jewish origin and culture, preferred the distant Peter (Cephas) for motives which were still human, i.e. because they thought of him as one of themselves. Instead the 'spiritual' principle on which St Paul insists, is to consider God as the only source of the Church's life. The Church is like a field: the apostles and preachers are only God's tools: the work of each is useful and necessary but God alone makes it fruitful. The Church is also a building founded on Christ's teaching: every preacher builds on this foundation and will have to give an account of his own work. As the preacher must not boast of his own work, so the faithful must not take a pride in their own preachers and cling to some rather than to others. The mention of fire shows, meta-phorically, the judgment of God on the work of the preachers of the Gospel: they may build with precious and lasting material, that is, eternal truth, or they may be tempted to do work of their own choice, for their own personal and petty glory (wood, hay, straw).

The last judgment ('that day') will be like a fire: all the work done for human motives will end by being burnt up.

It will be a great thing if the unfortunate preacher saves even himself, like one who barely escapes, while all his goods are destroyed by fire.

72 Contrast between the Apostle's humiliation and the Corinthians' presumption (4, 8-21)

[8] Already you are filled! Already you have become rich! Without us you have become kings! And would that you did reign, so that we might share the rule with you! [9] For I think that God has exhibited us apostles as last of all, like men sentenced to death; because we have become a spectacle to the world, to angels and to men. [10] We are fools for Christ's sake, but you are wise in Christ. We are weak, but you are strong. You are held in honour, but we in disrepute. [11] To the present hour we hunger and thirst, we are ill-clad and buffeted and homeless, [12] and we labour, working with our own hands. When reviled, we bless; when persecuted, we endure; [13] when slandered, we try to conciliate; we have become, and are now, as the refuse of the world, the offscouring of all things.

[14] I do not write this to make you ashamed, but to admonish you as my beloved children. [15] For though you have countless guides in Christ, you do not have many fathers. For I became your father in Christ Jesus through the gospel. [16] I urge you,

then, be imitators of me. [17] Therefore I sent to you Timothy, my beloved and faithful child in the Lord, to remind you of my ways in Christ, as I teach them everywhere in every church. [18] Some are arrogant, as though I were not coming to you. [19] But I will come to you soon, if the Lord wills, and I will find out not the talk of these arrogant people but their power. [20] For the kingdom of God does not consist in talk but in power. [21] What do you wish? Shall I come to you with a rod, or with love in a spirit of gentleness?

St Paul sometimes uses irony, with which he wishes to touch to the quick the hearts of his Christians, to whom he writes, by dictation, as if he had them before his eyes. Here the irony is truly bitted. Paul is for them as a father who has begotten them in the Christian faith, but now they believe they have out-distanced their old father: they have become wise ('full, rich, rulers') without him. 'Would that it were at least true!' says the Apostle sadly 'then I also might be able to have some small position by your side'. And in contrast with this vaunted spiritual well-being of the Corinthians he describes the humiliations of his own complete dedication to the apostolate as those of a poor vagabond, 'a fool' for Christ.

But after the sad irony and the tenderness of a father who sees himself set aside, we have the forceful affirmation of his own apostolic authority. May the great and small 'rebels' of our own day re-read these words.

73 Respect for the body as the temple of the Holy Spirit (6, 9-20)

[9] Do you not know that the unrighteous will not inherit the kingdom of God? Do not be deceived; neither the immoral, nor idolaters, nor adulterers, nor homosexuals, [10] nor thieves, nor the greedy, nor drunkards, nor revilers, nor robbers will inherit the kingdom of God. [11] And such were some of you. But you were washed, you were sanctified, you were justified in the name of the Lord Jesus Christ and in the Spirit of our God.

Ancient Corinth. Behind the columns of the Temple of Apollo appears the mountain of Acrocorinth, on the summit of which stood the famous sanctuary of Aphrodite, protectress of the city and goddess of sensual love. Therefore St Paul wrote to the Christians of this licentious city: **'The body is not meant for immorality but for the Lord'** (1 Cor. 6,13).

¹² "All things are lawful for me," but not all things are helpful. "All things are lawful for me," but I will not be enslaved by anything. ¹³ "Food is meant for the stomach and the stomach for food"—and God will destroy both one and the other. The body is not meant for immorality, but for the Lord, and the Lord for the body. ¹⁴ And God raised the Lord and will also raise us up by his power. ¹⁵ Do you not know that your bodies are members of Christ? Shall I therefore take the members of Christ and make them members of a prostitute? Never! ¹⁶ Do you not know that he who joins himself to a prostitute becomes one body with her? For, as it is written, "The two shall become one." ¹⁷ But he who is united to the Lord becomes one spirit with him. ¹⁸ Shun immorality. Every other sin which a man commits is outside the body; but the immoral man sins against his own body. ¹⁹ Do you not know that your body is a temple of the Holy Spirit within you, which you have from God? You are not your own; ²⁰ you were bought with a price. So glorify God in your body.

Corinth was proverbial for its corruption and for the thousand priestesses of Venus consecrated to temple prostitution. It is not to be wondered at that the Christians of the city, but lately converted, were again conscious of the temptations of the flesh and that some returned to their former vices.

The principles of individual or social utilitarianism are of little value against such bad habits. St Paul appeals firmly to the highest principles of the Christian faith. Our body is not a prison to scorn or a beast of burden to satisfy with whatever fodder pleases it. It is the temple of the Holy Spirit! By virtue of baptism it has a mysterious but real relationship with the body of the risen Christ, and is itself, this fleshly body, destined to rise, transformed and glorious.

Therefore the body deserves respect and reverence: if it is made the instrument of sin it is profaned and set in opposition to its sacred character and glorious destiny.

'All things are lawful for me' was probably a phrase dictated by St Paul to express the liberty of Christians by contrast with the coercive nature of the precepts of the Old Testament. But there were Corinthian Christians who misused this phrase to justify a certain carelessness with regard to sensual relationships. St Paul protested against such an interpretation: all things are permitted to the Christian, but not in such a way as to make him the slave of sin and place him in opposition to his freedom, which has its foundation in his relationship with Christ. Instead, true conjugal relations, symbols not of selfishness but of total dedication are

not only not harmful to his relationship with Christ, but are also a sacramental sign, a symbol of the fellowship of love and life between Christ and the faithful (see No. 127).

74 Marriage and virginity
(7, 1-17, 25-35, 39-40)

[1] Now concerning the matters about which you wrote. It is well for a man not to touch a woman. [2] But because of the temptation to immorality, each man should have his own wife and each woman her own husband. [3] The husband should give to his wife her conjugal rights, and likewise the wife to her husband. [4] For the wife does not rule over her own body, but the husband does; likewise the husband does not rule over his own body, but the wife does. [5] Do not refuse one another except perhaps by agreement for a season, that you may devote yourselves to prayer; but then come together again, lest Satan tempt you through lack of self-control. [6] I say this by way of concession, not of command. [7] I wish that all were as I myself am. But each has his own special gift from God, one of one kind and one of another.

[8] To the unmarried and the widows I say that it is well for them remain single as I do. [9] But if they cannot exercise self-control, they should marry. For it is better to marry than to be aflame with passion.

[10] To the married I give charge, not I but the Lord, that the wife should not separate from her husband [11] (but if she does, let her remain single or else be reconciled to her husband)—and that the husband should not divorce his wife.

[12] To the rest I say, not the Lord, that if any brother has a wife who is an unbeliever, and she consents to live with him, he should not divorce her. [13] If any woman has a husband who is an unbeliever, and he consents to live with her, she should not divorce him. [14] For the unbelieving husband is consecrated through his wife, and the unbelieving wife is consecrated through her husband. Otherwise, your children would be unclean, but as

it is they are holy. ¹⁵ But if the unbelieving partner desires to separate, let it be so; in such a case the brother or sister is not bound. For God has called us to peace. ¹⁶ Wife, how do you know whether you will save your husband? Husband, how do you know whether you will save your wife?

¹⁷ Only, let every one lead the life which the Lord has assigned to him, and in which God has called him. This is my rule in all the churches.

²⁵ Now concerning the unmarried, I have no command of the Lord, but I give my opinion as one who by the Lord's mercy is trustworthy. ²⁶ I think that in view of the impending distress it is well for a person to remain as he is. ²⁷ Are you bound to a wife? Do not seek to be free. Are you free from a wife? Do not seek marriage. ²⁸ But if you marry, you do not sin, and if a girl marries she does not sin. Yet those who marry will have worldly troubles, and I would spare you that. ²⁹ I mean, brethren, the appointed time has grown very short; from now on, let those who have wives live as though they had none, ³⁰ and those who mourn as though they were not mourning, and those who rejoice as though they were not rejoicing, and those who buy as though they had no goods, ³¹ and those who deal with the world as though they had no dealings with it. For the form of this world is passing away.

³² I want you to be free from anxieties. The unmarried man is anxious about the affairs of the Lord, how to please the Lord; ³³ but the married man is anxious about worldly affairs, how to please his wife, ³⁴ and his interests are divided. And the unmarried woman or girl is anxious about the affairs of the Lord, how to be holy in body and spirit; but the married woman is anxious about worldly affairs, how to please her husband. ³⁵ I say this for your own benefit, not to lay any restraint upon you, but to promote good order and to secure your undivided devotion to the Lord.

³⁹ A wife is bound to her husband as long as he lives. If the husband dies, she is free to be married to whom she wishes, only in the Lord. ⁴⁰ But in my judgment she is happier if she remains as she is. And I think that I have the Spirit of God.

Note that in this passage St Paul does not set out to discuss the whole doctrine of marriage *which he will have occasion to deal with in the Letter to the Ephesians (see No. 127) but is* replying to queries of a practical nature which the Corinthians had put to him by letter.

A careful reading of the passage, already clear in itself, brings out the following points:

(1) Virginity is better than marriage if it is embraced not for selfish reasons but so as to have complete liberty to dedicate oneself to God and works of charity. St Paul advises celibacy to the unmarried and to widows who are capable of it, on condition that this is 'God's gift' to them.

(2) Marriage is a good and honourable thing. Married people have mutual and exclusive rights and duties. St Paul generally advises against abstention from cohabitation for motives of perfection, though it may be practised prudently with a religious purpose, but only 'by agreement and for a season'.

However married life, as in general every other aspect of the present, ephemeral life, must be considered in the light of eternal values.

(3) Marriage is indissoluble until the death of one of the partners, and this is a command of the Lord, that is a 'word' spoken by Jesus himself and recorded as such in the Gospels. Therefore if separation occurs it does not give the right to contract a new marriage.

(4) But there is a special case on which Jesus made no pronouncement ('I have no command of the Lord but I give my opinion'), that of a marriage contracted in paganism after which one of the partners becomes a Christian. In that case St Paul advises them not to part: such a marriage becomes hallowed by the Christian profession of one of the partners and prepares the way for the conversion of the other. But if the pagan partner no longer wishes to cohabit, St Paul declares that the Christian partner is no longer bound by the marriage contracted before his conversion. This abrogation of indissolubility is called the 'Pauline privilege' (i.e. a doctrine authoritatively taught by St Paul) and was always interpreted in the sense that the Christian partner in such a case is free to contract a new marriage. This rule is still observed in missionary territory.

75   Zeal and unselfishness in St Paul's apostolate
(9, 1-27)

[1] Am I not free? Am I not an apostle? Have I not seen Jesus our Lord? Are not you my workmanship in the Lord? [2] If to others I am not an apostle, at least I am to you; for you are the seal of my apostleship in the Lord.

³ This is my defence to those who would examine me. ⁴ Do we not have the right to our food and drink? ⁵ Do we not have the right to be accompanied by a wife, as the other apostles and the brethren of the Lord and Cephas? ⁶ Or is it only Barnabas and I who have no right to refrain from working for a living? ⁷ Who serves as a soldier at his own expense? Who plants a vineyard without eating any of its fruit? Who tends a flock without getting some of the milk?

⁸ Do I say this on human authority? Does not the law say the same? ⁹ For it is written in the law of Moses, "You shall not muzzle an ox when it is treading out the grain." Is it for oxen that God is concerned? ¹⁰ Does he not speak entirely for our sake? It was written for our sake, because the ploughman should plough in hope and the thresher thresh in hope of a share in the crop. ¹¹ If we have sown spiritual good among you, is it too much if we reap your material benefits? ¹² If others share this rightful claim upon you, do not we still more?

Nevertheless, we have not made use of this right, but we endure anything rather than put an obstacle in the way of the gospel of Christ. ¹³ Do you not know that those who are employed in the temple service get their food from the temple, and those who serve at the altar share in the sacrificial offerings? ¹⁴ In the same way, the Lord commanded that those who proclaim the gospel should get their living by the gospel.

¹⁵ But I have made no use of any of these rights, nor am I writing this to secure any such provision. For I would rather die than have any one deprive me of my ground for boasting. ¹⁶ For if I preach the gospel, that gives me no ground for boasting. For necessity is laid upon me. Woe to me if I do not preach the gospel! ¹⁷ For if I do this of my own will, I have a reward; but if not of my own will, I am entrusted with a commission ¹⁸ What then is my reward? Just this: that in my preaching I may make the gospel free of charge, not making full use of my right in the gospel.

¹⁹ For though I am free from all men, I have made myself a slave to all, that I might win the more. ²⁰ To the Jews I became as a Jew, in order to win Jews; to those under the law I became as one under the law—though not being myself under the law—that I might win those under the law. ²¹ To those outside the law I became as one outside the law—not being without law toward God but under the law of Christ—that I might win those outside the law. ²² To the weak I became weak, that I might win the weak. I have become all things to all men, that I might by all means save some. ²³ I do it all for the sake of the gospel, that I may share in its blessings.

²⁴ Do you not know that in a race all the runners compete,

Another important centre in Corinth was the stadium in which the 'Isthmian Games' were celebrated every two years. In the photograph, the starting-line for the races: to these races St Paul refers: **'All the runners compete but only on receives the prize... I do not run aimlessly'** (1 Cor. 9,24-26).

but only one receives the prize? So run that you may obtain it. [25] Every athlete exercises self-control in all things. They do it to receive a perishable wreath, but we an imperishable. [26] Well, I do not run aimlessly, I do not box as one beating the air; [27] but I pommel my body and subdue it, lest after preaching to others I myself should be disqualified.

This digression shows a very attractive aspect of St Paul's personality: a sort of pride making him desire to be self-supporting, earning his own living by manual labour; he was a military tent-maker using goats' wool or sackcloth. This was a craft for which his country Cilicia was renowned. He would not let himself be kept by his spiritual children, as would have been his right, and as was the right, confirmed by him, of all preachers of the Gospel, so that they might be free for their spiritual work. St Paul renounced this right, seeing in this attitude a way of facilitating the credibility of his preaching: 'To the weak I became weak that I might win the weak'.

This digression was intended to teach, by his own example, that in certain cases, in order not to give scandal or make difficulties for the brethren, the Christian must know how to live a stricter life, e.g., refuse meats offered to idols. Christians who are 'strong', i.e. of enlightened faith, will eat them without scruples, but the 'weak' will regard them as contaminated (see in No. 43 the rule included in the Jerusalem decision). The explanation of this will be found in No. 76 which follows.

76 You canont partake of the table of the Lord and the table of devils
(10, 1-22)

[1] I want you to know, brethren, that our fathers were all under the cloud, and all passed through the sea, [2] and all were baptized into Moses in the cloud and in the sea, [3] and all ate the same supernatural food [4] and all drank the same supernatural drink. For they drank from the supernatural Rock which followed them, and the Rock was Christ. [5] Nevertheless with most of them God was not pleased; for they were overthrown in the wilderness.

⁶ Now these things are warnings for us, not to desire evil as they did. ⁷ Do not be idolaters as some of them were; as it is written, "The people sat down to eat and drink and rose up to dance." ⁸ We must not indulge in immorality as some of them did, and twenty-three thousand fell in a single day. ⁹ We must not put the Lord to the test, as some of them did and were destroyed by serpents; ¹⁰ nor grumble, as some of them did and were destroyed by the Destroyer. ¹¹ Now these things happened to them as a warning, but they were written down for our instruction, upon whom the end of the ages has come. ¹² Therefore let any one who thinks that he stands take heed lest he fall. ¹³ No temptation has overtaken you that is not common to man. God is faithful, and he will not let you be tempted beyond your strength, but with the temptation will also provide the way of escape, that you may be able to endure it.

¹⁴ Therefore, my beloved, shun the worship of idols. ¹⁵ I speak as to sensible men; judge for yourselves what I say. ¹⁶ The cup of blessing which we bless, is it not a participation in the blood of Christ? The bread which we break, is it not a participation in the body of Christ? ¹⁷ Because there is one bread, we who are many are one body, for we all partake of the one bread. ¹⁸ Consider the practice of Israel; are not those who eat the sacrifices partners in the altar? ¹⁹ What do I imply then? That food offered to idols is anything, or that an idol is anything? ²⁰ No, I imply that what pagans sacrifice they offer to demons and not to God. I do not want you to be partners with demons. ²¹ You cannot drink the cup of the Lord and the cup of demons. You cannot partake of the table of the Lord and the table of demons. ²² Shall we provoke the Lord to jealousy? Are we stronger than he?

In the markets in pagan cities like Corinth meat sacrificed to idols was for sale. Were the Christians allowed to eat it or not? This was the question raised by the Corinthians. St Paul replies that the idol is nothing and therefore the meat sacrificed has nothing evil about it. Anyone who knows this can eat of it freely, in private. If however he finds himself in the company of someone who thinks such meat to be forbidden, he should be very careful not to scandalize him and not to persuade him to do what he believes to be wrong. This respect for another's conscience is required by charity which forces one to forego even a right, if that would cause spiritual harm to a brother (see above No. 75).

But there was another case to be judged very differently; some allowed themselves actually to share in the sacred feasts which followed pagan sacrifices. St Paul condemns such licence as idolatry and so as to dissuade the Corinthian Christians puts forward two arguments:

(1) The example of the Hebrews escaping from Egypt: they had been surrounded by miraculous events which were the 'type', i.e.

the prophetic image, of the Christian sacraments, yet because of their arrogance and idolatry they perished in great numbers in the desert. It is not therefore enough to have been baptized and to eat the spiritual food of the Eucharist, it is also necessary to refrain from the vices of the pagans.

(2) The Eucharistic feast and idolatrous feasts are absolutely irreconcilable. In this passage, most noteworthy for its teaching on the eucharist, it is asserted: (a) that the eucharist is the sharing in the sacrifice of Christ and has therefore its own sacrificial value; (b) sharing in the eucharist is entering into communion with the Body and Blood of Christ who therefore is really present in the 'Cup of blessing' and in the 'Bread which we break'; (c) the 'one Bread' which is the Body of Christ makes the 'many' who share it become 'one body'.

77   The celebration of the Eucharist (11, 17-34)

[17] But in the following instructions I do not commend you, because when you come together it is not for the better but for the worse. [18] For, in the first place, when you assemble as a church, I hear that there are divisions among you; and I partly believe it, [19] for there must be factions among you in order that those who are genuine among you may be recognized. [20] When you meet together, it is not the Lord's supper that you eat. [21] For in eating, each one goes ahead with his own meal, and one is hungry and another is drunk. [22] What! Do you not have houses to eat and drink in? Or do you despise the church of God and humiliate those who have nothing? What shall I say to you? Shall I commend you in this? No, I will not.

The celebration of the Eucharist. Early Christian mosaic at Ravenna (Sant'Apollinare Nuovo). The sanctity of the eucharistic celebration is forcefully recalled by St Paul in 1 Corinthians.

²³ For I received from the Lord what I also delivered to you, that the Lord Jesus on the night when he was betrayed took bread, ²⁴ and when he had given thanks, he broke it, and said, "This is my body which is for you. Do this in remembrance of me." ²⁵ In the same way also the cup, after supper, saying, "This cup is the new covenant in my blood. Do this, as often as you drink it, in remembrance of me." ²⁶ For as often as you eat this bread and drink the cup, you proclaim the Lord's death until he comes.

²⁷ Whoever, therefore, eats the bread or drinks the cup of the Lord in an unworthy manner will be guilty of profaning the body and blood of the Lord. ²⁸ Let a man examine himself, and so eat of the bread and drink of the cup. ²⁹ For any one who eats and drinks without discerning the body eats and drinks judgment upon himself. ³⁰ That is why many of you are weak and ill, and some have died. ³¹ But if we judged ourselves truly, we should not be judged. ³² But when we are judged by the Lord, we are chastened so that we may not be condemned along with the world.

³³ So then, my brethren, when you come together to eat, wait for one another—³⁴ if any one is hungry, let him eat at home—lest you come together to be condemned. About the other things I will give directions when I come.

At Corinth, as in the whole Church, the eucharist was celebrated from the beginning. Then the celebration was in the evening at the end of a fraternal meal. But at Corinth that meal was no longer truly fraternal: the assembly served rather to show up the divisions among them and their disdain for the humblest. Those who acted in such a way showed themselves 'unworthy' of the eucharist, and while distinguishing it materially from the repast which preceded it, did not 'discern the Body of Christ', i.e. did not take account of the corporate value of the eucharist as a sign and instrument of the unity of all in charity. To demonstrate this St Paul refers to the words of institution, already well-known at Corinth, which repeatedly mention the idea of 'death for others', the generous self-sacrifice of Christ which ought to be reflected in the generous charity of anyone who shares in the eucharist. Further, he puts forward an argument which establishes two sets of identity (a) the identity of the bread consecrated by Jesus Christ with his Body (and similarly as regards the Blood); (b) the identity of that bread with this bread (and similarly as regards the cup). The argument is based on the words 'do this in remembrance of me' repeated twice. It is as if he says: we do the same thing which Jesus did: we do not merely repeat the same action, we bring about the same reality. In consequence this bread and this cup are that Body and that Blood. Therefore whoever approaches it unworthily is 'guilty' and 'eats and drinks judgment upon himself'. In the context the unworthiness is that of the man who spurns communal charity in the very act of approaching the sacrament of charity.

However, the expression, which is based upon faith in the real presence of Christ in the Eucharist, has a more general application to any serious opposition to the Christian ideal.

78 Varieties of gifts and unity of the Church (12, 1 - 4-30)

[1] Now concerning spiritual gifts, brethren, I do not want you to be uninformed.

[4] Now there are varieties of gifts, but the same Spirit; [5] and there are varieties of service, but the same Lord; [6] and there are varieties of working, but it is the same God who inspires them all in every one. [7] To each is given the manifestation of the Spirit for the common good. [8] To one is given through the Spirit the utterance of wisdom, and to another the utterance of knowledge according to the same Spirit, [9] to another faith by the same Spirit, to another gifts of healing by the one Spirit, [10] to another the working of miracles, to another prophecy, to another the ability to distinguish between spirits, to another various kinds of tongues, to another the interpretation of tongues. [11] All these are inspired by one and the same Spirit, who apportions to each one individually as he wills.

[12] For just as the body is one and has many members, and all the members of the body, though many, are one body, so it is with Christ. [13] For by one Spirit we were all baptized into

one body—Jews or Greeks, slaves or free— and all were made to drink of one Spirit.

[14] For the body does not consist of one member but of many. [15] If the foot should say, "Because I am not a hand, I do not belong to the body," that would not make it any less a part of the body. [16] And if the ear should say, "Because I am not an eye, I do not belong to the body," that would not make it any less a part of the body. [17] If the whole body were an eye, where would be the hearing? If the whole body were an ear, where would be the sense of smell? [18] But as it is, God arranged the organs in the body, each one of them, as he chose. [19] If all were a single organ, where would the body be? [20] As it is, there are many parts, yet one body. [21] The eye cannot say to the hand, "I have no need of you," nor again the head to the feet, "I have no need of you." [22] On the contrary, the parts of the body which seem to be weaker are indispensable, [23] and those parts of the body which we think less honourable we invest with the greater honour, and our unpresentable parts are treated with greater modesty, [24] which our more presentable parts do not require. But God has so adjusted the body, giving the greater honour to the inferior part, [25] that there may be no discord in the body, but that the members may have the same care for one another. [26] If one member suffers, all suffer together; if one member is honoured, all rejoice together.

[27] Now you are the body of Christ and individually members of it. [28] And God has appointed in the church first apostles, second prophets, third teachers, then workers of miracles, then healers, helpers, administrators, speakers in various kinds of tongues. [29] Are all apostles? Are all prophets? Are all teachers? Do all work miracles? [30] Do all possess gifts of healing? Do all speak with tongues? Do all interpret?

The Holy Spirit, the third Person of the Trinity, is called Spirit because he is like the soul of our soul, a power of knowledge and of life which unites us to the Risen Christ (He is the Spirit of Christ), which makes us like him, which makes us think and judge like him, which makes us live and work with him. In the primitive Church this presence of the Holy Spirit sometimes made itself manifest in the 'charisms' or gifts of the Spirit which operated like miraculous signs of the presence of God among the Christ-

ians (see Nos. 22 and 30) and furthermore were to serve the spiritual good of the community.

However, the Corinthian Christians were so prone to discord that the 'charisms' became for them an excuse for creating schisms. Therefore St Paul compares individual Christians, endowed with different gifts, to the individual members of the same body, which, each member having its own function, are all necessary and work together for the good of all. The Apostle, with authority, regulates the use of the charisms and so shows that there is in the Church an authority which is superior to them, though the Church cannot reach its full vitality without charisms. These still exist and are evident in special vocations, in the extraordinary deeds of the Saints and in heroic charity. Authority cannot create charisms, which depend on God's free initiative, but it is its task to recognize their authenticity and regulate their use with a view to the common good of the whole Church.

79 Hymn to Love
(12, 31; 13, 1-13)

12, ³¹ But earnestly desire the higher gifts. And I will show you a still more excellent way.

13, ¹ If I speak in the tongues of men and of angels, but have not love, I am a noisy gong or a clanging cymbal. ² And if I have prophetic powers, and understand all mysteries and all knowledge, and if I have all faith, so as to remove mountains, but have not love, I am nothing. ³ If I give away all I have, and if I deliver my body to be burned, but have not love, I gain nothing.

⁴ Love is patient and kind; love is not jealous or boastful; ⁵ it is not arrogant or rude. Love does not insist on its own way; it is not irritable or resentful; ⁶ it does not rejoice at wrong, but rejoices in the right. ⁷ Love bears all things, believes all things, hopes all things, endures all things.

⁸ Love never ends; as for prophecies, they will pass away; as for tongues, they will cease; as for knowledge, it will pass away. ⁹ For our knowledge is imperfect and our prophecy is

imperfect; [10] but when the perfect comes, the imperfect will pass away. [11] When I was a child, I spoke like a child, I thought like a child, I reasoned like a child; when I became a man, I gave up childish ways. [12] For now we see in a mirror dimly, but then face to face. Now I know in part; then I shall understand fully, even as I have been fully understood. [13] So faith, hope, love abide, these three; but the greatest of these is love.

The Corinthian Christians were tempted to admire most the more ostentatious charisms, like the gift of tongues by which the 'charismatic person' as though possessed by the Spirit, began suddenly to praise the Lord in some unknown tongue.

St Paul criticizes the childish preferences of the Corinthians. He forbids speaking 'with tongues' in the liturgical assembly, unless there be present one who has the gift of interpreting these exotic expressions of enthusiasm. He teaches that the gift of prophecy is more useful, and finally shows

'a still more excellent way', that is love. Let these words be pondered by those who, under the pretext of charisms, i.e. of having been given special gifts by God, sin against love by making divisions in the Church!

This marvellous praise of love shows that all the charisms, even prophecy and so called theological science, are in some sense provisional, and will seem childish prattlings when we see God. Love, on the other hand, begins down here and 'never ends', continuing without interruption into eternal life.

80 The resurrection of the dead (15, 1-58)

[1] Now I would remind you, brethren, in what terms I preached to you the gospel, which you received, in which you stand, [2] by which you are saved, if you hold it fast—unless you believed in vain.

³ For I delivered to you as of first importance what I also received, that Christ died for our sins in accordance with the scriptures, ⁴ that he was buried, that he was raised on the third day in accordance with the scriptures, ⁵ and that he appeared to Cephas, then to the twelve. ⁶ Then he appeared to more than five hundred brethren at one time, most of whom are still alive, though some have fallen asleep. ⁷ Then he appeared to James, then to all the apostles. ⁸ Last of all, as to one untimely born, he appeared also to me. ⁹ For I am the least of the apostles, unfit to be called an apostle, because I persecuted the church of God. ¹⁰ But by the grace of God I am what I am, and his grace toward me was not in vain. On the contrary, I worked harder than any of them, though it was not I, but the grace of God which is with me. ¹¹ Whether then it was I or they, so we preach and so you believed.

¹² Now if Christ is preached as raised from the dead, how can some of you say that there is no resurrection of the dead? ¹³ But if there is no resurrection of the dead, then Christ has not been raised; ¹⁴ If Christ has not been raised, then our preaching is in vain and your faith is in vain. ¹⁵ We are even found to be misrepresenting God, because we testified of God that he raised Christ, whom he did not raise if it is true that the dead are not raised. ¹⁶ For if the dead are not raised, then Christ has not been raised. ¹⁷ If Christ has not been raised, your faith is futile and you are still in your sins. ¹⁸ Then those also who have fallen asleep in Christ have perished. ¹⁹ If for this life only we have hoped in Christ, we are of all men most to be pitied.

²⁰ But in fact Christ has been raised from the dead, the first fruits of those who have fallen asleep. ²¹ For as by a man came death, by a man has come also the resurrection of the dead. ²² For as in Adam all die, so also in Christ shall all be made alive. ²³ But each in his own order: Christ the first fruits, then at his coming those who belong to Christ. ²⁴ Then comes the end, when he delivers the kingdom to God the Father after destroying every rule and every authority and power. ²⁵ For he must reign until he has put all his enemies under his feet. ²⁶ The last enemy to be destroyed is death. ²⁷ "For God has put all things in subjection under his feet." But when it says, "All things are put in subjection under him," it is plain that he is excepted who

put all things under him. [28] When all things are subjected to him, then the Son himself will also be subjected to him who put all things under him, that God may be everything to every one.

[29] Otherwise, what do people mean by being baptized on behalf of the dead? If the dead are not raised at all, why are people baptized on their behalf? [30] Why am I in peril every hour? [31] I protest, brethren, by my pride in you which I have in Christ Jesus our Lord, I die every day! [32] What do I gain if, humanly speaking, I fought with beasts at Ephesus? If the dead are not raised, "Let us eat and drink, for tomorrow we die." [33] Do not be deceived: "Bad company ruins good morals." [34] Come to your right mind, and sin no more. For some have no knowledge of God. I say this to your shame.

[35] But some one will ask, "How are the dead raised? With what kind of body do they come?" [36] You foolish man! What you sow does not come to life unless it dies. [37] And what you sow is not the body which is to be, but a bare kernel, perhaps of wheat or of some other grain. [38] But God gives it a body as he has chosen, and to each kind of seed its own body. [39] For not all flesh is alike, but there is one kind for men, another for animals, another for birds, and another for fish. [40] There are celestial bodies and there are terrestrial bodies; but the glory of the celestial is one, and the glory of the terrestrial is another. [41] There is one glory of the sun, and another glory of the moon, and another glory of the stars; for star differs from star in glory.

[42] So it is with the resurrection of the dead. What is sown is perishable, what is raised is imperishable. [43] It is sown in dishonour, it is raised in glory. It is sown in weakness, it is raised in power. [44] It is sown a physical body, it is raised a spiritual body. If there is a physical body, there is also a spiritual body. [45] Thus it is written, "The first man Adam became a living being;" the last Adam became a life-giving spirit. [46] But it is not the spiritual which is first but the physical, and then the spiritual. [47] The first man was from the earth, a man of dust; the second man is from heaven. [48] As was the man of dust, so are those who are of the dust; and as is the man of heaven, so are those who are of heaven. [49] Just as we have borne the image of the man of dust, we shall also bear the image of the man of heaven. [50] I tell you this, brethren; flesh and blood

Jerusalem, Basilica of the Holy Sepulchre. Interior of the shrine of the Holy Sepulchre: the woman is kissing the slab of marble which covers the ledge, cut out of the rock, on which the body of Jesus lay for several hours before it came to life again, transformed, in the glory of the resurrection.

'Christ has been raised from the dead, the first fruits of those who have fallen asleep' (1 Cor. 15,20).

cannot inherit the kingdom of God, nor does the perishable inherit the imperishable.

[51] Lo! I tell you a mystery. We shall not all sleep, but we shall all be changed, [52] in a moment, in the twinkling of an eye, at the last trumpet. For the trumpet will sound, and the dead will be raised imperishable, and we shall be changed. [53] For this perishable nature must put on the imperishable, and this mortal nature must put on immortality. [54] When the perishable puts on the imperishable, and the mortal puts on immortality, then shall come to pass the saying that is written:

"Death is swallowed up in victory."
[55] "O death, where is thy victory?
O death, where is thy sting?"
[56] The sting of death is sin, and the power of sin is the law.
[57] But thanks be to God, who gives us the victory through our Lord Jesus Christ.

[58] Therefore, by beloved brethren, be steadfast, immovable, always abounding in the work of the Lord, knowing that in the Lord your labour is not in vain.

The Corinthians did not deny Christ's resurrection, which was among the fundamental articles of the apostolic preaching, but they had difficulties about the general resurrection of the dead, either because they did not think it necessary, in view of the idea of the immortality of the soul, held by the Greeks, or because they did not understand how a body with material needs could last for ever.

St Paul replies in this very important chapter which completes what he had already explained to the Thessalonians (see No. 57). Note the fundamental points of the explanation which is quite clear:

(1) Christ is risen; this is a basic fact of faith for which there are irrefutable witnesses. Many who had seen the risen Jesus were *still alive when Paul wrote these words.*

(2) But why should he have risen if the resurrection is unnecessary or impossible? He is risen in order that we too may rise. That is the meaning of our salvation: the forgiveness of sins and the total redemption of man in soul and body. There is no substitute for this redemption nor any alternative to the salvation brought by Christ. Without him we should still be in sin and of what use would be an immortality of soul if it did no more than prolong for ever our alienation from God? But Christ's redemption is complete, it is victory over death, because death is the consequence and image of sin.

(3) But how can 'flesh and blood' subsist in an eternal life?

This is the other difficulty with which perhaps the Apostle had never before had occasion to deal. Here is his answer: we shall not rise in the same condition as before, we shall not retain human appetites in the sphere of glorified realities. There are different sorts of 'flesh', i.e. of bodies. Even our body exists in two different conditions: before death and after resurrection.

(4) This entrance of the body into a new and different state affects not only the dead, already dissolved into dust, but also those who will still be alive at the moment when Christ comes. In the instant which sees the dead arise, they will feel themselves radically changed, and clothed with the characteristics of immortal bodies.

(5) The risen Christ is the cause and pattern of the resurrection of the elect. Once risen, he became a quickening Spirit, that is to say, able to pour into a Christian a spiritual power which transforms him into a 'new creature' (see Nos. 89 and 93) in the deepest roots of his being. At the moment of the general resurrection that transformation will reach even the body, which will be renewed in the image of the risen Christ. The material creation also will take part in this transformation of totally redeemed man, as St Paul himself teaches when writing to the Romans (see No. 98).

81 The collection for the poor at Jerusalem: conclusion of the Letter
(16, 1-24)

[1] Now concerning the contribution for the saints: as I directed the churches of Galatia, so you also are to do. [2] On the first day of every week, each of you is to put something aside and store it up, as he may prosper, so that contributions need not be made when I come. [3] And when I arrive, I will send those whom you accredit by letter to carry your gift to Jerusalem. [4] If it seems advisable that I should go also, they will accompany me. [5] I will visit you after passing through Macedonia, for I intend to pass through Macedonia, [6] and perhaps I will stay with you or even spend the winter, so that you may speed me on my journey, wherever I go. [7] For I do not want to see you now just in passing; I hope to spend some time with you, if the Lord permits. [8] But I will stay in Ephesus until Pentecost, [9] for

a wide door for effective work has opened to me, and there are many adversaries.

[10] When Timothy comes, see that you put him at ease among you, for he is doing the work of the Lord, as I am. [11] So let no one despise him. Speed him on his way in peace, that he may return to me; for I am expecting him with the brethren.

[12] As for our brother Apollos, I strongly urged him to visit you with the other brethren, but it was not at all his will to come now. He will come when he has opportunity.

[13] Be watchful, stand firm in your faith, be courageous, be strong. [14] Let all that you do be done in love.

[15] Now, brethren, you know that the household of Stephanas were the first converts in Achaia, and they have devoted themselves to the service of the saints; [16] I urge you to be subject to such men and to every fellow worker and labourer. [17] I rejoice at the coming of Stephanas and Fortunatus and Achaicus, because they have made up for your absence; [18] for they refreshed my spirit as well as yours. Give recognition to such men.

[19] The churches of Asia send greetings. Aquila and Prisca, together with the church in their house, send you hearty greetings in the Lord. [20] All the brethren send greetings. Greet one another with a holy kiss.

[21] I, Paul, write this greeting with my own hand. [22] If any one has no love for the Lord, let him be accursed. Our Lord, come! [23] The grace of the Lord Jesus be with you. [24] My love be with you all in Christ Jesus. Amen.

The 'saints', that is the Christians for whom St Paul collected alms in the Churches he had evangelized, were those of the Church of Jerusalem, made up in great part of very poor people. In fact The Acts speak of the arrival of Paul at Jerusalem with abundant help for the poor (see Nos. 101 and 107). This fraternal aid was a sign of the communion of faith and charity between the communities originating in paganism and the Jewish-Christian community of the Holy City (see No. 100). For Paul's journey to Macedonia and then to Corinth see No. 65.

Apollos (see Introduction to No. 70) had returned from Corinth to Ephesus with St Paul; perhaps he did not share St Paul's optimism about the settlement of the dissensions at Corinth and feared to provoke new disorders if he were to return among those unruly admirers of his.

The Dardanelles Strait: in the background the European coasts seen from the shores of Asia Minor. We remember St Paul's mysterious call into Europe: **'A man of Macedonia was standing, beseeching him and saying "Come over to Macedonia and help us"'** (Acts 16,9).

Stephanas was a person of high rank in the community at Corinth. Being one of the first to be baptized (see No. 70), he was responsible for the Church in Corinth and with Fortunatus and Achaicus had brought the Apostle the latest news and the questions to be dealt with. Probably he was the bearer of this present letter.

Aquila and Prisca (or Priscilla), the married couple who had so generously entertained Paul, had returned from Corinth (see No. 51) to Ephesus with him at the end of the second missionary journey and had taken up residence there (see No. 53).

Writing his usual greeting in his own hand St Paul adds an invocation which sums up his whole message: Christ ('the Lord') is everything to us: whoever does not love him cannot be a Christian, he will be 'anathema', i.e. excommunicated, excluded from the Communion with the faithful.

'Maran atha' or better 'Marana tha' in Aramaic (the language of Jesus and the Apostles) means 'Come, Lord'. It had entered into the liturgy and expressed the ardent desire for the second coming of Jesus (see the end of the Apocalypse, No. 180).

EVENTS AFTER THE FIRST LETTER TO THE CORINTHIANS

1) The first Letter to the Corinthians, and Timothy's visit at the same time, produced no good result. Further, the situation was worsened by the arrival at Corinth of certain Christians of Jewish origin who took to themselves the title of apostle and belittled Paul in every way.

2) Probably St Paul made a very short visit to Corinth which was a sad disappointment to him: he was even publicly insulted by a quarrelsome member of that community.

3) From Ephesus St Paul wrote a Letter 'with many tears' which he entrusted to his disciple, Titus; this must have moved the Corinthians and induced them to see their faults. This Letter has not been preserved for us.

4) The riot of the silversmiths of Ephesus (see No. 64) caused St Paul to anticipate his departure with the result that he did not find at Troas Titus, who ought to have met him there with the news of Corinth. Not being able to put up with this worrying uncertainty he crossed to Macedonia.

5) In Macedonia, probably at Philippi, he succeeded in meeting Titus who brought him quite good news. But the community at Corinth was still much disturbed. So, before returning there in person, St Paul wrote another Letter to prepare for his arrival and had it delivered by Titus again. This is our second Letter to the Corinthians written about the year 57.

Neapolis, today Kavalla, the natural harbour of Ancient Philippi. Neapolis was the first European City visited by St Paul (see Acts 16, 11). The old city cannot have been very different from that of the present day, with its white houses overlooking the sea.

From St Paul's Second Letter to the Corinthians

The second Letter to the Corinthians is divided into three parts. In the first Paul defends himself against certain accusations brought against him by the Corinthians and describes the tragic and paradoxical aspects of the life of an apostle (Chapters 1 - 7).

In the second he speaks again of the method of organizing the collection for the poor in Jerusalem (see No. 81; chapters 8 and 9); in the third he attacks his detractors, sets out the facts which give him the prestige and authority of an apostle, and announces his early visit to Corinth.

The letter served its purpose, as is shown by Paul's peaceful stay at Corinth for three months towards the end of the third journey (see No. 65).

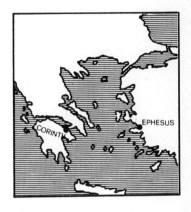

The district of Corinth.

82 The Apostle's tribulations and hopes
(4, 5-18; 5, 1-10)

4, ⁵ For what we preach is not ourselves, but Jesus Christ as Lord, with ourselves as your servants for Jesus' sake. ⁶ For it is the God who said, "Let light shine out of darkness," who has shone in our hearts to give the light of the knowledge of the glory of God in the face of Christ.

⁷ But we have this treasure in earthen vessels, to show that the transcendent power belongs to God and not to us. ⁸ We are afflicted in every way, but not crushed; perplexed, but not driven to despair; ⁹ persecuted, but not forsaken; struck down, but not destroyed; ¹⁰ always carrying in the body the death of Jesus, so that the life of Jesus may also be manifested in our bodies. ¹¹ For while we live we are always being given up to

The beginning of 2 Corinthians in the Vatican Codex (fourth century).

death for Jesus' sake, so that the life of Jesus may be manifested in our mortal flesh. ¹² So death is at work in us, but life in you.

¹³ Since we have the same spirit of faith as he had who wrote, "I believed, and so I spoke," we too believe, and so we speak, ¹⁴ knowing that he who raised the Lord Jesus will raise us also with Jesus and bring us with you into his presence. ¹⁵ For it is all for your sake, so that as grace extends to more and more people it may increase thanksgiving, to the glory of God.

¹⁶ So we do not lose heart. Though our outer nature is wasting away, our inner nature is being renewed every day. ¹⁷ For this slight momentary affliction is preparing for us an eternal weight of glory beyond all comparison, ¹⁸ because we look not to the things that are seen but to the things that are unseen; for the things that are seen are transient, but the things that are unseen are eternal.

5, ¹ For we know that if the earthly tent we live in is destroyed, we have a building from God, a house not made with hands, eternal in the heavens. ² Here indeed we groan, and long to put on our heavenly dwelling, ³ so that by putting it on we may not be found naked. ⁴ For while we are still in this tent, we sigh with anxiety; not that we would be unclothed, but that we would be further clothed, so that what is mortal may be swallowed up by life. ⁵ He who has prepared us for this very thing is God, who has given us the Spirit as a guarantee.

⁶ So we are always of good courage; we know that while we are at home in the body we are away from the Lord, ⁷ for we walk by faith, not by sight. ⁸ We are of good courage, and we would rather be away from the body and at home with the Lord. ⁹ So whether we are at home or away, we make it our aim to please him. ¹⁰ For we must all appear before the judgment seat of Christ, so that each one may receive good or evil, according to what he has done in the body.

The second Letter to the Corinthians written towards the end of the year 69 is very rich in personal touches, which give us a glimpse of St Paul's mind. He expresses very frankly to these turbulent Christians of his, poisoned as they are by the calumnies of certain intriguers against him, his most intimate feelings, his sufferings, anxiety and hopes. The passage here quoted is very important also for the doctrine of 'individual eschatology', that is, of the state of the soul after death but before the general resurrection.

St Paul has experienced the progressive breaking up of the body, caused more by the labours of the apostolate and by persecutions than by advancing years. He admits that the deep desire of his whole being would not be to be 'unclothed' of his mortal body, but to be 'further clothed'

by the transformed and immortal body without passing through death, and this will happen at the instant of the Lord's coming (see No. 80). The body is thus compared to a garment and also to a tent to dwell in. However, the prospect of death does not frighten him. Indeed, from a certain point of view he would rather die than remain too long in 'exile' far from his final meeting with the Lord. He asserts that dying ('being away from the body') he will go to live with the Lord. It is thus not necessary to wait till the moment of the resurrection to be with the risen Jesus; death changes the relationship with the mortal body but it does not change the relationship with Christ, except to make it more evident. He was to express the same idea when he wrote to the Philippians (see No. 117).

83 Paul defends his authority as an Apostle (11, 1-21)

¹ I wish you would bear with me in a little foolishness. Do bear with me! ² I feel a divine jealousy for you, for I betrothed you to Christ to present you as a pure bride to her one husband.

A weaver at work on a loom similar to those of two thousand years ago. St Paul himself ('a tent-maker') worked on a loom like this one so as not to be a burden to anyone. '**So I refrained and will refrain from burdening you in any way... this boast of mine shall not be silenced**' (2 Cor. 11, 9-10).

³ But I am afraid that as the serpent deceived Eve by his cunning, your thoughts will be led astray from a sincere and pure devotion to Christ. ⁴ For if some one comes and preaches another Jesus than the one we preached, or if you receive a different spirit from the one you received, or if you accept a different gospel from the one you accepted, you submit to it readily enough. ⁵ I think that I am not in the least inferior to these superlative apostles. ⁶ Even if I am unskilled in speaking, I am not in knowledge; in every way we have made this plain to you in all things.

⁷ Did I commit a sin in abasing myself so that you might be exalted, because I preached God's gospel without cost to you? ⁸ I robbed other churches by accepting support from them in order to serve you. ⁹ And when I was with you and was in want, I did not burden any one, for my needs were supplied by the brethren who came from Macedonia. So I refrained and will refrain from burdening you in any way. ¹⁰ As the truth of Christ is in me, this boast of mine shall not be silenced in the regions of Achaia. ¹¹ And why? Because I do not love you? God knows I do!

¹² And what I do I will continue to do, in order to undermine the claim of those who would like to claim that in their boasted mission they work on the same terms as we do. ¹³ For such men are false apostles, deceitful workmen, disguising themselves as apostles of Christ. ¹⁴ And no wonder, for even Satan disguises himself as an angel of light. ¹⁵ So it is not strange if his servants also disguise themselves as servants of righteousness. Their end will correspond to their deeds.

¹⁶ I repeat, let no one think me foolish; but even if you do, accept me as a fool, so that I too may boast a little. ¹⁷ (What I am saying I say not with the Lord's authority but as a fool, in this boastful confidence; ¹⁸ since many boast of worldly things, I too will boast.) ¹⁹ For you gladly bear with fools, being wise yourselves! ²⁰ For you bear it if a man makes slaves of you, or preys upon you, or takes advantage of you, or puts on airs, or strikes you in the face. ²¹ To my shame, I must say, we were too weak for that!

At Corinth there had arrived certain Christians of Jewish origin who wrongly called themselves 'apostles' and belittled St Paul, saying that he was not a true apostle and had no authority.

Detail of the present walls of Damascus with a tower adapted for habitation. St Paul reminds the Corinthians of the humiliation he had suffered when he had to flee from Damascus, lowered from a window on the wall.

Among other things they used the argument that St Paul did not claim maintenance from the Christians as did 'true' apostles. St Paul felt obliged to defend himself against this calumny. His 'jealousy' is really a fear that these false apostles would alienate the Corinthians not only from love and esteem for him but also from the true Gospel. And the Corinthians, fickle and unruly as they were, would be capable even of this.

Note the irony and paradox: the Corinthians reproach Paul with not having made himself chargeable to them, and yet run after those false prophets who exploit and cheat them.

84 Paul gives his reasons for boasting
(11, 21-33; 12, 1-10)

11, [21] But whatever any one dares to boast of—I am speaking as a fool—I also dare to boast of that. [22] Are they Hebrews? So am I. Are they Israelites? So am I. Are they descendants of Abraham? So am I. [23] Are they servants of Christ? I am a better one—I am talking like a madman—with far greater labours, far more imprisonments, with countless beatings, and often near death. [24] Five times I have received at the hands of the Jews the forty lashes less one. [25] Three times I have been beaten with rods; once I was stoned. Three times I have been shipwrecked; a night and a day I have been adrift at sea; [26] on frequent journeys, in danger from rivers, danger from robbers, danger from my own people, danger from Gentiles, danger in the city, danger in the wilderness, danger at sea, danger from false brethren; [27] in toil and hardship, through many a sleepless night, in hunger and thirst, often without food, in cold and exposure. [28] And, apart from other things, there is the daily pressure upon me of my anxiety for all the churches. [29] Who is weak, and I am not weak? Who is made to fall, and I am not indignant?

[30] If I must boast, I will boast of the things that show my weakness. [31] The God and Father of the Lord Jesus, he who is blessed for ever, knows that I do not lie. [32] At Damascus, the governor under King Aretas guarded the city of Damascus in order to seize me, [33] but I was let down in a basket through a window in the wall, and escaped his hands.

12, [1] I must boast; there is nothing to be gained by it, but I will go on to visions and revelations of the Lord. [2] I know a man in Christ who fourteen years ago was caught up to the third heaven—whether in the body or out of the body I do not know, God knows. ³ And I know that this man was caught up into Paradise—whether in the body or out of the body I do not know, God knows—⁴ and he heard things that cannot be told, which man may not utter. ⁵ On behalf of this man I will boast, but on my own behalf I will not boast, except of my weaknesses. ⁶ Though if I wish to boast, I shall not be a fool, for I shall be speaking the truth. But I refrain from it, so that no one may think more of me than he sees in me or hears from me. ⁷ And to keep me from being too elated by the abundance of revelations, a thorn was given me in the flesh, a messenger of Satan, to harass me, to keep me from being too elated. ⁸ Three times I besought the Lord about this, that it should leave me; ⁹ but he said to me, "My grace is sufficient for you, for my power is made perfect in weakness." I will all the more gladly boast of my weaknesses, that the power of Christ may rest upon me. ¹⁰ For the sake of Christ, then, I am content with weaknesses, insults, hardships, persecutions, and calamities; for when I am weak, then I am strong.

St Paul knows very well that boasting is madness, foolishness. But he is obliged by the Corinthians to boast because that is the only argument they understand. They believe Paul's detractors, though they have so many reasons for respecting the apostle. So Paul must enumerate all the reasons which give him authority, his credentials as it were. So we have this wonderful page of autobiography.

Note: 'Forty lashes less one' refers to the Jewish custom of inflicting the punishment of flogging; since the law of Moses forbade giving more than forty

lashes, for fear of breaking it they gave thirty-nine only. The incident at Damascus took place a little after the conversion (see No. 25). Aretas IV, king of the Nabatean Arabs, had ruled Damascus for some time. It was a great humiliation for Paul to have to flee in that way.

The 'thorn in the flesh' was not a temptation on the moral plane but a physical disability, perhaps a recurring illness which troubled the apostle, perhaps a very painful physiological reaction to those mystical experiences (raptures, visions) to which Paul had referred a little earlier.

From St Paul's Letter to the Galatians

The region of Galatia.

Galatia properly so-called was the district inhabited by the Galatians, who were a group of Gauls who in the fourth century B.C. invaded Asia Minor and settled at Ancyra (today Ankara) and in the surrounding mountains. But Galatia was also the name of the Roman province which included the regions further south called Pisidia and Lycaonia where St Paul had founded churches during the first missionary journey (see Nos. 38, 39 and 40). Probably we are here concerned not with those churches but with the Galatians properly so-called. St Paul had stayed among them because of an illness during the second journey; they were a simple and extremely friendly race who received the Gospel gladly.

St Paul must soon have left them, but he saw them again when he revisited them during the third journey (see No. 61). Some time afterwards these Galatians were however visited by some Jewish-Christians of the kind who taught 'Unless you are circumcized according to the custom of Moses, you cannot be saved'. This question had already been decided but the Galatians knew nothing of it and believed the new preachers, or at least were much perturbed by this doctrine, which was new to them.

St Paul heard of these matters during his three months' stay at Corinth towards the end of the third journey (see No. 65). He wrote this Letter in a vigorous and emotional style.

The almost exclusive subject of the Letter is justification by means of faith in Christ without recourse to the practices of the Mosaic Law. In certain ways it is the preface to the basic subject of the letter to the Romans which he was to write a little later. This was in the winter of the year 57-58.

A shepherd camp near Kayseri, the ancient Caesarea in Cappadocia. On the vast plateau, scorched by the sun, the inhabitants today are still shepherds and get their living from the pastures. St Paul referred to these pastoral scenes in his speech to the elders of Miletus (Acts 20,28-29; see No. 68).

85 Introduction (1, 1-10)

¹ Paul, an apostle—not from men nor through man, but through Jesus Christ and God the Father, who raised him from the dead— ² and all the brethren who are with me,

To the churches of Galatia:

³ Grace to you and peace from God the Father and our Lord Jesus Christ, ⁴ who gave himself for our sins to deliver us from the present evil age, according to the will of our God and Father; ⁵ to whom be the glory for ever and ever. Amen.

⁶ I am astonished that you are so quickly deserting him who called you in the grace of Christ and turning to a different gospel—⁷ not that there is another gospel, but there are some who trouble you and want to pervert the gospel of Christ. ⁸ But even if we, or an angel from heaven, should preach to you a gospel contrary to that which we preached to you, let him be accursed. ⁹ As we have said before, so now I say again, If any one is preaching to you a gospel contrary to that which you received, let him be accursed.

¹⁰ Am I now seeking the favour of men, or of God? Or am I trying to please men? If I were still pleasing men, I should not be a servant of Christ.

The beginning of the Letter to the Galatians in the Vatican Codex (fourth century).

86 St Paul's Gospel comes from revelation
(1, 11-24)

[11] For I would have you know, brethren, that the gospel which was preached by me is not man's gospel. [12] For I did not receive it from man, or was I taught it, but it came through a revelation of Jesus Christ. [13] For you have heard of my former life in Judaism, how I persecuted the church of God violently and tried to destroy it; [14] and I advanced in Judaism beyond many of my own age among my people, so extremely zealous was I for the traditions of my fathers. [15] But when he who had set me apart before I was born, and had called me through his grace, [16] was pleased to reveal his Son to me, in order that I might preach him among the Gentiles, I did not confer with flesh and blood, [17] nor did I go up to Jerusalem to those who were apostles before me, but I went away into Arabia; and again I returned to Damascus.

[18] Then after three years I went up to Jerusalem to visit Cephas, and remained with him fifteen days. [19] But I saw none of the other apostles except James the Lord's brother. [20] (In what I am writing to you, before God, I do not lie!) [21] Then I went into the regions of Syria and Cilicia. [22] And I was still not known by sight to the churches of Christ in Judea; [23] they only heard it said, "He who once persecuted us is now preaching the faith he once tried to destroy." [24] And they glorified God because of me.

The first part of the Letter to the Galatians is autobiographical: the Apostle tells of the first events after his conversion to show the authenticity of his apostolic mission and the genuineness of 'his Gospel' that is, of his way of interpreting the call of pagans to faith in Christ without submitting to circumcision and the Jewish law. It was a direct *revelation received at the very beginning of his conversion. The others could add nothing to it. For the facts to which he refers see Nos. 24, 25 and 26. Cephas, or better Kephas (a rock), is the Aramaic name of Peter: this 'visit' shows his pre-eminent position in the Church. James, called 'the Lord's brother' was Jesus' cousin; his mother, called 'Mary of*

James' was among the devout women who were present at the crucifixion of Jesus: that this was probably the apostle James, called the Less, follows from this passage where he is mentioned with Peter and, a little earlier, with Peter and John.

87 Paul's Gospel is recognized by the Apostles (2, 1-10)

[1] Then after fourteen years I went up—again to Jerusalem with Barnabas, taking Titus along with me. [2] I went up by revelation; and I laid before them (but privately before those who were of repute) the gospel which I preach among the Gentiles, lest somehow I should be running or had run in vain. [3] But even Titus, who was with me, was not compelled to be circumcised. though he was a Greek. [4] But because of false brethren secretly brought in, who slipped in to spy out our freedom which we have in Christ Jesus, that they might bring us into bondage—[5] to them we did not yield submission even for a moment, that the truth of the gospel might be preserved for you. [6] And from those who were reputed to be something (what they were makes no difference to me; God shows no partiality)—those, I say, who were of repute added nothing to me; [7] but on the contrary, when they saw that I had been entrusted with the gospel to the uncircumcised, just as Peter had been entrusted with the gospel to the circumcised [8] (for he who worked through Peter for the mission to the circumcised worked through me also for the Gentiles), [9] and when they perceived the grace that was given to me, James and Cephas and John, who were reputed to be pillars, gave to me and Barnabas the right hand of fellowship, that we should go to the Gentiles and they to the circumcised; [10] only they would have us remember the poor, which very thing I was eager to do.

St Paul puts on record the fact that on the occasion of the Council of Jerusalem (see No. 42) the responsible leaders of the Church found themselves in agreement with Paul's teaching, and with his programme of evangelizing the pagans. Certainly,

Iconium, today Konya. This city of Asia Minor was a scene of Paul's missionary activity. Today the only memory of his stay that remains is this Catholic Church dedicated in honour of the Apostle.

there were some 'false brethren', that is obstinate Judaizers who, knowing of the pagan origin of Paul's disciple, Titus, insisted that he should be circumcised. But Paul did not yield and the Apostles took his side. In this text there is reference again to the collection for the poor in Jerusalem (see No. 81) which demonstrates the bonds of charity between the two communities, converted pagan and Jewish-Christian, in spite of their difference of origin and customs.

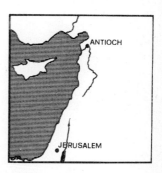

Antioch in Syria where Peter, coming from Jerusalem, met Paul.

88 The meeting with Peter at Antioch (2, 11-21)

[11] But when Cephas came to Antioch I opposed him to his face, because he stood condemned. [12] For before certain men came from James, he ate with the Gentiles; but when they came he drew back and separated himself, fearing the circumcision party. [13] And with him the rest of the Jews acted insincerely, so that even Barnabas was carried away by their insincerity. [14] But when I saw that they were not straightforward about the truth of the gospel, I said to Cephas before them all, "If you, though a Jew, live like a Gentile and not like a Jew, how can you compel the Gentiles to live like Jews?" [15] We ourselves, who are Jews by birth and not Gentile sinners, [16] yet who know that a man is not justified by works of the law but through faith in Jesus

Ancyra, today Ankara. This city, now the capital of Turkey, was an important commercial centre and, in the time of Augustus, became the chief town of the Roman province of Galatia.

Christ, even we have believed in Christ Jesus, in order to be justified by faith in Christ, and not by works of the law, because by works of the law shall no one be justified. [17] But if, in our endeavour to be justified in Christ, we ourselves were found to be sinners, is Christ then an agent of sin? Certainly not! [18] But if I build up again those things which I tore down, then I prove myself a transgressor. [19] For I through the law died to the law, that I might live to God. [20] I have been crucified with Christ; it is no longer I who live, but Christ who lives in me; and the life I now live in the flesh I live by faith in the Son of God, who loved me and gave himself for me. [21] I do not nullify the grace of God; for if justification were through the law, then Christ died to no purpose.

In this passage the 'pagans' are Christians converted from paganism while the 'Jews' are Christians of Jewish origin. In the community at Jerusalem over which the apostle James (the 'Lord's brother') presided the Jewish-Christians followed the practices laid down by the Law of Moses, specially with regard to clean and unclean foods and the obligation to avoid contact with the pagans. By contrast, even the Jewish-Christians at Antioch associated with other Christians of pagan origin, disregarding as unnecessary and worthless the Jewish rules about 'clean' and 'unclean'. Even the Apostle Peter (Cephas), when he came to Antioch, immediately adapted himself to this custom, all the more readily since to him individually, in the vision at Joppa (see Nos. 29 and 31) it had been revealed that these legal distinctions between clean and unclean,

circumcised and uncircumcised should no longer persist between Christians. Yet when certain Judeo-Christians arrived from Jerusalem, whom Peter knew well for their fanatical attachment to Jewish customs, he no longer went to table with Christians who had come from paganism, so as not to irritate their susceptibility. Other Jewish-Christians at Antioch, and even Barnabas, followed his example.

The matter in itself was merely disciplinary and contained no statement of principle. But, in addition to resulting in a lack of brotherly love (Christians divided into two groups which did not eat together), this way of behaving could be interpreted as the acknowledgement of a difference between circumcised and uncircumcised on the doctrinal plane, as though the former were more perfect or more in order than the latter. Therefore

Iconium, today Konya. This was one of the largest commercial centres of the Anatolian plateau and is mentioned many times in the Acts. In the places where St Paul had founded his flourishing communities, Christianity has today almost completely disappeared. In the photograph: the Melana Mosque, an ancient monastery of the dancing Dervishes.

Paul, who had immediately seen the danger of such consequences, withstood Peter in the face of all, in public debate, and complained both of his practical behaviour and of the claims of the Judaizers, about which Peter had no need to be convinced. Peter humbly acknowledged his fault.

Paul repeated his arguments in very precise form to the Galatians. They can be summarized thus:

1) Pagans and Jews are equally sinners and need to be saved, to be 'justified', that is to become 'righteous'.

2) The Old Testament Law could not bring this salvation.

3) Therefore pagans and Jews, equally described as sinners, without any other remedy, find salvation in faith in Jesus Christ (see No. 95).

4) By belonging to Jesus Christ, pagans and Jews become new beings, purified and inwardly transformed. It would be nonsense for the Jews to go back to look for something positive in the old Law, still more nonsensical to try to force converted pagans to keep that Law which had been unable to save the Jews.

To this basic reasoning St Paul added two arguments 'ex absurdo' i.e. based on the absurdity of the conclusions which would be drawn:

a) If we were mistaken in abandoning the Law to seek salvation in Christ, then Christ would be the cause ('agent') of our sin.

b) If there had been a Law truly capable of giving justification, then it would have been unnecessary for Christ to come and die on the Cross for our sins.

In the second part of the Letter, doctrinal in character, these arguments are repeated and developed, so as to persuade the Galatians to give up the errors of the Judaizers.

89 Baptized in Christ, you have put on Christ
(3, 23-29)

[23] Now before faith came, we were confined under the law, kept under restraint until faith should be revealed. [24] So that the law was our custodian until Christ came, that we might be justified by faith. [25] But now that faith has come, we are no longer under a custodian; [26] for in Christ Jesus you are all sons of God, through faith. [27] For as many of you as were baptized into Christ have put on Christ. [28] There is neither Jew nor Greek, there is neither slave nor free, there is neither male

Silla, near Konya. In the poor Turkish village an ancient Byzantine Church, abandoned and now in ruins, recalls St Paul's journey through these places.

nor female; for you are all one in Christ Jesus. ²⁹ And if you are Christ's, then you are Abraham's offspring, heirs according to promise.

The Law, that is the collection of the enactments of the Old Testament, had not become worthless, but it had a preparatory character; its external and coercive rules were a sort of prison, which prevented God's people from escaping, mingling with the pagans and so losing their ability to receive the Messiah. St Paul compares the Law to a 'custodian', that is to that servant who had the task of leading the pupils to the master and looking after them until his arrival. But once *the Messiah, Jesus Christ, has come, there is no further need for a custodian, that is for the Law. Nor can its function of imprisoning, i.e. segregating God's people, continue. In fact baptism radically transforms the pagans as it does the Jews into children of God, spiritually united to Christ. So the descendants of Abraham, the father of the multitudinous people of God, are not the Jews only, but all those who belong to the perfect 'seed of Abraham', Jesus.*

90 You are no longer a slave, but a son
(4, 1-7)

¹ I mean that the heir, as long as he is a child, is no better than a slave, though he is the owner of all the estate; ² but he is under guardians and trustees until the date set by the father. ³ So with us; when we were children, we were slaves to the elemental spirits of the universe. ⁴ But when the time had fully come God sent forth his Son, born of woman, born under the law, ⁵ to redeem those who were under the law, so that we might receive adoption as sons. ⁶ And because you are sons, God has sent the Spirit of his Son into our hearts, crying, "Abba! Father!" ⁷ So through God you are no longer a slave but a son, and if a son then an heir.

An argument parallel to the preceding one. The 'elemental *spirits of the universe' are the external and coercive rules of*

A typical view of the Anatolian plateau in the region of ancient Galatia, made up of broad plains bordered by rounded hills. The grazing of flocks, often nomadic, is still widely practised. Long treks over these desolate lands may have been the cause of the illness which forced St Paul to stay among the Galatians (see Gal, 4,13).

Jewish and pagan institutions.

They corresponded to the period of minority of the future sons of God. But the coming of Christ inaugurated the period of maturity and so of freedom. The Incarnation is portrayed as the beginning of redemption; the Son of God became son of a woman so that we might become sons of God: he became subject to the Law of Moses to free us from the slavery of the Law. It is his sharing in our poverty which makes us capable of sharing in his wealth. The Holy Spirit who dwells in the baptized obliges them to address the Father as 'Abba', either inwardly or using the gift of tongues (see No. 78), and in Palestinian language this was the familiar name for 'father' (see No. 98).

91   'I could wish to be present with you' (4, 12-20)

¹² Brethren, I beseech you, become as I am, for I also have become as you are. You did me no wrong; ¹³ you know it was because of a bodily ailment that I preached the gospel to you at first; ¹⁴ and though my condition was a trial to you, you did not scorn or despise me, but received me as an angel of God, as Christ Jesus. ¹⁵ What has become of the satisfaction you felt? For I bear you witness that, if possible, you would have plucked out your eyes and given them to me. ¹⁶ Have I then become your enemy by telling you the truth? ¹⁷ They make much of you, but for no good purpose; they want to shut you out, that you may make much of them. ¹⁸ For a good purpose it is always good to be made much of, and not only when I am present with you. ¹⁹ My little children, with whom I am again in travail until Christ be formed in you! ²⁰ I could wish to be present with you now and to change my tone, for I am perplexed about you.

A moving memory of the generous welcome the Galatians had given Paul. The mutual attachment of the faithful and their pastor is a good thing but only if it is born of a right intention. Such was their attachment to Paul but this is not the case of these new teachers. 'Become as I am ...' St Paul had renounced

the advantages which he might have been given among his fellow-citizens if he had remained attached to the Mosaic Law and the traditions of the fathers (see No. 73).

92 True liberty in charity
(5, 13-26)

[13] For you were called to freedom, brethren; only do not use your freedom as an opportunity for the flesh, but through love be servants of one another. [14] For the whole law is fulfilled in one word, "You shall love your neighbour as yourself." [15] But if you bite and devour one another take heed that you are not consumed by one another.

[16] But I say, walk by the Spirit, and do not gratify the desires of the flesh. [17] For the desires of the flesh are against the Spirit, and the desires of the Spirit are against the flesh; for these are opposed to each other, to prevent you from doing what you would. [18] But if you are led by the Spirit you are not under the law. [19] Now the works of the flesh are plain: immorality, impurity, licentiousness, [20] idolatry, sorcery, emnity, strife, jealousy, anger, selfishness, dissension, party spirit, [21] envy, drunkenness, carousing, and the like. I warn you, as I warned you before, that those who do such things shall not inherit the kingdom of God. [22] But the fruit of the Spirit is love, joy, peace, patience, kindness, goodness, faithfulness, [23] gentleness, self-control; against such there is no law. [24] And those who belong to Christ Jesus have crucified the flesh with its passions and desires.

[25] If we live by the Spirit, let us also walk by the Spirit. [26] Let us have no self-conceit, no provoking of one another, no envy of one another.

The third part of the Letter is a series of moral precepts. The

freedom to which St Paul often refers is not licence to do what one likes, but an aptitude for doing good by the power of the Holy Spirit. With this freedom is contrasted a two-fold slavery, the slavery of sin by which he who is under the power of sin can never succeed in freeing himself, and the slavery of the Law, which threatens external punishment and shows the evil to be avoided, but does not give one the spiritual power to conquer the evil (see No. 97).

'Flesh and Spirit', not only in this context but generally in St Paul's language, are not the body and the soul; they are respectively the human mentality ('flesh') and the supernatural mentality ('spirit'), the instinct of faith coming from grace and from the presence of the Holy Spirit. 'Flesh' is not therefore merely sin which expresses itself in the body, impurity, drunkenness, etc. but also and even more, pride, selfishness and malice, as we see in his list of 'works of the flesh' contrasted with 'the fruit of the Spirit'.

The Pauline text of the Letter to the Galatians, 5,13-14 (first column on the left) in the Vatican Codex (4th century).

93 Conclusion of the Letter
(6, 7-18)

[7] Do not be deceived; God is not mocked, for whatever a man sows, that he will also reap. [8] For he who sows to his own flesh will from the flesh reap corruption; but he who sows to the Spirit will from the Spirit reap eternal life. [9] And let us not grow weary in welldoing, for in due season we shall reap, if we do not lose heart. [10] So then, as we have opportunity, let us do good to all men, and especially to those who are of the household of faith.

[11] See with what large letters I am writing to you with my own hand. [12] It is those who want to make a good showing in the flesh that would compel you to be circumcised, and only in order that they may not be persecuted for the cross of Christ. [13] For even those who receive circumcision do not themselves keep the law, but they desire to have you circumcised that they may glory in your flesh. [14] But far be it from me to glory except in the cross of our Lord Jesus Christ, by which the world has been crucified to me, and I to the world. [15] For neither circumcision counts for anything, nor uncircumcision, but a new creation. [16] Peace and mercy be upon all who walk by this rule, upon the Israel of God.

[17] Henceforth let no man trouble me; for I bear on my body the marks of Jesus.

[18] The grace of our Lord Jesus Christ be with your spirit, brethren. Amen.

St Paul adds with his own hand the final greeting, with some vigorous and impassioned assertions which summarize the basic teaching of the Letter. The 'marks of Jesus' to which the Apostle refers are the scars of scourging and the signs of sufferings borne for the Gospel: as the brand impressed by red-hot iron stamps the slave as belonging to his master, so these 'marks' prove that Paul belonged to Christ, and authenticate all his apostolic work.

From St Paul's Letter to the Romans

The beginning of the Letter to the Romans in the Vatican Codex (fourth century).

The Letter to the Romans was written by St Paul during his three months' stay at Corinth, a little before the spring of the year 58, when he was setting out for Jerusalem at the end of the third missionary journey (see No. 65). Rome, the celebrated capital of the Empire, had a flourishing Christian community, already of long standing and 'known in all the world'.

Paul spoke with respect of the Roman Christians: they were not 'his' and perhaps by that time St Peter had already been at work in the organization of that Church. On the other hand St Paul had no cause for controversy with them, as is seen from the discursive nature of the long doctrinal exposition which occupies a great part of the Letter. For a long time St Paul had wished to visit the heart of the Empire and now the time for realizing his plan was approaching. Returning from Jerusalem he was to repair to Rome and thence to Spain in the far west (see No. 100). The Letter then was intended as a sort of introduction. On this occasion he compiled it in a form which was, as it were, the exposition and theological demonstration of 'his Gospel', embodied in his most characteristic message; that is, that Christ is the only hope of salvation for all men, without distinction of Jews and pagans.

After the preface in which he announces his subject (No. 94) the Letter divides into two parts, the former of a doctrinal character (Chapters 1-11), the second of a moral content (12, 1 - 15, 13). The epilogue (15, 14 - 16, 27) contains personal news and greetings.

Rome. The Roman forum with the Capitol in the background. St Paul who, when writing to the Romans, expresses his wish to go and visit them, did not look with contempt on these monuments of paganism for he judged the Jews as sinners no less than the pagans: '**All have sinned and fall short of the glory of God**' (Rom. 3,23).

94 Introduction
(1, 1-15)

¹ Paul, a servant of Jesus Christ, called to be an apostle, set apart for the gospel of God ² which he promised beforehand through his prophets in the holy scriptures, ³ the gospel concerning his Son, who was descended from David according to the flesh ⁴ and designated Son of God in power according to the Spirit of holiness by his resurrection from the dead, Jesus Christ our Lord, ⁵ through whom we have received grace and apostleship to bring about the obedience of faith for the sake of his name among all the nations, ⁶ including yourselves who are called to belong to Jesus Christ;

⁷ To all God's beloved in Rome, who are called to be saints: Grace to you and peace from God our Father and the Lord Jesus Christ.

⁸ First, I thank my God through Jesus Christ for all of you, because your faith is proclaimed in all the world. ⁹ For God is my witness, whom I serve with my spirit in the gospel of his Son, that without ceasing I mention you always in my prayers, ¹⁰ asking that somehow by God's will I may now at last succeed in coming to you. ¹¹ For I long to see you, that I may impart to you some spiritual gift to strengthen you, ¹² that is, that we may be mutually encouraged by each other's faith, both yours and mine. ¹³ I want you to know, brethren, that I have often intended to come to you (but thus far have been prevented) in order that I may reap some harvest among you as well as among the rest of the Gentiles. ¹⁴ I am under obligation both to Greeks and to barbarians, both to the wise and to the foolish: ¹⁵ so I am eager to preach the gospel to you also who are in Rome.

95 Justification by faith
(1, 16-17; 3, 20-30)

1, ¹⁶ For I am not ashamed of the gospel: it is the power of God for salvation to every one who has faith, to the Jew first and also to the Greek. ¹⁷ For in it the righteousness of God is

Rome, Roman forum: the Curial building, the hall in which sat the Senate, with, in the background, the Mamertine prison. St Paul, a Roman citizen, was always loyal in his encounters with authority. He wrote to Timothy: '**Let prayers be made for all men, for kings and all who are in high positions**' (1 Tim. 2,1-2).

revealed through faith for faith; as it is written, "He who through faith is righteous shall live."

3, ²⁰ For no human being will be justified in his sight by works of the law, since through the law comes knowledge of sin.

²¹ But now the righteousness of God has been manifested apart from law, although the law and the prophets bear witness to it, ²² the righteousness of God through faith in Jesus Christ for all who believe. For there is no distinction; ²³ since all have sinned and fall short of the glory of God, ²⁴ they are justified by his grace as a gift, through the redemption which is in Christ Jesus, ²⁵ whom God put forward as an expiation by his blood, to be received by faith. This was to show God's righteousness, because in his divine forbearance he had passed over former sins; ²⁶ it was to prove at the present time that he himself is righteous and that he justifies him who has faith in Jesus.

²⁷ Then what becomes of our boasting? It is excluded. On what principle? On the principle of works? No, but on the principle of faith. ²⁸ For we hold that a man is justified by faith apart from works of law. ²⁹ Or is God the God of Jews only? Is he not the God of Gentiles also? Yes, of Gentiles also, ³⁰ since God is one; and he will justify the circumcised on the ground of their faith and the uncircumcised through their faith.

A passage from the prophet Habakkuk (2, 4): 'The righteous shall live (i.e. be saved) by his faith' gives St Paul the starting point for stating his subject, which he puts forward as the keystone of the Gospel. In fact the 'gospel' is the joyful announcement of the plan of salvation willed by God and is also the 'power of God' since by inspiring faith it brings about salvation. The 'justice of God' in St Paul's language is not 'revengeful justice' which punishes, but 'saving just-ice', that is God's fidelity to his promises, to his benevolent plan of leading men to salvation. St Paul shows that God's way of 'making man righteous', that is, enabling him to emerge from sin and become what He wishes him to be, is not the Law, but Faith.

If God had chosen order, the system of the Law, he would have given the description 'righteous' and the reward of eternal life to every man who had obeyed the

Law of God. In that case man would have been able to boast of being himself the author of his own salvation, of having made himself 'righteous' by his own efforts.

But God did not wish to choose this system, for nothing is further from the divine plan than the pride of a man who claims to become God's creditor. There is also here an actual disproportion; however much a man does to make himself righteous, at best he will be a good man (in the natural order); he cannot leap the chasm to become a 'son of God', that is in a living communion with God, which is the only 'salvation', the 'eternal life' prepared by God for men (in the supernatural order).

Instead God chose the system of faith, the only means by which man enters into God's plan and so crosses the chasm from the natural to the supernatural order. 'Faith' means that man recognizes in the first place his own incapacity to attain justification and the 'salvation' willed by God,

and trusts entirely in the divine goodness, believing in the plan revealed by God and recognizing that God wishes to make him 'righteous' as a free gift, out of pure kindness, since man did not deserve this. That is what is meant by the word 'grace', a free gift. The Gospel shows more clearly the divine plan which is centred in the redemptive work of Christ. 'Justification' first of all means passing from the state of sin to the state of friendship with God: so Jesus with his Blood is the 'propitiation', that is the instrument of the expiation of the sins of the world. The word 'propitiation' indicates the golden cover of the Ark of the Covenant, on which the High Priest sprinkled the blood of expiatory sacrifices for all the sins of the people. This was a purely symbolical rite (see No. 142) whereas, instead, the death of Jesus on the Cross is the only sacrifice which can truly expiate the sins of all those who adhere to him by faith. Faith in the divine plan is therefore also faith in the person and work of Christ.

Reconstruction of the Ark of the Covenant with the 'Propitiation' above it.

The Law in this context is the sum total of the prescriptions of the Old Testament, including the Decalogue, but stands also for all moral laws which impose duty from without, as an obligation sanctioned by punishment.

Such a Law does not lead to salvation because, although it exposes evil, it does not give the power to avoid it (see No. 97). The error of a section of Judaism and of Judaizing Christians was the over-valuation of the Law of the Old Testament as being the means given by God to man so that he might work out his own justification. St Paul demonstrates the falsity of that claim with the words of Psalm 142 (143) verse 2: 'No man living is righteous before thee' and refers to our sad experience of the universality of sin.

We must understand precisely what St Paul means when he asserts that justification is ensured by means of faith 'without the works of the Law'. The reference here is to the starting-point for becoming 'righteous': now the starting-point is sin, that is, the breaking of God's Law. But even supposing that a person had not yet begun to sin

(there is always original sin, see No. 96) the works of the Law without faith, cannot enable him to cross the gulf that divides the natural from the supernatural order. All those who in the Old Testament were 'justified', were saved by 'grace', by God's free gift, by virtue of their more or less explicit faith and not by virtue of the Mosaic Law. So Abraham was counted 'righteous' for his act of faith, before circumcision and before any institution of the Mosaic Law, and, like Abraham, every one else, for the divine plan has always remained the same.

But this 'without the works of the Law' does not mean that the Christian, once 'justified', does not need to practise good works. That would go against two very distinct statements of St Paul: first, that the man who is justified is inwardly transformed and becomes the temple of the Holy Spirit (see Nos. 89, 90 and 98); secondly, that the Christian must continually strive to be worthy of the vocation to holiness, to which he has been called, by means of the exercise of charity and of all good works (see No. 99 and the moral teaching of all the Letters).

96   Liberation from the sin of Adam and from death (5, 12-21)

[12] Therefore as sin came into the world through one man and death through sin, and so death spread to all men because all men sinned—[13] sin indeed was in the world before the law was given, but sin is not counted where there is no law. [14] Yet death reigned from Adam to Moses, even over those whose sins were not like the transgression of Adam, who was a type of the one who was to come.

[15] But the free gift is not like the trespass. For if many died through one man's trespass, much more have the grace of God and the free gift in the grace of that one man Jesus Christ abounded for many. [16] And the free gift is not like the effect of that one man's sin. For the judgment following one trespass brought condemnation, but the free gift following many trespasses brings justification. [17] If, because of one man's trespass, death reigned through that one man, much more will those who receive the abundance of grace and the free gift of righteousness reign in life through the one man Jesus Christ. [18] Then as one man's trespass led to condemnation for all men, so one man's act of righteousness leads to acquittal and life for all men. [19] For as by one man's disobedience many were made sinners, so by one man's obedience many will be made righteous. [20] Law came in, to increase the trespass; but where sin increased, grace abounded all the more, [21] so that, as sin reigned in death, grace also might reign through righteousness to eternal life through Jesus Christ our Lord.

This is the most important passage for demonstrating the doctrine of original sin. It is set however in a context which brings *out pre-eminently the greatness of Christ's redemption and the generosity of God's plan: man's sin cannot prevent God from realizing his plan of salvation. These ideas are interwoven here:*

1) The personal conduct of Adam (fall, disobedience, transgression) introduced into the world 'sin', by which 'all were made sinners'. It is a state of estrangement from God (in contrast to the 'righteousness' brought by Christ), which works like a leaven of evil and causes the multiplication of actual sins. The result of sin was death, understood in its fullest sense: physical death which is a sign of estrangement from God and which would be final but for the coming of redemption. It is a case of original sin existing in every man born of Adam by reason of the personal (originating) sin of Adam, the father of the human race.

2) Christ is the new Adam, the Head of redeemed mankind, and in the order of salvation He exercizes a power similar to that of the old Adam. Over against

Adam's act of disobedience is set Christ's act of obedience; over against damnation, grace; over against 'sin', righteousness; over against death, eternal life.

3) But St Paul does not say that the efficacy of the act by which Christ brought salvation is equal to the efficacy of the act by which Adam brought ruin. He repeatedly asserts and proves that the efficacy of Christ was incomparably greater: good decisively overcomes evil because it is 'God's gift'.

4) There are periods in the history of sin: before the Mosaic Law there was a certain ignorance, but that did not prevent the domination of sin and death. The Law could not provide a remedy; in fact, the knowledge of sin makes sins more deliberate and more serious (see No. 97). With Christ begins the age of victory over sin and death.

97   Liberation from the Law
       (7, 5-25)

[5] While we were living in the flesh, our sinful passions, aroused by the law, were at work in our members to bear fruit for death. [6] But now we are discharged from the law, dead to that which held us captive, so that we serve not under the old written code but in the new life of the Spirit.

[7] What then shall we say? That the law is sin? By no means! Yet, if it had not been for the law, I should not have known sin. I should not have known what it is to covet if the law had not said, "You shall not covet." [8] But sin, finding opportunity

in the commandment, wrought in me all kinds of covetousness. Apart from the law sin lies dead. ⁹ I was once alive apart from the law, but when the commandment came, sin revived and I died; ¹⁰ the very commandment which promised life proved to be death to me. ¹¹ For sin, finding opportunity in the commandment, deceived me and by it killed me. ¹² So the law is holy, and the commandment is holy and just and good.

¹³ Did that which is good, then, bring death to me? By no means! It was sin, working death in me through what is good, in order that sin might be shown to be sin, and through the commandment might become sinful beyond measure. ¹⁴ We know that the law is spiritual; but I am carnal, sold under sin. ¹⁵ I do not understand my own actions. For I do not do what I want, but I do the very thing I hate. ¹⁶ Now if I do what I do not want, I agree that the law is good. ¹⁷ So then it is no longer I that do it, but sin which dwells within me. ¹⁸ For I know that nothing good dwells within me, that is, in my flesh. I can will what is right, but I cannot do it. ¹⁹ For I do not do the good I want, but the evil I do not want is what I do. ²⁰ Now if I do what I do not want, it is no longer I that do it, but sin which dwells within me.

²¹ So I find it to be a law that when I want to do right, evil lies close at hand. ²² For I delight in the law of God, in my immost self, ²³ but I see in my members another law at war with the law of my mind and making me captive to the law of sin which dwells in my members. ²⁴ Wretched man that I am! Who will deliver me from this body of death? ²⁵ Thanks be to God through Jesus Christ our Lord! So then, I of myself serve the law of God with my mind, but with my flesh I serve the law of sin.

In this passage it is first stated that by virtue of our redemption in Christ we have been liberated from the painful situation in which we found ourselves as the result of our submission to the Law. Then to make us understand the value of this aspect of redemption, there is a description of the desperate situation of a man faced with the Law but without the help of grace coming from Christ.

Note carefully, St Paul is not speaking of his present situation, for which indeed he thanks God, but of the condition in which he found himself before his conversion. He personalizes in himself the experience of all mankind, beginning with Adam. The Law here is not only the sum of the Mosaic prescriptions, but also the Decalogue and the moral law itself presented as an imposition from without.

The purpose of the Law is to make us know what is good and what is bad, in the form of precepts and prohibitions. It is therefore good in itself and indeed necessary for the moral education of mankind. But it has no power in itself to direct the will in the right way. So it collides with the innermost proclivities of man and thus exasperates him, for we are most inclined to things which are forbidden. So instead of curbing sin it makes it more deliberate and more serious. 'Sin' in this passage is personified: it is the possibility of evil, already present in Adam when he was innocent, 'apart from the law sin lies dead... but when the commandment came, sin revived'. It

is then the positive tendency to evil, which follows from original sin and from sins previously committed.

Thus the Law reveals an inner schism in man. It speaks to his reason and man understands the authority of the Law. But he feels 'another law' in himself, contrary to God's law, and ends by choosing sin. St Paul does not deny that in these circumstances freedom of choice persists — otherwise the sinner would not be responsible — but speaks of the ordinary experience of one who is discomfited by the power of evil and so finds himself the slave of sin and also the slave of the Law which continues to threaten him without being able to give him the help he needs.

This passage has a great importance for teachers: Christian education must not be primarily the presentation of an external law, but the bringing about of a lively encounter with Jesus, the source of grace and the incarnation of every ideal of goodness.

98 Object and motives of our hope
(8, 12-39)

¹² So then, brethren, we are debtors, not to the flesh, to live according to the flesh—¹³ for if you live according to the flesh you will die, but if by the Spirit you put to death the deeds of the body you will live. ¹⁴ For all who are led by the Spirit of God are sons of God. ¹⁵ For you did not receive the spirit

of slavery to fall back into fear, but you have received the spirit of sonship. When we cry, "Abba! Father!" [16] it is the Spirit himself bearing witness with our spirit that we are children of God, [17] and if children, then heirs, heirs of God and fellow heirs with Christ, provided we suffer with him in order that we may also be glorified with him.

[18] I consider that the sufferings of this present time are not worth comparing with the glory that is to be revealed to us. [19] For the creation waits with eager longing for the revealing of the sons of God; [20] for the creation was subjected to futility, not of its own will but by the will of him who subjected it in hope; [21] because the creation itself will be set free from its bondage to decay and obtain the glorious liberty of the children of God. [22] We know that the whole creation has been groaning in travail together until now; [23] and not only the creation, but we ourselves, who have the first fruits of the Spirit, groan inwardly as we wait for adoption as sons, the redemption of our bodies. [24] For in this hope we were saved. Now hope that is seen is not hope. For who hopes for what he sees? [25] But if we hope for what we do not see, we wait for it with patience.

[26] Likewise the Spirit helps us in our weakness; for we do not know how to pray as we ought, but the Spirit himself intercedes for us with sighs too deep for words. [27] And he who searches the hearts of men knows what is the mind of the Spirit. because the Spirit intercedes for the saints according to the will of God.

[28] We know that in everything God works for good with those who love him, who are called according to his purpose. [29] For those whom he foreknew he also predestined to be conformed to the image of his Son, in order that he might be the first-born among many brethren. [30] And those whom he predestined he also called; and those whom he called he also justified; and those whom he justified he also glorified.

[31] What then shall we say to this? If God is for us, who is against us? [32] He who did not spare his own Son but gave him up for us all, will he not also give us all things with him? [33] Who shall bring any charge against God's elect? It is God

who justifies; ³⁴ who is to condemn? Is it Christ Jesus, who died, yes, who was raised from the dead, who is at the right hand of God, who indeed intercedes for us? ³⁵ Who shall separate us from the love of Christ? Shall tribulation, or distress, or persecution, or famine, or nakedness, or peril, or sword? ³⁶ As it is written,

"For thy sake we are being killed all the day long;
we are regarded as sheep to be slaughtered."

³⁷ No, in all these things we are more than conquerors through him who loved us. ³⁸ For I am sure that neither death, nor life, nor angels, nor principalities, nor things present, nor things to come, nor powers, ³⁹ nor height, nor depth, nor anything else in all creation, will be able to separate us from the love of God in Christ Jesus our Lord.

The contrast of 'spirit' and 'flesh' in the Christian still remains (see No. 92) because the final transformation of the body has not yet occurred; in fact there still remain the instinctive motions and psychological reflexes bound up with our psycho-physical being. Hence the necessity of 'mortification', that is continually putting to death whatever opposes life 'in the Spirit'. To this moral suffering are added the physical sufferings inherent in the state of the body in a world not yet redeemed.

But the struggle and the suffering are sustained by a joyful hope because:

1) The Spirit who is in us gives us the assurance that we are sons of God (for 'Abba' see No. 90), therefore we already have allotted to us our inheritance, the final possession of glory with Christ.

2) 'Creation', that is the material world which also has a share in our physical being, is in eager expectation of total renewal: it will be the birth of 'new heavens and a new earth' (see the Apocalypse, No. 179). This material world, in so far as it is a part and instrument of man, is in a state of subjection to sin and its consequences: man is the Lord of creation, so that by serving sin he puts creation under the domination of evil.

But the 'redemption of our body', that is the final resurrection, will be accompanied by the liberation of creation. That liberation is by virtue of Christ's redemption, but man, with the help of grace, already anticipates it by living according to the Spirit, and by using his own body and the material forces at his disposal in the service of charity. Such is the cosmic value of Christ's redemption.

3) Our ignorance of prayer must not cut us off from hope, for the Spirit within us intercedes: he is like the soul of our soul and arouses in us aspirations which

cannot be translated into words.
4) We love God and therefore are already predestined for glory and God makes everything serve to bring us to that end. No ex- *ternal power will be able to separate us from the love of God. So there is nothing to fear, so long as we remain in union with Christ.*

99 The Christian's moral duties
(12, 1-21; 13, 8-10)

12. [1] I appeal to you therefore, brethren, by the mercies of God, to present your bodies as a living sacrifice, holy and acceptable to God, which is your spiritual worship. [2] Do not be conformed to this world but be transformed by the renewal of your mind, that you may prove what is the will of God, what is good and acceptable and perfect.

[3] For by the grace given to me I bid every one among you not to think of himself more highly than he ought to think, but to think with sober judgment, each according to the measure of faith which God has assigned him. [4] For as in one body we have many members, and all the members do not have the same function, [5] so we, though many, are one body in Christ, and individually members one of another. [6] Having gifts that differ according to the grace given to us, let us use them: if prophecy, in proportion to our faith; [7] if service, in our serving; he who teaches, in his teaching; [8] he who exhorts, in his exhortation; he who contributes, in liberality; he who gives aid, with zeal; he who does acts of mercy, with cheerfulness.

[9] Let love be genuine; hate what is evil, hold fast to what is good; [10] love one another with brotherly affection; outdo one another in showing honour. [11] Never flag in zeal, be aglow with the Spirit, serve the Lord. [12] Rejoice in your hope, be patient in tribulation, be constant in prayer. [13] Contribute to the needs of the saints, practise hospitality.

[14] Bless those who persecute you; bless and do not curse them. [15] Rejoice with those who rejoice, weep with those who weep. [16] Live in harmony with one another; do not be haughty,

but associate with the lowly; never be conceited. ¹⁷ Repay no one evil for evil, but take thought for what is noble in the sight of all. ¹⁸ If possible, so far as it depends upon you, live peaceably with all. ¹⁹ Beloved, never avenge yourselves, but leave it to the wrath of God; for it is written, "Vengeance is mine, I will repay, says the Lord." ²⁰ No, "if your enemy is hungry, feed him; if he is thirsty, give him drink; for by so doing you will heap burning coals upon his head." ²¹ Do not be overcome by evil, but overcome evil with good.

13, ⁸ Owe no one anything, except to love one another; for he who loves his neighbour has fulfilled the law. ⁹ The commandments, "You shall not commit adultery, You shall not kill, You shall not steal, You shall not covet," and any other commandment, are summed up in this sentence, "You shall love your neighbour as yourself." ¹⁰ Love does no wrong to a neighbour; therefore love is the fulfilling of the law.

The third part of the Letter is composed of moral exhortations. In the passage included here it insists on the unity of souls and on charity which goes so far as to include the love of one's enemies according to the Gospel ideal. In the exhortation to live in peace he again uses the illustration of the body and its members as in the first Letter to the Corinthians (see No. 78).

Here too we have a list of 'charisms', that is, of special gifts and vocations: he is dealing not only with extraordinary phenomena but also with the gifts of serving the community, of helping those in need, of taking up the burden of office and of teaching.

The Church is not a homogeneous lump like a rock of crystal, but a living organism in which the parts, as in every living being, are different, so as to fulfil different functions. No one can live by himself: each receives from others an incalculable amount of good and is expected to give to the community the fruit of his own particular gift.

100 Plans for journeys
(15, 22-33)

²² This is the reason why I have so often been hindered from coming to you. ²³ But now, since I no longer have any room for work in these regions, and since I have longed for many

Jerusalem: the Holy City became St Paul's goal in this last part of his third journey. An obscure presentiment warned him that at Jerusalem he was to undergo many sufferings.
'The Holy Ghost testifies to me that in that city imprisonment and afflictions await me' (Acts 20,23).

years to come to you, [24] I hope to see you in passing as I go to Spain, and to be sped on my journey there by you, once I have enjoyed your company for a little. [25] At present, however, I am going to Jerusalem with aid for the saints. [26] For Macedonia and Achaia have been pleased to make some contribution for the poor among the saints at Jerusalem; [27] they were pleased to do it, and indeed they are in debt to them, for if the Gentiles have come to share in their spiritual blessings, they ought also to be of service to them in material blessings. [28] When therefore I have completed this, and have delivered to them what has been raised, I shall go on by way of you to Spain; [29] and I know that when I come to you I shall come in the fulness of the blessing of Christ.

[30] I appeal to you, brethren, by our Lord Jesus Christ and by the love of the Spirit, to strive together with me in your prayers to God on my behalf, [31] that I may be delivered from the unbelievers in Judea, and that my service for Jerusalem may be acceptable to the saints, [32] so that by God's will I may come to you with joy and be refreshed in your company. [33] The God of peace be with you all. Amen.

St Paul's plan was not to be realized in the way he expected. He was to arrive in Jerusalem with the money collected for the poor of the community, and he found the atmosphere hostile to him. Even among the 'saints' (the Christians) there were those who had reserves about Paul's activities; therefore he desired prayers to be offered that his service 'might be acceptable to the saints'.

At Jerusalem he was to be arrested (see No. 102) and only after two years of imprisonment at Caesarea would he see the realization of his desire to go to Rome, but he was to go there as a prisoner awaiting trial (see Nos. 108 and 112).

END OF ST PAUL'S LETTERS WRITTEN DURING THE THIRD JOURNEY

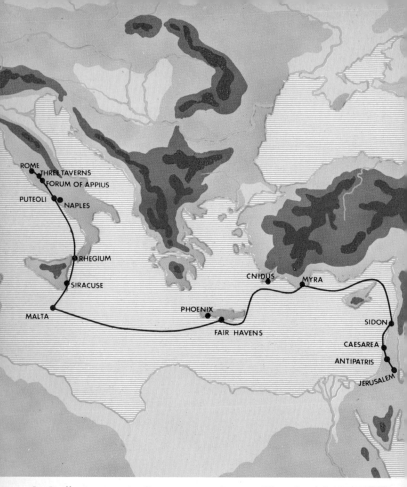

St Paul's journey to Rome as a prisoner. When he left Jerusalem, after a halt at Antipatris, he reached Caesarea where he remained as a prisoner for two years. At Caesarea he took ship and, having touched Sidon and rounded Cyprus, he went ashore at Myra where he was transferred to another ship. Setting sail for Italy, he sailed under the lee of Crete and landed at Fair Havens. In an attempt to reach the harbour of Myra, more suitable for wintering in, the ship was caught in a storm and carried towards Malta where she ran aground. When winter was over, he sailed in another ship for Syracuse and, having called at Rhegium, disembarked at Puteoli whence, by land, he reached Rome.

V. St Paul's arrest, and his trial, from Jerusalem to Caesarea and Rome

101 Arrival at Jerusalem
(Acts 21, 15-26)

[15] After these days we made ready and went up to Jerusalem. [16] And some of the disciples from Caesarea went with us, bringing us to the house of Mnason of Cyprus, an early disciple, with whom we should lodge.

[17] When we had come to Jerusalem, the brethren received us gladly. [18] On the following day Paul went in with us to James; and all the elders were present. [19] After greeting them, he related one by one the things that God had done among the Gentiles through his ministry. [20] And when they heard it, they glorified God. And they said to him, "You see, brother, how many thousands there are among the Jews of those who have believed; they are all zealous for the law, [21] and they have been told about you that you teach all the Jews who are among the Gentiles to forsake Moses, telling them not to circumcise their children or observe the customs. [22] What then is to be done? They will certainly hear that you have come. [23] Do therefore what we tell you. We have four men who are under a vow; [24] take these men and purify yourself along with them and pay their expenses, so that they may shave their heads. Thus all will know that there is nothing in what they have been told about you but that you yourself live in observance of the law. (1) [25] But as for the Gentiles who have believed, we have sent a letter with our judgment that they should abstain from what has been sacrificed to idols and from blood and from what is strangled and from unchastity."

²⁶ Then Paul took the men, and the next day he purified himself with them and went into the temple, to give notice when the days of purification would be fulfilled and the offering presented for every one of them.

(1) The rulers of the Church of Jerusalem, a very conservative group, (see p. 115, the early church in Jerusalem) were concerned to prevent the creation of divisions, at least in practical matters. The vow which is referred to is the vow of the Nazirite (see Note to No. 53). It might happen that, when the period of the vow was accomplished, poor Jews did not have the means to bear the considerable expenses involved (offering of a lamb, a sheep and a ram: see Numbers 6,14 ff.). In this case richer people were proud to intervene with an act of generosity. This is precisely what it was suggested that Paul should do. At this point also a 'we-section' ends, one of those passages, that is, in which Luke speaks in the first person plural (see Nos 45, 65 and 112).

Jerusalem, the sacred area of the Temple was separated from the 'Court of the Gentiles' by a rectangular balustrade which forbade access to pagans on pain of death.

102 Paul arrested in the Temple
(Acts 21, 27-40)

²⁷ When the seven days were almost completed, the Jews from Asia, who had seen him in the temple, stirred up all the crowd, and laid hands on him, ²⁸ crying out, "Men of Israel,

Fragment of a Greek inscription forbidding pagans to enter the sacred precinct of the Temple, on pain of death.

help! This is the man who is teaching men everywhere against the people and the law and this place; moreover he also brought Greeks into the temple, and he has defiled this holy place." ²⁹ For they had previously seen Trophimus the Ephesian with him in the city, and they supposed that Paul had brought him into the temple. ³⁰ Then all the city was aroused, and the people ran together; they seized Paul and dragged him out of the temple, and at once the gates were shut. ³¹ And as they were trying to kill him, word came to the tribune of the cohort that all Jerusalem was in confusion. ³² He at once took soldiers and centurions, and ran down to them; and when they saw the tribune and the soldiers, they stopped beating Paul. ³³ Then the tribune came up and arrested him, and ordered him to be bound with two chains. He inquired who he was and what he had done (1). ³⁴ Some in the crowd shouted one thing, some another; and as he could not learn the facts because of the uproar, he ordered him to be brought into the barracks. ³⁵ And when he came to the steps, he was actually carried by the soldiers because of the violence of the crowd; ³⁶ for the mob of the people followed, crying, "Away with him!"

Jerusalem: Detail of the Temple esplanade. It is the place on which the Antonia Tower probably stood. This tower, built by Herod and afterwards used by the Roman procurators, was destroyed with the rest of the city in 70 A.D. The Roman soldiers imprisoned St Paul there to rescue him from the fury of the crowd (see Acts 21,34).

[37] As Paul was about to be brought into the barracks, he said to the tribune, "May I say something to you?" And he said, "Do you know Greek? [38] Are you not the Egyptian, then, who recently stirred up a revolt and led the four thousand men of the Assassins out into the wilderness?" [39] Paul replied, "I am a Jew, from Tarsus in Cilicia, a citizen of no mean city; I beg you, let me speak to the people." [40] And when he had given him leave, Paul, standing on the steps, motioned with his hand to the people; and when there was a great hush, he spoke to them in the Hebrew language, saying:

(1) The Temple, properly so-called (see "Gospel of Jesus", page 25), was reserved for Jews only. The entrance of a non-Jew was considered so grave a sacrilege as to be legally punishable by death. The arrival of the tribune with his cohort was due to the fear that the riot might swell into a more open rebellion.

The character to whom the tribune alluded was a certain Ben-Stada of Egyptian origin. The Jewish historian Josephus Flavius relates that this man, giving himself out as Messiah, had been followed by a great many Jews of the extreme nationalist party called 'Sicari' (Assassins) (from the word 'sica', the name of the dagger they carried hidden beneath their cloaks). This false Messiah had been defeated by the procurator Felix (52-59 A.D.).

103 Paul's speech to the people
(Acts 22, 1-21)

[1] "Brethren and fathers, hear the defence which I now make before you."

[2] And when they heard that he addressed them in the Hebrew language, they were the more quiet. And he said: [3] "I am a Jew, born at Tarsus in Cilicia, but brought up in this city at the feet of Gamaliel, educated according to the strict manner of the law of our fathers, being zealous for God as you all are this day. [4] I persecuted this Way to the death, binding and delivering to prison both men and women, [5] as the high priest and the whole council of elders bear me witness. From them I received letters to the brethren, and I journeyed to Damascus to take those also who were there and bring them in bonds to Jerusalem to be punished.

[6] "As I made my journey and drew near to Damascus, about

Jerusalem. Of the majestic Temple of Herod there remains today only the great esplanade whose area gives us an idea of the vastness of the building: in the shape of an irregular trapeze, it measures 491 metres on the west side and 462 metres on the east. In the photograph is the Mosque of Omar seen from the south.

noon a great light from heaven suddenly shone about me. [7] And I fell to the ground and heard a voice saying to me, 'Saul, Saul, why do you persecute me?' [8] And I answered, 'Who are you, Lord?' And he said to me, 'I am Jesus of Nazareth whom you are persecuting.' [9] Now those who were with me saw the light but did not hear the voice of the one who was speaking to me. [10] And I said, 'What shall I do, Lord?' And the Lord said to me, 'Rise, and go into Damascus, and there you will be told all that is appointed for you to do.' [11] And when I could not see because of the brightness of that light, I was led by the hand by those who were with me, and came into Damascus.

[12] "And one Ananias, a devout man according to the law, well spoken of by all the Jews who lived there, [13] came to me, and standing by me said to me, 'Brother Saul, receive your sight.' And in that very hour I received my sight and saw him. [14] And he said, 'The God of our fathers appointed you to know his will, to see the Just One and to hear a voice from his mouth; [15] for you will be a witness for him to all men of what you have seen and heard. [16] And now why do you wait? Rise and be baptized, and wash away your sins, calling on his name.'

[17] "When I had returned to Jerusalem and was praying in the temple, I fell into a trance [18] and saw him saying to me, 'Make haste and get quickly out of Jerusalem, because they will not accept your testimony about me.' [19] And I said, 'Lord, they themselves know that in every synagogue I imprisoned and beat those who believed in thee. [20] And when the blood of Stephen thy witness was shed, I also was standing by and approving, and keeping the garments of those who killed him.' [21] And he said to me, 'Depart; for I will send you far away to the Gentiles.'"

104 A prisoner in the Antonia barracks
(Acts 22, 22-29)

[22] Up to this word they listened to him; then they lifted up their voices and said, "Away with such a fellow from the earth! For he ought not to live." [23] And as they cried out and waved their garments and threw dust into the air, [24] the tribune commanded him to be brought into the barracks, and ordered

Jerusalem. Another view on the Temple esplanade towards the minaret which stands on the probable site of the Antonia Tower, which from its size was also called 'Fortress'.

'As Paul was about to be brought into the barracks he said to the tribune ..."I beg you, let me speak to the people"' (Acts 21,37 and 39).

him to be examined by scourging, to find out why they shouted thus against him. ²⁵ But when they had tied him up with the thongs, Paul said to the centurion who was standing by, "Is it lawful for you to scourge a man who is a Roman citizen, and uncondemned?" ²⁶ When the centurion heard that, he went to the tribune and said to him, "What are you about to do? For this man is a Roman citizen." ²⁷ So the tribune came and said to him, "Tell me, are you a Roman citizen?" And he said, "Yes." ²⁸ The tribune answered, "I bought this citizenship for a large sum." Paul said, "But I was born a citizen." ²⁹ So those who were about to examine him withdrew from him instantly; and the tribune also was afraid, for he realized that Paul was a Roman citizen and that he had bound him. (1)

(1) Concerning the privileged penal treatment reserved for Roman citizens see the note to No. 46.

105 Paul before the Sanhedrim
(Acts 22, 30; 23, 1-11)

22, ³⁰ But on the morrow, desiring to know the real reason why the Jews accused him, he unbound him, and commanded the chief priests and all the council to meet, and he brought Paul down and set him before them.

23, ¹ And Paul, looking intently at the council, said, "Brethren, I have lived before God in all good conscience up to this day." ² And the high priest Ananias (1) commanded those who stood by him to strike him on the mouth. ³ Then Paul said to him, "God shall strike you, you whitewashed wall! Are you sitting to judge me according to the law, and yet contrary to the law you order me to be struck?" ⁴ Those who stood by said, "Would you revile God's high priest?" ⁵ And Paul said, "I did not know, brethren, that he was the high priest; for it is written, 'You shall not speak evil of a ruler of your people.'"

⁶ But when Paul perceived that one part were Sadducees and the other Pharisees, he cried out in the council, "Brethren, I am a Pharisee, a son of Pharisees; with respect to the hope and the resurrection of the dead I am on trial." ⁷ And when he had said this, a dissension arose between the Pharisees and the

In the neighbourhood of the ancient Antipatris, the place where the escort which accompanied St Paul from Jerusalem to Caesarea made a halt.

'So the soldiers, according to their instructions, took Paul and brought him by night to Antipatris' (Acts 23,31).

Sadducees; and the assembly was divided. ⁸ For the Sadducees say that there is no resurrection, nor angel, nor spirit; but the Pharisees acknowledge them all. ⁹ Then a great clamour arose; and some of the scribes of the Pharisees' party stood up and contended, "We find nothing wrong in this man. What if a spirit or an angel spoke to him?" ¹⁰ And when the dissension became violent, the tribune, afraid that Paul would be torn in pieces by them, commanded the soldiers to go down and take him by force from among them and bring him into the barracks.

¹¹ The following night the Lord stood by him and said, "Take courage, for as you have testified about me at Jerusalem, so you must bear witness also at Rome."

(1) Ananias was High Priest in the years from 47 to 59 A.D. He had the reputation of being a very violent man and was killed by the 'Sicari' (see note to No. 102) in the year 66.

106 Jewish plot: Paul is transferred to Caesarea
(Acts 23, 12-35)

¹² When it was day, the Jews made a plot and bound themselves by an oath neither to eat nor drink till they had killed Paul. ¹³ There were more than forty who made this conspiracy. ¹⁴ And they went to the chief priests and elders, and said, "We have strictly bound ourselves by an oath to taste no food till we have killed Paul. ¹⁵ You therefore, along with the council, give notice now to the tribune to bring him down to you, as though you were going to determine his case more exactly. And we are ready to kill him before he comes near."

¹⁶ Now the son of Paul's sister (1) heard of their ambush; so he went and entered the barracks and told Paul. ¹⁷ And Paul called one of the centurions and said, "Bring this young man to the tribune; for he has something to tell him." ¹⁸ So he took him and brought him to the tribune and said, "Paul the prisoner

called me and asked me to bring 'this young man to you, as he has something to say to you." [19] The tribune /took him by the hand, and going aside asked him privately, "What is it that you have to tell me?" [20] And he said, "The Jews have agreed to ask you to bring Paul down to the council tomorrow, as though they were going to inquire somewhat more closely about him. [21] But do not yield to them; for more than forty of their men lie in ambush for him, having bound themselves by an oath neither to eat nor drink till they have killed him; and now they are ready, waiting for the promise from you." [22] So the tribune dismissed the young man, charging him, "Tell no one that you have informed me of this."

[23] Then he called two of the centurions and said, "At the third hour of the night get ready two hundred soldiers with seventy horsemen and two hundred spearmen to go as far as Caesarea. [24] Also provide mounts for Paul to ride, and bring him safely to Felix the governor." (2) [25] And he wrote a letter to this effect:

[26] "Claudius Lysias to his Excellency the governor Felix, greeting. [27] This man was seized by the Jews, and was about to be killed by them, when I came upon them with the soldiers and rescued him, having learned that he was a Roman citizen. [28] And desiring to know the charge on which they accused him, I brought him down to their council. [29] I found that he was accused about questions of their law, but charged with nothing deserving death or imprisonment. [30] And when it was disclosed to me that there would be a plot against the man, I sent him to you at once, ordering his accusers also to state before you what they have against him."

[31] So the soldiers, according to their instructions, took Paul and brought him by night to Antipatris. [32] And on the morrow they returned to the barracks, leaving the horsemen to go on with him. [33] When they came to Caesarea and delivered the letter to the governor, they presented Paul also before him. [34] On reading the letter, he asked to what province he belonged. When he learned that he was from Cilicia [35] he said, "I will hear you when your accusers arrive." And he commanded him to be guarded in Herod's praetorium.

(1) The expression 'the son of Paul's sister' is the only mention of the Apostle's family that we have in the whole of the New Testament.
(2) The procurator, Antonius Felix, (see chronological diagram on page 43) was a freedman of the Imperial household. Backed by the protection he enjoyed at court, he ruled with insolence, licentiousness

and venality. Of him the Roman historian Tacitus wrote: 'he exercised the power of a king with the spirit of a slave'. Because of his bad government he was dismissed.

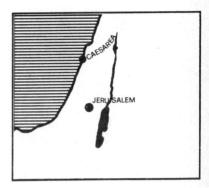

The position of Jerusalem and Caesarea.

107 The trial before Felix
(Acts 24, 1-27)

¹ And after five days the high priest Ananias came down with some elders and a spokesman, one Tertullus. They laid before the governor their case against Paul; ² and when he was called, Tertullus began to accuse him, saying:

"Since through you we enjoy much peace, and since by your provision, most excellent Felix, reforms are introduced on behalf of this nation, ³ in every way and everywhere we accept this with all gratitude. ⁴ But, to detain you no further, I beg you in your kindness to hear us briefly. ⁵ For we have found this man a pestilent fellow, an agitator among all the Jews throughout the world, and a ringleader of the sect of the Nazarenes. ⁶ He even tried to profane the temple, but we seized him. [⁷] ⁸ By examining him yourself you will be able to learn from him about everything of which we accuse him."

⁹ The Jews also joined in the charge, affirming that all this was so.

Caesarea. The city was built by Herod who called it Caesarea in honour
of Caesar Augustus. Because of its beauty and mild Mediterranean
climate it became the seat of the Roman governors who, for reasons
of security, went up to Jerusalem with their escort only on the occasion
of great Feasts.

[10] And when the governor had motioned to him to speak, Paul replied:

"Realizing that for many years you have been judge over this nation, I cheerfully make my defence. [11] As you may ascertain, it is not more than twelve days since I went up to worship at Jerusalem; [12] and they did not find me disputing with any one or stirring up a crowd, either in the temple or in the synagogues, or in the city. [13] Neither can they prove to you what they now bring up against me. [14] But this I admit to you, that according to the Way, which they call a sect, I worship the God of our fathers, believing everything laid down by the law or written in the prophets, [15] having a hope in God which these themselves accept, that there will be a resurrection of both the just and the unjust. [16] So I always take pains to have a clear conscience toward God and toward men. [17] Now after some years I came to bring to my nation alms and offerings. [18] As I was doing this, they found me purified in the temple, without any crowd or tumult. But some Jews from Asia—[19] they ought to be here before you and to make an accusation, if they have anything against me. [20] Or else let these men themselves say what wrong-doing they found when I stood before the council, [21] except this one thing which I cried out while standing among them, 'With respect to the resurrection of the dead I am on trial before you this day.'"

[22] But Felix, having a rather accurate knowledge of the Way, put them off, saying, "When Lysias the tribune comes down, I will decide your case." [23] Then he gave orders to the centurion that he should be kept in custody but should have some liberty, and that none of his friends should be prevented from attending to his needs.

[24] After some days Felix came with his wife Drusilla, who was a Jewess; and he sent for Paul and heard him speak upon faith in Christ Jesus. [25] And as he argued about justice and self-control and future judgment, Felix was alarmed and said, "Go away for the present; when I have an opportunity I will summon you." [26] At the same time he hoped that money would be given him by Paul. So he sent for him often and conversed with him. [27] But when two years had elapsed, Felix was succeeded by Porcius Festus; (1) and desiring to do the Jews a favour, Felix left Paul in prison.

[⁷] 'We would have judged him according to our Law. But the chief captain Lysias came and with great violence took him out of our hands [⁸] commanding his accusers to come before you'.

These verses are omitted in the best codices.

(1) Porcius Festus was procurator in Judea from the year 60 till his death in 62 (see chronological diagram on page 43). He was of the 'Porcius family' of which other members were Cato the Censor and Cato the Less. He is presented to us by Josephus Flavius as an active and honourable officer.

108 Paul and the Procurator Festus. The appeal to Caesar (Acts 25, 1-12)

¹ Now when Festus had come into his province, after three days he went up to Jerusalem from Caesarea. ² And the chief priests and the principal men of the Jews informed him against Paul; and they urged him, ³ asking as a favour to have the man sent to Jerusalem, planning an ambush to kill him on the way. ⁴ Festus replied that Paul was being kept at Caesarea, and that he himself intended to go there shortly. ⁵ "So," said he, "Let the men of authority among you go down with me, and if there is anything wrong about the man, let them accuse him."

⁶ When he had stayed among them not more than eight or ten days, he went down to Caesarea; and the next day he took his seat on the tribunal and ordered Paul to be brought. ⁷ And when he had come, the Jews who had gone down from Jerusalem stood about him, bringing against him many serious charges which they could not prove. ⁸ Paul said in his defence, "Neither against the law of the Jews, nor against the temple, nor against Caesar have I offended at all." ⁹ But Festus, wishing to do the Jews a favour, said to Paul, "Do you wish to go up to Jerusalem, and there be tried on these charges before me?" ¹⁰ But Paul said, "I am standing before Caesar's tribunal, where I ought to be tried; to the Jews I have done no wrong, as you know very well. ¹¹ If then I am a wrongdoer, and have committed anything for which I deserve to die, I do not seek to escape death; but if there is nothing in their charges against me, no one can give me up to them. I appeal to Caesar." ¹² Then Festus, when he had conferred with his council, answered, "You have appealed to Caesar; to Caesar you shall go."

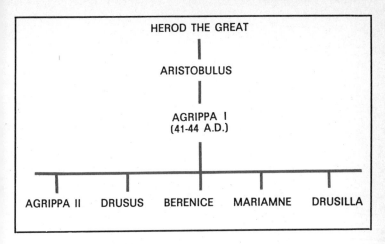

Genealogy of Agrippa II.

109 Festus explains Paul's case to King Agrippa II (Acts 25, 13-27)

[13] Now when some days had passed, Agrippa the king and Bernice arrived at Caesarea to welcome Festus. [14] And as they stayed there many days, Festus laid Paul's case before the king, saying, "There is a man left prisoner by Felix; [15] and when I was at Jerusalem, the chief priests and the elders of the Jews gave information about him, asking for sentence against him. [16] I answered them that it was not the custom of the Romans to give up any one before the accused met the accusers face to face, and had opportunity to make his defence concerning the charge laid against him. [17] When therefore they came together here, I made no delay, but on the next day took my seat on the tribunal and ordered the man to be brought in. [18] When the accusers stood up, they brought no charge in his case of such evils as I supposed; [19] but they had certain points of dispute with him about their own superstition and about one Jesus, who was dead, but whom Paul asserted to be alive. [20] Being at a

Caesarea Philippi. Here at the sources of the Jordan (shown in the photograph) stood the ancient city which Philip, son of Herod, had built as the capital of his kingdom. It was so called to distinguish it from Caesarea on the coast. In the time of the Apostle Paul it was the seat of King Agrippa II.

The place where Caesarea Philippi was built was called 'Panion' because of ancient rock temples to the god Pan. In the photograph: the niches in which small statues of the god were placed.

loss how to investigate these questions, I asked whether he wished to go to Jerusalem and be tried there regarding them. ²¹ But when Paul had appealed to be kept in custody for the decision of the emperor, I commanded him to be held until I could send him to Caesar." ²² And Agrippa said to Festus, "I should like to hear the man myself." "Tomorrow," said he, "you shall hear him."

²³ So on the morrow Agrippa and Bernice came with great pomp, and they entered the audience hall with the military tribunes and the prominent men of the city. Then by command of Festus Paul was brought in. ²⁴ And Festus said, "King Agrippa and all who are present with us, you see this man about whom the whole Jewish people petitioned me, both at Jerusalem and here, shouting that he ought not to live any longer. ²⁵ But I found that he had done nothing deserving death; and as he himself appealed to the emperor, I decided to send him. ²⁶ But I have nothing definite to write to my lord (2) about him. Therefore I have brought him before you, and, especially before you, King Agrippa, that, after we have examined him, I may have something

to write. [27] For it seems to me unreasonable, in sending a prisoner, not to indicate the charges against him."

(1) Agrippa II, son of Agrippa I (see note to No. 33), lived incestuously with his sister, Bernice. Brought up and educated in Rome at the court of Claudius, he became king in the year 48 and was always most loyal to the Empire. Of weak character, he was always completely dominated by his sister. Their conduct was known even in Rome and provoked sarcastic references from Juvenal in his satires (Satire 6).
Agrippa II was not king of Judea but of the territories to the north-east of Galilee; however he had the supervision of the Temple with the right of nominating the High Priest.
(2) Note the divine title 'Lord' given by Festus to the Emperor. Whereas such a usage was a long-standing tradition in the east, it was introduced in Rome by the Emperors Caligula and Nero.

110 Paul before King Agrippa II
(Acts 26, 1-23)

[1] Agrippa said to Paul, "You have permission to speak for yourself." Then Paul stretched out his hand and made his defence:
[2] "I think myself fortunate that it is before you, King Agrippa, I am to make my defence today against all the accusations of the Jews, [3] because you are especially familiar with all customs and controversies of the Jews; therefore I beg you to listen to me patiently.
[4] "My manner of life from my youth, spent from the beginning among my own nation and at Jerusalem, is known by all the Jews. [5] They have known for a long time, if they are willing to testify, that according to the strictest party of our religion I have lived as a Pharisee. [6] And now I stand here on trial for hope in the promise made by God to our fathers, [7] to which our twelve tribes hope to attain, as they earnestly worship night and day. And for this hope I am accused by Jews, O king! [8] Why is it thought incredible by any of you that God raises the dead?
[9] "I myself was convinced that I ought to do many things in opposing the name of Jesus of Nazareth. [10] And I did so in Jerusalem; I not only shut up many of the saints in prison, by authority from the chief priests, but when they were put to

death I cast my vote against them. [11] And I punished them often in all the synagogues and tried to make them blaspheme; and in raging fury against them, I persecuted them even to foreign cities.

[12] "Thus I journeyed to Damascus with the authority and commission of the chief priests. [13] At midday, O king, I saw on the way a light from heaven, brighter than the sun, shining round me and those who journeyed with me. [14] And when we had all fallen to the ground, I heard a voice saying to me in the Hebrew language, 'Saul, Saul, why do you persecute me? It hurts you to kick against the goads.' [15] And I said, 'Who are you, Lord?' And the Lord said, 'I am Jesus whom you are persecuting. [16] But rise and stand upon your feet; for I have appeared to you for this purpose, to appoint you to serve and bear witness to the things in which you have seen me and to those in which I will appear to you, [17] delivering you from the people and from the Gentiles—to whom I send you [18] to open their eyes, that they may turn from darkness to light (1) and from the power of Satan to God, that they may receive forgiveness of sins and a place among those who are sanctified by faith in me.'

[19] "Wherefore, O King Agrippa, I was not disobedient to the heavenly vision, [20] but declared first to those at Damascus, then at Jerusalem and throughout all the country of Judea, and also to the Gentiles, that they should repent and turn to God and perform deeds worthy of their repentance. [21] For this reason the Jews seized me in the temple and tried to kill me. [22] To this day I have had the help that comes from God, and so I stand here testifying both to small and great, saying nothing but what the prophets and Moses said would come to pass: [23] that the Christ must suffer, and that, by being the first to rise from the dead, he would proclaim light both to the people and to the Gentiles."

(1) See Isaiah 42, 7 and 16.

111 Agrippa acknowledges Paul's innocence
(Acts 26, 24-32)

[24] And as he thus made his defence, Festus said with a loud voice, "Paul, you are mad; your great learning is turning you

Caesarea (on the coast). The remains of the Tower of Strato, a fort built on the coast to defend the harbour. The city, founded in the year 25 B.C., because of its favourable situation soon acquired great importance as the port of Jerusalem. Here St Paul was put on board ship as a prisoner for his dramatic voyage to Rome.

mad." [25] But Paul said, "I am not mad, most excellent Festus, but I am speaking the sober truth. [26] For the king knows about these things, and to him I speak freely; for I am persuaded that none of these things has escaped his notice, for this was not done in a corner. [27] King Agrippa, do you believe the prophets? I know that you believe." [28] And Agrippa said to Paul, "In a short time you think to make me a Christian!" [29] And Paul said, "Whether short or long, I would to God that not only you but also all who hear me this day might become such as I am—except for these chains."

[30] Then the king rose, and the governor and Bernice and those who were sitting with them; [31] and when they had withdrawn, they said to one another, "This man is doing nothing to deserve death or imprisonment." [32] And Agrippa said to Festus, "This man could have been set free if he had not appealed to Caesar."

112 The departure for Rome
(Acts 27, 1-12)

[1] And when it was decided that we should sail (1) for Italy, they delivered Paul and some other prisoners to a centurion of the Augustan Cohort, named Julius. [2] And embarking in a ship of Adramyttium, which was about to sail to the ports along the coast of Asia, we put to sea, accompanied by Aristarchus, a Macedonian from Thessalonica. [3] The next day we put in at Sidon; and Julius treated Paul kindly, and gave him leave to go to his friends and be cared for. [4] And putting to sea from there we sailed under the lee of Cyprus, because the winds were against us. [5] And when we had sailed across the sea which is off Cilicia and Pamphylia, we came to Myra in Lycia. [6] There the centurion found a ship of Alexandria sailing for Italy, and put us on board. [7] We sailed slowly for a number of days, and arrived with difficulty off Cnidus, and as the wind did not allow us to go on, we sailed under the lee of Crete off Salmone. [8] Coasting along it with difficulty, we came to a place called Fair Havens, near which was the city of Lasaea.

Sidon (today Saida). A very old Phoenician city; it was in the Apostles'
time still a big centre of commerce because of its flourishing port.
It was a port of call for St Paul when a prisoner, accompanied by
St Luke.
'**The next day we put in at Sidon; and Julius treated Paul kindly, and
gave him leave to go to his friends and be cared for**' (Acts 27,3).

⁹ As much time had been lost, and the voyage was already dangerous because the fast (2) had already gone by, Paul advised them, ¹⁰ saying, "Sirs, I perceive that the voyage will be with injury and much loss, not only of the cargo and the ship, but also of our lives." ¹¹ But the centurion paid more attention to the captain and to the owner of the ship than to what Paul said. ¹² And because the harbour was not suitable to winter in, the majority advised to put to sea from there, on the chance that somehow they could reach Phoenix, a harbour of Crete, looking northeast and southeast, and winter there.

(1) St Luke, who during St Paul's captivity at Caesarea, must have been collecting material for his Gospel and the Acts, at this point joined Paul (the third 'we-section' begins, see Nos. 45 and 65) and accompanied him to Rome.

(2) The great fast was on the occasion of the Day of Atonement which fell about the end of September or beginning of October. That was a little before navigation was suspended. With the means then available it was in fact very unwise to put to sea during the winter.

Fragment of a bas-relief, depicting a Roman ship. The ship in which St Paul sailed as a prisoner was like this one.

Tyre was already a very ancient city at the end of the Phoenician era and had a big harbour. In the photograph: stone anchors of the Phoenician period found in the excavations of the old city.

113 The storm and the shipwreck
(Acts 27, 13-44)

¹³ And when the south wind blew gently, supposing that they had obtained their purpose, they weighed anchor and sailed along Crete, close inshore. ¹⁴ But soon a tempestuous wind, called the northeaster, struck down from the land; ¹⁵ and when the ship was caught and could not face the wind, we gave way to it and were driven. ¹⁶ And running under the lee of a small island called Cauda, we managed with difficulty to secure the boat; ¹⁷ after hoisting it up, they took measures to undergird the ship; then, fearing that they should run on the Syrtis, they lowered the gear, and so were driven. ¹⁸ As we were violently storm-tossed, they began next day to throw the cargo overboard; ¹⁹ and the third day they cast out with their own hands the tackle of the ship. ²⁰ And when neither sun nor stars appeared for many a day, and no small tempest lay on us, all hope of our being saved was at last abandoned.

²¹ As they had been long without food, Paul then came forward among them and said, "Men, you should have listened to me, and should not have set sail from Crete and incurred this injury and loss. ²² I now bid you to take heart; for there will be no loss of life among you, but only of the ship. ²³ For this very night there stood by me an angel of the God to whom I belong and whom I worship, ²⁴ and he said, 'Do not be afraid, Paul; you must stand before Caesar; and lo, God has granted you all those who sail with you.' ²⁵ So take heart, men, for I have faith in God that it will be exactly as I have been told. ²⁶ But we shall have to run on some island."

²⁷ When the fourteenth night had come, as we were drifting across the sea of Adria (1), about midnight the sailors suspected that they were nearing land. ²⁸ So they sounded and found twenty fathoms; a little farther on they sounded again and found fifteen fathoms. ²⁹ And fearing that we might run on the rocks, they let out four anchors from the stern, and prayed for day to come. ³⁰ And as the sailors were seeking to escape from the ship, and had lowered the boat into the sea, under pretence of laying out anchors from the bow, ³¹ Paul said to

Malta. A church in St Paul's Bay, many times rebuilt, on the ruins of a Roman villa (Publius' house?) recalls the scene of St Paul's shipwreck.

the centurion and the soldiers, "Unless these men stay in the ship, you cannot be saved." [32] Then the soldiers cut away the ropes of the boat, and let it go.

[33] As day was about to dawn, Paul urged them all to take some food, saying, "Today is the fourteenth day that you have continued in suspense and without food, having taken nothing. [34] Therefore I urge you to take some food; it will give you strength, since not a hair is to perish from the head of any of you." (2) [35] And when he had said this, he took bread, and giving thanks to God in the presence of all he broke it and began to eat. [36] Then they all were encouraged and ate some food themselves. [37] (We were in all two hundred and seventy-six persons in the ship.) [38] And when they had eaten enough, they lightened the ship, throwing out the wheat into the sea.

[39] Now when it was day, they did not recognize the land, but they noticed a bay with a beach, on which they planned if possible to bring the ship ashore. [40] So they cast off the anchors and left them in the sea, at the same time loosening the ropes that tied the rudders; then hoisting the foresail to the wind they made for the beach. [41] But striking a shoal they ran the vessel aground; the bow stuck and remained immovable, and the stern was broken up by the surf. [42] The soldiers' plan was to kill the prisoners, lest any should swim away and escape; [43] but the centurion, wishing to save Paul, kept them from carrying out their purpose. He ordered those who could swim to throw themselves overboard first and make for the land, [44] and the rest on planks or on pieces of the ship. And so it was that all escaped to land.

(1) By the name 'Sea of Adria' the ancients meant the sea between Greece, Italy and Africa.
(2) Similar words had been used by Jesus (see Luke 12,7 and 21,18).

114 Paul and the shipwrecked mariners all given hospitality in Malta
(Acts 28, 1-10)

[1] After we had escaped, we then learned that the island was called Malta. [2] And the natives showed us unusual kindness, for they kindled a fire and welcomed us all, because it had begun

The ancient city of Puteoli (now Pozzuoli) was the chief commercial port of Italy and one of the most important in the whole of the Mediterranean. When St Paul arrived there as a prisoner with St Luke he found a Christian community which welcomed him joyfully.

'... **we came to Puteoli. There we found brethren and were invited to stay with them for seven days**' (Acts 28,13-14).

to rain and was cold. ³ Paul had gathered a bundle of sticks and put them on the fire, when a viper came out because of the heat and fastened on his hand. ⁴ When the natives saw the creature hanging from his hand, they said to one another, "No doubt this man is a murderer. Though he has escaped from the sea, justice (1) has not allowed him to live." ⁵ He, however, shook off the creature into the fire and suffered no harm. ⁶ They waited, expecting him to swell up or suddenly fall down dead; but when they had waited a long time and saw no misfortune come to him, they changed their minds and said that he was a god.

⁷ Now in the neighbourhood of that place were lands belonging to the chief man of the island, named Publius, who received us and entertained us hospitably for three days. ⁸ It happened that the father of Publius lay sick with fever and dysentery; and Paul visited him and prayed, and putting his hands on him healed him. ⁹ And when this had taken place, the rest of the people on the island who had diseases also came and were cured. ¹⁰ They presented many gifts to us; and when we sailed, they put on board whatever we needed.

(1) The 'Justice' of which the Maltese spoke among themselves is the goddess 'Dike' (which means precisely Justice) of Greek mythology. The island of Malta was administered by the Praetor of Sicily whose representative on the island was in fact called 'Chief man of the Island', a title which is confirmed by ancient inscriptions which have been found.

115 From Malta to Rome
(Acts 28, 11-15)

¹¹ After three months we set sail in a ship which had wintered in the island, a ship of Alexandria, with the Twin Brothers (1) as figurehead. ¹² Putting in at Syracuse, we stayed there for three days. ¹³ And from there we made a circuit and arrived at Rhegium; and after one day a south wind sprang up, and on the second day we came to Puteoli. ¹⁴ There we found brethren, and were invited to stay with them for seven days. And so we came to Rome. ¹⁵ And the brethren there, when

A stretch of the old Appian Way paved with great slabs of stone. The Appian Way was the most impressive as well as the most important of the old Roman roads. The great noble families of Rome had built their tombs along it. St Paul walked on these stones on his way to the imperial city.

they heard of us, came as far as the Forum of Appius and Three Taverns to meet us. On seeing them Paul thanked God and took courage.

(1) It was a common custom for ships to bear on their prows the image or at least the name of a tutelary divinity. The ship on which St Paul embarked bore the figure-head of Castor and Pollux (the Dioscuri, 'Twins') who were protectors of sea-farers in peril.

The ship which carried St Paul from Malta to Puteoli carried as a mascot the sign of the Twins, Castor and Pollux (see Acts 28. 11). In the photograph: The remains of the Temple of the Dioscuri in the Roman forum.

116 Paul in the Capital of the Empire
(Acts 28, 16-31)

[16] And when we came into Rome, Paul was allowed to stay by himself, with the soldier that guarded him. (1)
[17] After three days he called together the local leaders of the Jews; and when they had gathered, he said to them, "Brethren, though I had done nothing against the people or the customs of our fathers, yet I was delivered prisoner from Jerusalem into the hands of the Romans. [18] When they had examined me, they wished to set me at liberty, because there was no reason for the death penalty in my case. [19] But when the Jews objected, I was compelled to appeal to Caesar—though I had no charge to bring against my nation. [20] For this reason therefore I have

Rome. The Basilica of St Paul-outside-the-Walls, reconstructed in 1823 after the fire which destroyed the fourth century Basilica. Under the altar of the Confession it preserves the tomb of St Paul, the Apostle of the Gentiles.

Rome. Detail of the Arch of Septimius Severus. The Roman soldier who leads a handcuffed prisoner gives us an idea of St Paul's entry into Rome.

asked to see you and speak with you, since it is because of the hope of Israel that I am bound with this chain." ²¹ And they said to him, "We have received no letters from Judea about you, and none of the brethren coming here has reported or spoken any evil about you. ²² But we desire to hear from you what your views are; for with regard to this sect we know that everywhere it is spoken against."

²³ When they had appointed a day for him, they came to him at his lodging in great numbers. And he expounded the matter to them from morning till evening, testifying to the kingdom of God and trying to convince them about Jesus both from the law of Moses and from the prophets. ²⁴ And some were convinced by what he said, while others disbelieved. ²⁵ So, as they disagreed among themselves, they departed, after Paul had made one statement: "The Holy Spirit was right in saying to your fathers through Isaiah the prophet:

²⁶ 'Go to this people, and say,

You shall indeed hear but never understand,

and you shall indeed see but never perceive.

27 For this people's heart has grown dull,
and their ears are heavy of hearing,
and their eyes they have closed;
lest they should perceive with their eyes,
and hear with their ears,
and understand with their heart,
and turn for me to heal them.' (2)

28 Let it be known to you then that this salvation of God has been sent to the Gentiles; they will listen." [29]

30 And he lived there two whole years at his own expense, and welcomed all who came to him, 31 preaching the kingdom of God and teaching about the Lord Jesus Christ quite openly and unhindered.

(1) The type of custody which Paul the prisoner had to endure was very lenient: the prisoner could freely choose the house in which he was to live. But his right hand was always fastened with a chain to the soldier who guarded him.

(2) The quotation is from the Prophet Isaiah 6, 9 ff. used also by Jesus (see Matthew 13,14; Mark 4,12 and John 12,40).

[29] 'And when he had said these things, the Jews departed, holding much dispute among themselves'.

This verse is omitted in the best codices.

 END OF THE BOOK OF THE ACTS OF THE APOSTLES

VI. St Paul's Letters written during his captivity in Rome

From St Paul's Letter to the Philippians

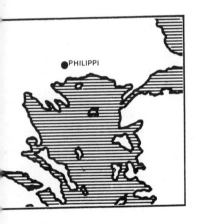

The position of Philippi.

Philippi, so called after Philip II, father of Alexander the Great, was made famous by the victory of Anthony and Octavian (later Caesar Augustus) over Brutus and Cassius, the murderers of Julius Caesar, in 42 B.C. With the Macedonian inhabitants lived many Roman colonists, veterans of the army, whom Augustus settled there with many privileges. It was the first European city evangelised by St Paul, in 50-51 during his second journey (see No. 46). The Apostle returned there twice during the third journey (see No. 65).

The Christian community of Philippi, always full of affection for St Paul, was the only one which gave him no anxieties and the only one from which he accepted material help.

The occasion for the Letter to the Philippians was in fact the sending of financial help by means of Epaphroditus while St Paul was a prisoner in Rome between 61 and 63 A.D. Epaphroditus took the letter when he returned to Philippi. It is entirely an outpouring of paternal affection and gratitude on the part of St Paul who gives news of his captivity, expresses the hope of soon being released so as to be able to see the Philippians again, and takes the opportunity to exhort them to live in peace and beware of the Judaizers.

Philippi. The ruins of the ancient 'agora' (central market place). Here St Paul was brought before the magistrates on the charge of having provoked disturbances in the city.

'**These men ... are disturbing our city. They advocate customs which it is not lawful for us Romans to accept or practise**' (Acts 16,20-21, see No. 46).

The beginning of St Paul's Letter to the Philippians in the Vatican Codex (fourth century).

117 Introduction
(1, 1-26)

¹ Paul and Timothy, servants of Christ Jesus,
To all the saints in Christ Jesus who are at Philippi, with the bishops and deacons:
² Grace to you and peace from God our Father and the Lord Jesus Christ.
³ I thank my God in all my remembrance of you, ⁴ always in every prayer of mine for you all making my prayer with joy, ⁵ thankful for your partnership in the gospel from the first day until now. ⁶ And I am sure that he who began a good work in you will bring it to completion at the day of Jesus Christ. ⁷ It is right for me to feel thus about you all, because I hold you in my heart, for you are all partakers with me of grace, both in my imprisonment and in the defence and confirmation of the gospel. ⁸ For God is my witness, how I yearn for you all with the affection of Christ Jesus. ⁹ And it is my prayer that your love may abound more and more, with knowledge and all discernment, ¹⁰ so that you may approve what is excellent, and may be pure and blameless for the day of Christ, ¹¹ filled with the fruits of righteousness which come through Jesus Christ, to the glory and praise of God.
¹² I want you to know, brethren, that what has happened

Philippi. The remains of the ancient Roman theatre. St Paul arrived at Philippi from the nearby port Neapolis (see No. 46) walking along the Egnatian Way. It was here that for the first time he preached Christianity on the continent of Europe.

to me has really served to advance the gospel, [13] so that it has become known throughout the whole praetorian guard and to all the rest that my imprisonment is for Christ; [14] and most of the brethren have been made confident in the Lord because of my imprisonment, and are much more bold to speak the word of God without fear.

[15] Some indeed preach Christ from envy and rivalry, but others from good will. [16] The latter do it out of love, knowing that I am put here for the defence of the gospel; [17] the former proclaim Christ out of partisanship, not sincerely but thinking to afflict me in my imprisonment. [18] What then? Only that in every way, whether in pretence or in truth, Christ is proclaimed; and in that I rejoice.

[19] Yes, and I shall rejoice. For I know that through your prayers and the help of the Spirit of Jesus Christ this will turn out for my deliverance, [20] as it is my eager expectation and hope that I shall not be at all ashamed, but that with full courage now as always Christ will be honoured in my body, whether by life or by death. [21] For to me to live is Christ, and to die is gain. [22] If it is to be life in the flesh, that means fruitful labour for me. Yet which I shall choose I cannot tell. [23] I am hard pressed between the two. My desire is to depart and be with Christ, for that is far better. [24] But to remain in the flesh is more necessary on your account. [25] Convinced of this, I know that I shall remain and continue with you all, for your progress and joy in the faith, [26] so that in me you may have ample cause to glory in Christ Jesus, because of my coming to you again.

118 Christ the supreme example of humility
(2, 1-13)

[1] So if there is any encouragement in Christ, any incentive of love, any participation in the Spirit, any affection and sympathy, [2] complete my joy by being of the same mind, having the same love, being in full accord and of one mind. [3] Do nothing

from selfishness or conceit, but in humility count others better than yourselves. [4] Let each of you look not only to his own interests, but also to the interests of others. [5] Have this mind among yourselves, which was in Christ Jesus, [6] who, though he was in the form of God, did not count equality with God a thing to be grasped, [7] but emptied himself, taking the form of a servant, being born in the likeness of men. [8] And being found in human form he humbled himself and became obedient unto death, even death on a cross. [9] Therefore God has highly exalted him and bestowed on him the name which is above every name, [10] that at the name of Jesus every knee should bow, in heaven and on earth and under the earth, [11] and every tongue confess that Jesus Christ is Lord, to the glory of God the Father.

[12] Therefore, my beloved, as you have always obeyed, so now, not only as in my presence but much more in my absence, work out your own salvation with fear and trembling; [13] for God is at work in you, both to will and to work for his good pleasure.

In order to exhort the Philippians to humility, St Paul quotes the example of Christ, referring to the words of a hymn of the early Church which celebrated the humiliation and consequent exaltation of the Son of God. In this passage of great doctrinal importance the person of Christ is thought of in three successive stages:

1) Before the Incarnation Christ already existed, as Son of God, of the same nature as God and with all the glory which belongs to the immensity of God.

2) In the Incarnation the Son of God assumed human nature. When he did this he did not require that his humanity should be endowed with the glory that was his by right because it was united in one single person with him who is 'equal with God'. Christ rejected that glory, being content that his human nature should be of a very humble sort, like that of other men in all ways except sin. Thus on the way of humiliation he was subject not only to God but also to other men, even to the outrages of the passion and finally to death on the cross.

3) After the resurrection God has exalted Jesus, pouring down over his transformed humanity the immense splendour of the Godhead. The 'name which is above every name' is Christ's effective sovereignty over all created beings, which is expressed in the word 'Lord' ('Kyrios' in Greek). The phrase 'Christ is Lord' is an epitome of the Christian faith: it means not only that Christ is God, but that his glorified humanity has dominion over all creatures and has the power to save men from sin and death and to unite them with himself in adoration of the Father.

Philippi. The interior of St Paul's prison, hewn out of the rock. Here the Apostle was confined after having been scourged (see No. 46).

View of the site of the ancient city of Colossae whose ruins are very difficult to trace today. Colossae was probably the leader of the other Christian communities of Laodicea and Hierapolis founded by some disciples of St Paul's.

From St Paul's Letter to the Colossians

The position of Colossae.

Colossae was a city of Phrygia in Asia Minor evangelized not by St Paul in person but by Epaphras, a citizen of Colossae converted by the Apostle during his three years' stay at Ephesus between the years 54 and 57 (see No. 63).

Following St Paul's instructions, Epaphras had converted to Christianity a considerable number of pagans and organized the Church of Colossae, for which he was responsible.

When St Paul was a prisoner in Rome (61-63 A.D.), Epaphras came to visit him, bringing news of that Christian Church, and remained at hand to help him in prison. The news was not wholly good. False teachers had infiltrated among the Christians in Colossae and insisted on certain ascetic practices of Jewish origin and on a mistaken worship of Angels, with the result of obscuring or directly denying the universal sovereignty of Christ. To combat these errors and to establish bonds of affection with that Church, St Paul wrote the Letter to the Colossians and sent it to them by his disciple Tychicus. In the first, more dogmatic, part of the Letter St Paul expounds at length Christ's primacy and warns against the errors propagated by false teachers. In the second part, more concerned with morals, he explains what should be the virtues of Christians, whether in the pursuit of heavenly blessings or in the practice of communal and domestic virtues.

The beginning of the Letter to the Colossians in the Vatican Codex (fourth century).

119 Introduction
(1, 1-12)

[1] Paul, an apostle of Christ Jesus by the will of God, and Timothy our brother.
[2] To the saints and faithful brethren in Christ at Colossae: Grace to you and peace from God our Father.
[3] We always thank God, the Father of our Lord Jesus Christ, when we pray for you, [4] because we have heard of your faith in Christ Jesus and of the love which you have for all the saints, [5] because of the hope laid up for you in heaven. Of this you have heard before in the word of the truth, the gospel [6] which has come to you, as indeed in the whole world it is bearing fruit and growing—so among yourselves, from the day you heard and understood the grace of God in truth, [7] as you learned it from Epaphras our beloved fellow servant. He is a faithful minister of Christ on our behalf [8] and has made known to us your love in the Spirit.
[9] And so, from the day we heard of it, we have not ceased to pray for you, asking that you may be filled with the knowledge of his will in all spiritual wisdom and understanding, [10] to lead a life worthy of the Lord, fully pleasing to him, bearing fruit in every good work and increasing in the knowledge of God. [11] May you be strengthened with all power, according to his glorious might, for all endurance and patience with joy, [12] giving thanks to the Father, who has qualified us to share in the inheritance of the saints in light.

120 Universal primacy of Christ
(1, 13-23)

[13] He has delivered us from the dominion of darkness and transferred us to the kingdom of his beloved Son, [14] in whom we have redemption, the forgiveness of sins.

[15] He is the image of the invisible God, the first-born of all creation; [16] for in him all things were created, in heaven and on earth, visible and invisible, whether thrones or dominions or principalities or authorities—all things were created through him and for him. [17] He is before all things, and in him all things hold together. [18] He is the head of the body, the church; he is the beginning, the first-born from the dead, that in everything he might be pre-eminent. [19] For in him all the fulness of God was pleased to dwell, [20] and through him to reconcile to himself all things, whether on earth or in heaven, making peace by the blood of his cross.

[21] And you, who once were estranged and hostile in mind, doing evil deeds, [22] he has now reconciled in his body of flesh by his death, in order to present you holy and blameless and irreproachable before him, [23] provided that you continue in the faith, stable and steadfast, not shifting from the hope of the gospel which you heard, which has been preached to every creature under heaven, and of which I, Paul, became a minister.

In this passage of great doctrinal importance, St Paul restates the various reasons which assign to Jesus Christ a state and dignity absolutely unique in the universe. We select the following points:

1) By his divine nature Christ is the 'image of God' in the sense that he is of the same nature as the Father and also in the sense that he is the manifestation of God who remains 'invisible' and inaccessible in himself.

On the road from the modern towns of Silifke and Karaman in the Taurus Range, once stood the Byzantine Monastery of Alahan, of which only impressive ruins remain today.

In the early Christian Church of the Holy Evangelists, of about the fifth century, it is still possible to make out the cruciform baptistry. **'You were buried with him in baptism'** (Col. 2,12).

2) Because of his creative action he is in a situation entirely different from that of mere creatures, including the Angels who are here enumerated with the names which among the Jews specified the different ranks or types of their sovereignty: 'Thrones dominions, principalities, authorities'. Christ exists before all creatures as their Creator, and as the incarnate Son of God he is the 'first-born', that is, he to whom belong the primacy and the sovereignty over all created beings. Indeed, as true man Christ is to be found in the order of created entities, but at their head and in a completely different manner.

3) For his redemptive work he was filled with all the fullness of grace, i.e. of sanctifying and life-giving power; by means of his death on the cross, he has reconciled mankind with God and the whole universe, and has become the 'first-born from the dead', i.e. the first of those to be raised and the cause of the future resurrection of all men. In particular, he has become the Head of the Church, which is a Body, that is a living and continually growing organism, belonging to Christ, in a sacramental relationship with his risen Body. Here appears the doctrine of the Church as the 'mystical Body' of Christ, which completes the image of the body already mentioned in the Letters to the Corinthians (see No. 78) and the Romans (No. 99) and to be developed in the Letter to the Ephesians (see No. 125).

121 Christ associates us with his triumph (2, 9-14)

⁹ For in him the whole fulness of deity dwells bodily, ¹⁰ and you have come to fulness of life in him, who is the head of all rule and authority. ¹¹ In him also you were circumcised with a circumcision made without hands, by putting off the body of flesh in the circumcision of Christ; ¹² and you were buried with him in baptism, in which you were also raised with him through faith in the working of God, who raised him from the dead. ¹³ And you, who were dead in trespasses and the uncircumcision of your flesh, God made alive together with him, having forgiven us all our trespasses, ¹⁴ having cancelled the bond which stood against us with its legal demands; this he set aside, nailing it to the cross.

From the idea of the primacy of Christ we turn to that of his unique efficacy for our Salvation: we must not expect to be saved by 'Principalities' or 'Authorities', that is by Angels, whatever their sphere of influence may be, for Christ is the 'Head', that is the Sovereign even of angelic beings. Even less are we to look for salvation in the Jewish rite of circumcision.

St Paul is thus arguing against the 'false teachers' of Colossae but this gives him the opportunity to express very forcibly three fundamental truths: 1) the divinity of Christ: 'the whole fulness of the deity' dwells in Christ 'bodily', that is in the human nature (body and soul) of the risen Christ; 2) Baptism, accompanied by faith, makes us share in the mystery of the death and resurrection of Christ; by it we have passed from spiritual death to life, and we have become new men, putting off the old man and his vices; 3) the death of Christ on the Cross has cancelled the debt we have incurred by our sins; here St Paul uses the metaphor of a written document, containing details of the charges against us, which has been nailed to the Cross by Christ. This 'document' also contains an allusion to the Law of Moses with its rules which exclude pagans and with its sentences of death for all sinners.

122 Lesson in the christian life
(3, 1-15)

[1] If then you have been raised with Christ, seek the things that are above, where Christ is, seated at the right hand of God. [2] Set your minds on things that are above, not on things that are on earth. [3] For you have died, and your life is hid with Christ in God. [4] When Christ who is our life appears, then you also will appear with him in glory.

[5] Put to death therefore what is earthly in you: immorality, impurity, passion, evil desire, and covetousness, which is idolatry. [6] On account of these the wrath of God is coming. [7] In these you once walked, when you lived in them. [8] But now put them all away: anger, wrath, malice, slander, and foul talk from your mouth. [9] Do not lie to one another, seeing that you have put off the old nature with its practices [10] and have put on the new

nature, which is being renewed in knowledge after the image of its creator. [11] Here there cannot be Greek and Jew, circumcised and uncircumcised, barbarian, Scythian, slave, free man, but Christ is all, and in all.

[12] Put on then, as God's chosen ones, holy and beloved, compassion, kindness, lowliness, meekness, and patience, [13] forbearing one another and, if one has a complaint against another, forgiving each other; as the Lord has forgiven you, so you also must forgive. [14] And above all these put on love, which binds everything together in perfect harmony. [15] And let the peace of Christ rule in your hearts, to which indeed you were called in the one body. And be thankful.

Moral exhortations, which are never lacking in St Paul's Letters and need no comment, are always dependent on the truths of the faith. If we are already spiritually associated with Christ's resurrection our whole life has experienced a radical change of meaning and purpose. If we are risen it is because we have first 'died', that is, we have made a decisive break with our former sins and with the way of thinking out of which sins arise.

But whereas Christ, the source of our new life, is already in glory, our true life is still 'hidden'

until his coming. For this reason our carnal nature still makes us tend towards the sins to which we are already 'dead'. We need therefore continually to kill ('mortify') the tendencies which drive us towards evil and continually to exercize the virtues which we 'put on' when we 'put off' the old man in Baptism. Note the illustrations taken from the rite of baptism: the man who was being baptized took off his clothes and went down into the water as if into a tomb; then he came up out of it as if rising (from the dead) and was clothed in new white garments.

123 Epilogue and greetings
(4, 7-18)

[7] Tychicus will tell you all about my affairs; he is a beloved brother and faithful minister and fellow servant in the Lord. [8] I have sent him to you for this very purpose, that you may

known how we are and that he may encourage your hearts, [9] and with him Onesimus, the faithful and beloved brother, who is one of yourselves. They will tell you of everything that has taken place here.

[10] Aristarchus my fellow prisoner greets you, and Mark the cousin of Barnabas (concerning whom you have received instructions—if he comes to you, receive him), [11] and Jesus who is called Justus. These are the only men of the circumcision among my fellow workers for the kingdom of God, and they have been a comfort to me. [12] Epaphras, who is one of yourselves, a servant of Christ Jesus, greets you, always remembering you earnestly in his prayers, that you may stand mature and fully assured in all the will of God. [13] For I bear him witness that he has worked hard for you and for those in Laodicea and in Hierapolis. [14] Luke the beloved physician and Demas greet you. [15] Give my greetings to the brethren at Laodicea, and to Nympha and the church in her house. [16] And when this letter has been read among you, have it read also in the church of the Laodiceans. [17] And say to Archippus, "See that you fulfil the ministry which you have received in the Lord."

[18] I, Paul, write this greeting with my own hand. Remember my fetters. Grace be with you.

Note the interesting information contained in the last verses of the Letter. Mark, St Paul's young companion, on his first journey (see Nos. 37, 38 and 44) is in Rome helping the Apostle during his captivity; later he will be found also with St Peter (see No. 154) and will write the second Gospel.

Luke, the author of the third Gospel and of the Acts, arrives in Rome with St Paul (see No. 115 which is a 'we-section') and attends him faithfully. It is from this passage that we know that he was a doctor and was not of Jewish origin. Onesimus is the fugitive slave, converted by St Paul, who is the subject of the letter to Philemon (see No. 129); from this it appears that Philemon belonged to the Church at Colossae. Noteworthy also is St Paul's practice of circulating his letters among the different churches. The Letter to the Laodiceans, unless it is that which bears the heading 'To the Ephesians' (see No. 124), has been lost.

From St Paul's Letter to the Ephesians

The position of Ephesus.

Ephesus was the capital of the Roman province of Asia which covered the western part of Asia Minor or Anatolia. A very ancient city of some commercial importance because of its situation on the Aegean Sea, it became the centre of St Paul's apostolic activity during the third journey and was to be the first of the seven churches of Asia mentioned by St John in the Apocalypse (see No. 167).

St Paul's letter, called 'To the Ephesians' was not addressed to a single Christian community at Ephesus but is a sort of circular letter sent to all the communities in the Ephesian district. This explains its impersonal character, lacking references to actual situations and to people whom St Paul had known during his three years' stay at Ephesus. It may perhaps be that very letter to the Laodiceans (see No. 123) which the Colossians were told to receive from the nearby community of Laodicea. In fact this letter too was carried by the same Tychicus who took the letter to the Colossians to Colossae. St Paul wrote them both at about the same time, towards the end of his Roman captivity (62-63 A.D.). The letter to the Ephesians is not of a directly controversial character but treats the same subjects as the letter to the Colossians with a particular emphasis on praising God, praying and encouraging the faithful.

This letter too is divided into two parts, one mainly doctrinal, in which we note specially the theology of the Church in relation to God's plan of salvation, and the other devoted to moral exhortations. At the very beginning of the letter, we find these truly fundamental statements, in the form of a thanksgiving to God:

1) God the Father has determined from all eternity to 'restore'

Ephesus was a seaport and a commercial city of the first importance, being the junction of two great Roman roads and a port of access to the western part of Asia Minor. The Christian community at Ephesus was founded by St Paul (see Acts No. 63).

all things in Christ, that is to gather together all material and spiritual entities and put them under one Head, Christ.

2) In this scheme of his we also have a place: each of us has been individually chosen by God 'before the foundation of the world' and destined to become 'holy', that is consecrated to God, 'blameless', that is free from sin, and, adopted 'sons of God', 'heirs' of God's blessings which we shall finally enjoy 'in the heavenly places'.

3) All these blessings come to us from our being united with Christ. This has come about as a result of the redemption wrought by the Son of God, by means of which the Father 'has bestowed on us' every grace, that

is every free gift. We have received the 'forgiveness of our trespasses' and every blessing, not for our merits, but through 'his blood', that is through his death offered as a propitiatory sacrifice.

4) At the moment of our adherence to Christ through faith in the glad tidings (the 'Gospel') of the divine plan, we were given the Holy Spirit: He is the 'seal', that is the pledge, the manifestation of the blessings we have received and the 'guarantee' of those which belong to us by 'inheritance' but which we are not yet able to enjoy. In this way he refers to the inner light and charismatic phenomena (see Nos. 78, 90 and 98) which are due to the action of the Holy Spirit dwelling in us.

124 Introduction: God's plan in Christ (1, 1-14)

[1] Paul, an apostle of Christ Jesus by the will of God. To the saints who are also faithful in Christ Jesus: [2] Grace to you and peace from God our Father and the Lord Jesus Christ. [3] Blessed be the God and Father of our Lord Jesus Christ, who has blessed us in Christ with every spiritual blessing in the heavenly places, [4] even as he chose us in him before the foundation of the world, that we should be holy and blameless before him. [5] He destined us in love to be his sons through Jesus Christ, according to the purpose of his will, [6] to the praise of his glorious grace which he freely bestowed on us in the Beloved. [7] In him we have redemption through his blood, the forgiveness of our trespasses, according to the riches of his grace [8] which he lavished upon us. [9] For he has made known to us in all wisdom and insight the mystery of his will, according

to his purpose which he set forth in Christ ¹⁰ as a plan for the fulness of time, to unite all things in him, things in heaven and things on earth.

¹¹ In him, according to the purpose of him who accomplishes all things according to the counsel of his will, ¹² we who first hoped in Christ have been destined and appointed to live for the praise of his glory. ¹³ In him you also, who have heard the word of truth, the gospel of your salvation, and have believed in him, were sealed with the promised Holy Spirit, ¹⁴ who is the guarantee of our inheritance until we acquire possession of it, to the praise of his glory.

125 The Church as the Body of Christ
(1, 16-23; 4, 15-16)

1, ¹⁶ I do not cease to give thanks for you, remembering you in my prayers, ¹⁷ that the God of our Lord Jesus Christ, the Father of glory, may give you a spirit of wisdom and of revelation in the knowledge of him, ¹⁸ having the eyes of your hearts enlightened, that you may know what is the hope to which he has called you, what are the riches of his glorious inheritance in the saints, ¹⁹ and what is the immeasurable greatness of his power in us who believe, according to the working of his great might ²⁰ which he accomplished in Christ when he raised him from the dead and made him sit at his right hand in the heavenly places, ²¹ far above all rule and authority and power and dominion, and above every name that is named, not only in this age but also in that which is to come; ²² and he has put all things under his feet and has made him the head over all things for the church, ²³ which is his body, the fulness of him who fills all in all.

4, ¹⁵ Speaking the truth in love, we are to grow up in every way into him who is the head, into Christ, ¹⁶ from whom the whole body, joined and knit together by every joint with which it is supplied, when each part is working properly, makes bodily growth and upbuilds itself in love.

The risen Christ, 'at the right hand' of God, that is equal with the Father, not only because of his divine nature but also in the exercise of universal suzerainty, is Lord of angelic spirits ('all rule and authority and power and dominion'), and is Head of the Church. This is a Body, that is an entity of various parts, each with its own distinct functions, in continual progress towards an ever more perfect assimilation to Christ's perfection.

Every member of the Church is united to the vital power which *derives from Christ, the Head, so long as he remains attached to the 'joints' or members through which the grace of Christ works. But as he receives from other members, so also must he give, in order to grow with the rest and to make the whole Body grow in Christ. The Church is the Body of Christ because it belongs to him and because it is his 'fulness', that is to say the space, so to speak, which he fills with his grace (For the Church as the Body of Christ see also Nos. 78, 99 and 120).*

126 In the Church Jews and pagans become one single people
(2, 4-22)

⁴ God, who is rich in mercy, out of the great love with which he loved us, ⁵ even when we were dead through our trespasses, made us alive together with Christ (by grace you have been saved), ⁶ and raised us up with him, and made us sit with him in the heavenly place in Christ Jesus, ⁷ that in the coming ages he might show the immeasurable riches of his grace in kindness toward us in Christ Jesus. ⁸ For by grace you have been saved through faith; and this is not your own doing, it is the gift of God—⁹ not because of works, lest any man should boast. ¹⁰ For we are his workmanship, created in Christ Jesus for good works, which God prepared beforehand, that we should walk in them.

¹¹ Therefore remember that at one time you Gentiles in the flesh, called the uncircumcision by what is called the circumcision, which is made in the flesh by hands—¹² remember that you were at that time separated from Christ, alienated from the commonwealth of Israel, and strangers to the covenants of promise, having no hope and without God in the world. ¹³ But now in Christ Jesus you who once were far off have been brought near in the blood of Christ. ¹⁴ For he is our peace, who has made

us both one, and has broken down the dividing wall of hostility, [15] by abolishing in his flesh the law of commandments and ordinances, that he might create in himself one new man in place of the two, so making peace, [16] and might reconcile us both to God in one body through the cross, thereby bringing the hostility to an end. [17] And he came and preached peace to you who were far off and peace to those who were near; [18] for through him we both have access in one Spirit to the Father. [19] So then you are no longer strangers and sojourners, but you are fellow citizens with the saints and members of the household of God, [20] built upon the foundation of the apostles and prophets, Christ Jesus himself being the cornerstone, [21] in whom the whole structure is joined together and grows into a holy temple in the Lord; [22] in whom you also are built into it for a dwelling place of God in the Spirit.

One of the effects of Christ's redemption has been the supersession of the Law of Moses and the annulment of the arrangements which were intended to make Israel a people separated from all others. St Paul makes use of the illustration of a party wall which has been demolished by the death of Christ on the Cross. Salvation comes by faith, by God's gift, with no difference between Jews and pagans; united with Christ the two peoples become one people, 'one new man', 'one body', that is the Church.

This is described under the image of a building under construction in which new converts are incorporated as living stones to form the one Temple of God.

127 The sacred character of marriage
(5, 21-33)

[21] Be subject to one another out of reverence for Christ. [22] Wives, be subject to your husbands, as to the Lord, [23] For the husband is the head of the wife as Christ is the head of the church, his body, and is himself its Saviour. [24] As the church is subject to Christ, so let wives also be subject in everything to their husbands. [25] Husbands, love your wives, as Christ loved

the church and gave himself up for her, ²⁶ that he might sanctify her, having cleansed her by the washing of water with the word, ²⁷ that he might present the church to himself in splendour, without spot or wrinkle or any such thing, that she might be holy and without blemish. ²⁸ Even so husbands should love their wives as their own bodies. He who loves his wife loves himself. ²⁹ For no man ever hates his own flesh, but nourishes and cherishes it, as Christ does the church, ³⁰ because we are members of his body. ³¹ "For this reason a man shall leave his father and mother and be joined to his wife, and the two shall become one." ³² This is a great mystery, and I mean in reference to Christ and the church; ³³ however, let each one of you love his wife as himself, and let the wife see that she respects her husband.

The union of a man and woman, hallowed by an unbreakable pact, is a 'mystery', which means a sacred reality in the order of salvation. Marriage is the image of the union of Christ with the Church and so of the common life (i.e. grace) which flows between Christ and the Church. Therefore, the Church teaches, marriage according to Christ's will is an effective means of grace, i.e. a 'sacrament'. From this doctrine a very practical conclusion follows: the image must be like its sublime model; the love of husband and wife must draw its inspiration from Christ, who loved the Church and sacrificed himself for it. Note that this description of the Church as the Bride, and also as the Body of Christ, makes it clear that the Church's belonging to Christ as his Body, does not in any way remove the distinction between the Person of Christ, divine by nature, and the individuality of the members of the Church, each of whom is 'son' of God by incorporation and by grace and not by nature.

128 Duties of fathers and sons, of masters and servants (16, 1-9)

¹ Children, obey your parents in the Lord, for this is right. ² "Honour your father and mother" (this is the first command-

ment with a promise), [3] "that it may be well with you and that you may live long on the earth." [4] Fathers, do not provoke your children to angers but bring them up in the discipline and instruction of the Lord.

[5] Slaves, be obedient to those who are your earthly masters, with fear and trembling, in singleness of heart, as to Christ; [6] not in the way of eye-service, as men-pleasers, but as servants of Christ, doing the will of God from the heart, [7] rendering service with a good will as to the Lord and not to men, [8] knowing that whatever good any one does, he will receive the same again from the Lord, whether he is a slave or free. [9] Masters, do the same to them, and forbear threatening, knowing that he who is both their Master and yours is in heaven, and that there is no partiality with him.

Here is another example of the doctrinal formation of Christian morality, Christ is the point of reference for relations among men. One alone is truly Lord; to him must those who call themselves masters on earth render their account, just as those who perform the duties of servants must serve him. In the letter to Philemon this is brought out very clearly with regard to relations between the master and the Christian slave: 'In Christ Jesus there is 'neither slave nor free' (see No. 89 and No. 129 which follows).

St Paul's Letter to Philemon

This short Letter, full of warm human feeling, and of lively affection not without a trace of gentle irony ('I will repay it — to say nothing of your owing me even your own self') was written by St Paul as a note to accompany Onesimus the fugitive slave, who was sent back to his master, Philemon at Colossae, together with Tychicus, the bearer of the Letter to the Colossians. It was thus written towards the end of Paul's captivity (about 62-63 A.D.); in it he expresses the hope of soon being his friend's guest. Onesimus, the pagan slave of the Christian Philemon, had fled after having done 'some injury'. When he arrived in Rome he had been converted and baptized by St Paul. The latter did not keep the fugitive with him, nor does he directly command his friend to free the slave, but he recommends him to receive him 'no longer as a slave but... as a beloved brother'. So he calls Onesimus 'my child', 'my very heart'; he intervenes with the weight of his friendship and of the debts of gratitude which Philemon owes him, in order that the runaway may be pardoned and welcomed with generous kindliness. In this incident may be seen the influence of Christianity on the institutions of the day. It does not take up an external position of hostility to the institution of slavery on which the economy of the Graeco-Roman world was based. It does not proclaim an economic and social revolution, but destroys from within the mistaken assumptions of this institution, and replaces them by principles which, once they are understood and welcomed, will cause the collapse of the institution and in the meantime will radically transform relations between freemen and slaves in the bosom of the Christian community.

129

[1] Paul, a prisoner for Christ Jesus, and Timothy our brother. To Philemon our beloved fellow worker [2] and Apphia our sister and Archippus our fellow soldier, and the church in your house:

[3] Grace to you and peace from God our Father and the Lord Jesus Christ.

⁴ I thank my God always when I remember you in my prayers, ⁵ because I hear of your love and of the faith which you have toward the Lord Jesus and all the saints, ⁶ and I pray that the sharing of your faith may promote the knowledge of all the good that is ours in Christ. ⁷ For I have derived much joy and comfort from your love, my brother, because the hearts of the saints have been refreshed through you.

⁸ Accordingly, though I am bold enough in Christ to command you to do what is required, ⁹ yet for love's sake I prefer to appeal to you—I, Paul, an ambassador and now a prisoner also for Christ Jesus—¹⁰ I appeal to you for my child, Onesimus, whose father I have become in my imprisonment. ¹¹ (Formerly he was useless to you, but now he is indeed useful to you and to me.) ¹² I am sending him back to you, sending my very heart. ¹³ I would have been glad to keep him with me, in order that he might serve me on your behalf during my imprisonment for the gospel; ¹⁴ but I preferred to do nothing without your consent in order that your goodness might not be by compulsion but of your own free will.

¹⁵ Perhaps this is why he was parted from you for a while, that you might have him back for ever, ¹⁶ no longer as a slave but more than a slave, as a beloved brother, especially to me but how much more to you, both in the flesh and in the Lord. ¹⁷ So if you consider me your partner, receive him as you would receive me. ¹⁸ If he has wronged you at all, or owes you anything, charge that to my account. ¹⁹ I, Paul, write this with my own hand, I will repay it—to say nothing of your owing me even your own self. ²⁰ Yes, brother, I want some benefit from you in the Lord. Refresh my heart in Christ.

²¹ Confident of your obedience, I write to you, knowing that you will do even more than I say. ²² At the same time prepare a guest room for me, for I am hoping through your prayers to be granted to you.

²³ Epaphras, my fellow prisoner in Christ Jesus, sends greetings to you, ²⁴ and so do Mark, Aristarchus, Demas, and Luke, my fellow workers.

²⁵ The grace of the Lord Jesus Christ be with your spirit.

Third Period

THE APOSTOLIC WRITINGS FROM NERO'S PERSECUTION TILL THE DEATH OF ST JOHN

(64-104 A. D.)

Jerusalem. The Pinnacle of the Temple recalls the martyrdom of St James, Jesus' cousin. The south-eastern corner of the Herodian wall was generally called the 'Pinnacle'; it was about a hundred metres high. Excavations which are now being carried out at the foot of the south-eastern corner give rise to the opinion that the foundations of the Pinnacle itself are several metres below the present level.

From the time when the book of the Acts ends (in 63 A.D.) until the end of the apostolic age which closes with the death of St John the Evangelist (about the year 103) there was a succession of events of great importance in the history of the early Church. The essential points in these events are as follows:

62 A.D. MARTYRDOM OF ST JAMES, JESUS' COUSIN

In the year 62 the Procurator Festus, who had sent Paul for trial in Rome (see No. 108) died in office, and had no successor for some months until the arrival of the new Procurator Albinus. The High Priest, Ananias, son of that Annas, the father-in-law of Caiaphas, who had played a large part in the condemnation of Jesus, took advantage of the 'power vacuum' to bring some Christians to trial and condemn them to death. Among them was James, the 'brother' or cousin of Jesus (see Nos. 42 and 101) who was head of the Church in Jerusalem. Even many of the Jews deplored this killing, for James was held in considerable esteem for his ascetic life and was well known for his particular observance of all the rules of the Law of Moses. In fact the new Procurator Albinus accused Ananias of breaking the statute which forbade the Sanhedrim to carry out death sentences, and had him deposed. According to a tradition not to be lightly dismissed, James was cast down from the south-eastern side of the Temple into the valley of the Kedron and there stoned. While he was praying for his murderers, a blow on the head with a cudgel ended his life.

The death of St James marks the final estrangement of the Jewish Christians from official Judaism. St James had tried hard not to break these ties, by frequenting the Temple and praying for the conversion of his people.

64-67 A.D. NERO'S PERSECUTION

As the book of the Acts also shows, until the year 64 the Roman authorities had shown no bias against the Christians; in fact St Paul had chosen Nero's judgment in preference to that of the Sanhedrim (see No. 108).

But the situation changed without warning after the fire which devastated Rome in July, 64. Nero, who was accused by public opinion of having caused the fire, threw back the charge on to the Christians, who were unpopular because of their rejection of the national religion. The historian Tacitus writes that 'a huge crowd' of Christians was condemned to death to provide a public spectacle in Nero's gardens on the slopes of the Vatican hill.

They were clothed in animals' skins and torn to pieces by dogs or covered with inflammable materials and burnt alive to illuminate the nocturnal revelries. On this occasion the imperial decree 'It is not permitted to be a Christian' was promulgated: it formed the legal ground for the persecutions which followed.

67 A.D. THE MARTYRDOM OF ST PETER AND ST PAUL

The most distinguished victims of Nero's persecution were the apostles Peter and Paul, the former discovered to be head of the Roman church, the latter probably arrested at Troas and brought to Rome. According to a well-founded historical tradition, St Peter was crucified on the Vatican hill where his tomb has been constantly venerated until our own days. This tradition has been confirmed by recent archaeological excavations under the Basilica of St Peter.

St Paul, as a Roman citizen, died by the sword, being beheaded on the Ostian Way. The site of his martyrdom is shown in the Church of the Three Fountains: his tomb is in the Basilica of St Paul-outside-the-Walls.

Rome. Very early 'graffiti' and inscriptions by pilgrims, invoking Peter and Paul in the Catacombs of St Sebastian on the Old Appian Way.

66-70 A.D. THE JEWISH WAR

The insurrection of the Palestinian Jews against the Romans was caused by the greedy and provocative government of the Roman Procurator Gessius Florus (64-66).

The first acts of armed hostility were the massacre of the Roman garrison of Jerusalem, in spite of King Agrippa's attempt to pacify the insurgents, and the assassination of the high priest, Ananias, chief spokesman of the pacifists.

This happened in May-June 66. In the autumn the Legate (Governor) of Syria, Cestius Gallus, intervened with his Legion and auxiliary troops. He occupied the northern part of Jerusalem and made an unsuccessful assault on the Temple, which was like a great fortress. He then withdrew, pursued by the insurgents, who were by now determined to use every means against the colossal power of Rome. Nero, who was then in Greece, gave the command of Judea to Vespasian, who went there with three legions and allied forces, in all about 60,000 men.

Meanwhile the Christian community in Jerusalem, mindful of Jesus' prophecy, left the city destined for destruction, and took refuge in the free city of Pella on the other side of the Jordan.

The second year of war (67-68) marked for the insurgents the loss of Galilee and the victory of the extreme party, the Zealots, over the traditional aristocracy, inside Jerusalem. The ex-High Priest Ananias, slayer of St James, was also murdered, along with a great many others and lay for a long time unburied. Vespasian occupied the region round Jerusalem until, on the death of Nero (9 June 68), he broke off military operations, though remaining in the positions he had taken.

Rome. In the Roman forum: detail from the Arch of Triumph raised in honour of Titus, the victor of the Judean War. The seven-branched candlestick, in solid gold, which burned in the Temple of Jerusalem, is carried by Roman legionaries as a trophy of war.

329

Masada: a rocky height which stands alone in the volcanic desert of the Dead Sea. Because of its rugged nature it was often fortified in Jewish history. Here the survivors of the Jewish War took refuge and here, after a long resistance, they killed each other so as not to fall alive into the hands of the pagans (73 A.D.).

The war was at a standstill during the whole of the year 68-69 during which three emperors, Galba, Otto and Vitellius, succeeded one another. But within the city three factions of Zealots, led by John of Giscala, Simon bar Ghiosa and Eleazar, fought among themselves with bitter hatred, great loss of men and the destruction of provisions.

The war started again in July 69 when Vespasian was acclaimed emperor. His son, Titus, was given charge of military operations which he directed calmly and relentlessly until in May 70 he stationed his legions around Jerusalem. When Titus had surrounded the city on every side with a fortified rampart, hunger began to claim its victims among the besieged. But the city did not yield to hunger. Entrenched behind the great walls which protected the different quarters, the citizens defended their positions desperately but saw one quarter after another fall into enemy hands. On 6 August 70,

against the wishes of Titus, the soldiers set fire to the Temple, which was quickly devoured by the flames. On 2 September the high city on the western hill fell, and all of Jerusalem that still survived was destroyed by fire.

At Rome the victorious Titus celebrated his triumph. The arch, called in fact the Arch of Titus, (constructed later) still preserves its memory. After this John of Giscala was sent to the galleys and Simon bar Ghiora was beheaded in the Mamertine prison. Some of the 97,000 prisoners were condemned to forced labour in the quarries, others sold into slavery.

The last act of this terrible war was the fall of the fortress of Masada on the western shore of the Dead Sea, where a group of Zealots with their families resisted desperately until the spring of 73. When surrender became inevitable, they killed each other so as not to fall alive into the hands of the Romans.

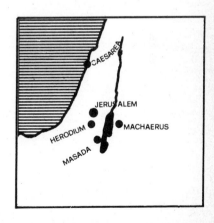

Sites of the Jewish war.

Patmos. The little island off the coast of Asia where St John in exile wrote the Apocalypse.

The fall of Jerusalem and particularly the destruction of the Temple, which was never rebuilt, marked the end of Biblical Judaism. It was not the cause of the Diaspora which had already been in existence for more than two centuries, but it deprived the scattered Jews of a single authoritative religious centre. By the Christians it was interpreted as a sign from God of the fall of the old religious system which had indeed prepared for the coming of the Messiah (in the Old Testament), but had no more reason for existing after the inauguration of the Kingdom of Christ.

A.D. 95-96 DOMITIAN'S PERSECUTION

The Emperor Domitian (81-96), successor of his brother Titus, in spite of his successful military enterprises, made himself hated by the tyranny of his rule to such an extent that he was killed by conspirators. Jews and Christians saw in him a second Nero, specially because of his craze for being given divine honours. Domitian renewed Nero's decree against the Christians, bringing to trial and sending to their deaths even distinguished people like the ex-consul Flavius Clemens, Flavia Domitilla, members of the Imperial family, and Acilius Glabrio, the senator. St John the Evangelist was banished to the island of Patmos where he wrote the Apocalypse in which there are obvious allusions to Domitian and the blood of the martyrs spilt in his reign. According to a tradition mentioned by Tertullian (third century) St John was plunged into boiling oil and when he emerged miraculously unhurt was sentenced to banishment.

The position of Patmos.

333

98-117 A.D. TRAJAN'S PERSECUTION

After the mild rule of Nerva (96-98) Trajan took the affairs of the Empire firmly in hand and renewed the persecution of the Christians, regulating the procedure by the famous rescript to Pliny the Younger. The police were not to seek out Christians nor were they to accept anonymous accusations. On a regular denunciation they were to take action, enquiring into the truth of the denunciation and trying to make those who turned out to be Christians renounce their religion. Those who persisted were to be sentenced to death.

In this persecution there perished St Ignatius of Antioch and St Simon Bishop of the Jewish Christians.

The Apostle St John died at Ephesus in Trajan's reign (probably in its sixth year, i.e. about 104 A.D.) but not by martyrdom. Already the Popes Linus, Cletus, Clement and Evaristus had succeeded to St Peter's Chair in Rome.

Seventy years after Pentecost the Christian Church had spread through Palestine, Syria, Asia Minor, Cyprus, Crete, Macedonia, Greece, southern Italy and in Rome, the centre of the Empire.

END OF THE HISTORICAL SUMMARY

I. St Paul's Pastoral Letters

Macedonia and Ephesus.

The letters to Timothy and Titus, St Paul's last writings, are called 'Pastoral Letters' because their chief content concerns the rules the two disciples must follow in the government of the Church entrusted to them by the Apostle for a period. In fact they seem to have been given full powers, as deputes or delegates of the Apostle, including the power of ordaining presbyters (that is, priests) and deacons, though they had not yet the authority of resident bishops, which they were to receive on the death of the Apostles.

From St Paul's First Letter to Timothy

The first of St Paul's pastoral letters was addressed to Timothy, the devoted disciple who had been the Apostle's constant companion since his second journey (see No. 45), and had also undertaken important and delicate missions (see Nos. 56, 63, 72 and 81).

Towards the end of 63 the trial of St Paul had ended in his acquittal. Freed from his Roman captivity, during which Timothy had lovingly assisted him, the Apostle was able to return with his disciple to visit his Christian communities.

It was probably at this time that Paul was also able to realize his desire to carry the Gospel into Spain (see No. 100) but he cannot have remained there long. During a visit to Ephesus he became aware of certain irregularities. He was particularly con-

335

Macedonian countryside. Macedonia was crossed by the Roman road called 'Egnatia' which joined the Bosphorüs with the Adriatic at Durazzo opposite Brindisi, so making an ideal connexion with the Appian Way and Rome. It was from Macedonia that St Paul wrote the first Letter to his disciple, Timothy.

cerned that some people, posing as masters of the Jewish Law, were teaching new doctrines foreign to the Gospel. As he was unable to stay at Ephesus, before leaving for Macedonia he left Timothy with all the powers and authority of an apostle in the Asian capital. He wrote the first Letter from Macedonia in 65 or 66 in order to advise and support him in his difficult task.

130 Introduction
(1, 1-7)

¹ Paul, an apostle of Christ Jesus by command of God our Saviour and of Christ Jesus our hope.

² To Timothy, my true child in the faith:

Grace, mercy, and peace from God the Father and Christ Jesus our Lord.

³ As I urged you when I was going to Macedonia, remain at Ephesus that you may charge certain persons not to teach any different doctrine, ⁴ nor to occupy themselves with myths and endless genealogies which promote speculations rather than the divine training that is in faith; ⁵ whereas the aim of our charge is love that issues from a pure heart and a good conscience and sincere faith. ⁶ Certain persons by swerving from these have wandered away into vain discussion, ⁷ desiring to be teachers of the law, without understanding either what they are saying or the things about which they make assertions.

131 The selection of bishops and deacons
(3, 1-16)

¹ The saying is sure; If any one aspires to the office of bishop, he desires a noble task. ² Now a bishop must be above reproach, the husband of one wife, temperate, sensible, dignified, hospitable, an apt teacher, ³ no drunkard, not violent but gentle, not quarrelsome, and no lover of money. ⁴ He must manage his own household well, keeping his children submissive and respectful in every way; ⁵ for if man does not know how to manage his own household, how can he care for God's church? ⁶ He must not be a recent convert, or he may be puffed up

with conceit and fall into the condemnation of the devil; [7] moreover he must be well thought of by outsiders, or he may fall into reproach and the snare of the devil.

[8] Deacons likewise must be serious, not double-tongued, not addicted to much wine, not greedy for gain; [9] they must hold the mystery of the faith with a clear conscience. [10] And let them also be tested first; then if they prove themselves blameless let them serve as deacons. [11] The women likewise must be serious, no slanderers, but temperate, faithful in all things. [12] Let deacons be the husband of one wife, and let them manage their children and their households well; [13] for those who serve well as deacons gain a good standing for themselves and also great confidence in the faith which is in Christ Jesus.

[14] I hope to come to you soon, but I am writing these instructions to you so that, [15] if I am delayed, you may know how one ought to behave in the household of God, which is the church of the living God, the pillar and bulwark of the truth. [16] Great indeed, we confess, is the mystery of our religion:

He was manifested in the flesh,
vindicated in the Spirit, seen by angels,
preached among the nations,
believed on in the world, taken up in glory.

The hierarchy of the several churches during the life of the Apostles was thus organized:

1) Supreme authority was held by the Apostle who had founded the local church, in this case at Ephesus. St Paul alone chose and appointed the presbyters and ruled the Church, even from a distance by means of delegates or deputies, like Timothy and Titus. These delegates had full powers and they also chose and appointed presbyters and deacons. They were thus like those who were later called 'bishops' and who, after the Apostles died, were their successors in the government of local churches.

2) In every church there was a college of 'presbyters'. This Greek word means 'elders' and from it is derived the English word 'priest'.

Concerning the appointment of presbyters see No. 40; for the presbyters of Jerusalem see Nos. 41 and 101. The task of the presbyters was to govern the community in the absence of the Apostles and to preside over the celebration of the Eucharist in liturgical assemblies. The presbyters were also called 'bishops', that is 'overseers' or 'supervisors' (see No. 68), but were probably not bishops in the modern sense, (the word 'bishop' is derived from the Greek 'episcopos') but simply priests.

3) In every church there was also an adequate number of

'deacons', that is 'ministers' (see their institution at No. 16). They had liturgical functions and tasks of charitable relief: it they were specially gifted, they preached the word of God.

Presbyters and deacons were men of mature age, respected by the community, and had shown wisdom and the power to govern the Christian community by the way they ordered their own families. So as to guide his disciple in the exercise of his authority St Paul tells Timothy what their gifts must be.

At the end of this passage St Paul quotes a verse of an ancient hymn to Christ, 'the mystery of our religion', that is the object of faith and the reason and foundation of all religious practice.

132 Timothy's pastoral tasks (4, 12-16)

¹² Let no one despise your youth, but set the believers an example in speech and conduct, in love, in faith, in purity. ¹³ Till I come, attend to the public reading of scripture, to preaching, to teaching. ¹⁴ Do not neglect the gift you have, which was given you by prophetic utterance when the elders laid their hands upon you. ¹⁵ Practise these duties, devote yourself to them, so that all may see your progress. ¹⁶ Take heed to yourself and to your teaching; hold to that, for by so doing you will save both yourself and your hearers.

This passage must be read in connection with the other passage in 2 Timothy 1, 6: 'I remind you to rekindle the gift of God that is within you through the laying on of my hands' (see No. 136).

St Paul encourages his disciple to undertake the heavy responsibilities of his pastoral office by reminding him of the grace, 'gift', which is his by the sacrament of Holy Order conferred through the laying on of the Apostle's hands, joined with those of the college of presbyters. The 'prophetic utterance' to which St Paul refers, concerns the choice of the candidate: people endowed with the gift of prophecy (see No. 78) had certified that Timothy's ordination was in accordance with God's will. This too must have encouraged Timothy if his still youthful age (he was about thirty-five) and his timid and gentle character put him in difficulties in dealing with presbyters who were older and yet had less authority.

133 Widows in the service of the Church
(5, 3-16)

³ Honour widows who are real widows. ⁴ If a widow has children or grandchildren, let them first learn their religious duty to their own family and make some return to their parents; for this is acceptable in the sight of God. ⁵ She who is a real widow, and is left all alone, has set her hope on God and continues in supplications and prayers night and day; ⁶ whereas she who is self-indulgent is dead even while she lives. ⁷ Command this, so that they may be without reproach. ⁸ If any one does not provide for his relatives, and especially for his own family, he has disowned the faith and is worse than an unbeliever.

⁹ Let a widow be enrolled if she is not less than sixty years of age, having been the wife of one husband; ¹⁰ and she must be well attested for her good deeds, as one who has brought up children, shown hospitality, washed the feet of the saints, relieved the afflicted, and devoted herself to doing good in every way. ¹¹ But refuse to enrol younger widows; for when they grow wanton against Christ they desire to marry, ¹² and so they incur condemnation for having violated their first pledge. ¹³ Besides that, they learn to be idlers, gadding about from house to house, and not only idlers but gossips and busybodies, saying what they should not. ¹⁴ So I would have younger widows marry, bear children, rule their households, and give the enemy no occasion to revile us. ¹⁵ For some have already strayed after Satan. ¹⁶ If any believing woman has relatives who are widows, let her assist them; let the church not be burdened, so that it may assist those who are real widows.

Widows who had no relatives who could take care of them were supported by the Church's charity. Those who were suitable served as 'deaconesses' without however belonging to the hierarchy. They were of great service in approaching and instructing other women who, in a Greek milieu, were difficult of access to strangers. Their delicate mission required wisdom and prudence: hence the rules for their selection which St Paul gives.

From St Paul's Letter to Titus

After his release from captivity in Rome (63 A.D.) St Paul again went to the island of Crete and organized a Christian community there. He left there his disciple Titus with full powers (like Timothy in Ephesus) to carry on the apostolic work. After a time he wrote this letter, probably from Macedonia, with valuable pastoral regulations about the *choice of the sacred ministers and the duties of various classes of person. Titus, a disciple from the very beginning, and a convert from paganism (see No. 87), had always been at St Paul's side; he was energetic and prudent and had brought his mission to the unruly community at Corinth to a satisfactory conclusion (see page 217).*

134 Duties of presbyters (1, 5-9)

⁵ This is why I left you in Crete, that you might amend what was defective, and appoint elders in every town as I directed you, ⁶ if any man is blameless, the husband of one wife, and his children are believers and not open to the charge of being profligate or insubordinate. ⁷ For a bishop, as God's steward, must be blameless; he must not be arrogant or quick-tempered or a drunkard or violent or greedy for gain, ⁸ but hospitable, a lover of goodness, master of himself, upright, holy, and self-controlled; ⁹ he must hold firm to the sure word as taught, so that he may be able to give instruction in sound doctrine and also to confute those who contradict it.

135 Latest news (3, 12-15)

¹² When I send Artemas or Tychicus to you, do your best to come to me at Nicopolis, for I have decided to spend the winter there. ¹³ Do your best to speed Zenas the lawyer and Apollos on their way; see that they lack nothing. ¹⁴ And let our people learn to apply themselves to good deeds, so as to help cases of urgent need, and not to be unfruitful.
¹⁵ All who are with me send greetings to you. Greet those who love us in the faith.
Grace be with you all.

Artemas, of whom we know nothing, and Tychicus who had been bearer of the letters to the Colossians and Ephesians (see No. 123 and p. 315) would appear to have been replaced by Titus who must have joined St Paul in the city of Nicopolis in Epirus. Thence, before St Paul was imprisoned for the last time, he left for Dalmatia (see No. 139); according to tradition he returned to Crete after St Paul's death and became its first bishop. Zenas, who is unknown, and the famous Apollos, the great preacher at Corinth, (see Nos. 62, 70 and 81) were bearers of the letter to Titus, who must have provided for their return journey.

From St Paul's Second Letter to Timothy

The Neronian persecution of the Christians was raging. Beginning in Rome in 64 it spread with varying degrees of speed and violence in the Eastern provinces of the Empire. St Paul had been arrested while he was at Troas, probably in the summer of the year 66. Taken to Rome by virtue of his status as a Roman citizen, he had the benefit of a regular trial which went on for a long time. But he had no illusions: this time he felt he was near the end. In these circumstances he wanted to have the company of Timothy, his faithful disciple from the first years of his apostleship, and wrote this letter in which he does not fail to include valuable advice but in which he frankly opens his heart in a retrospective survey of his long and arduous apostolic work.

Worthy of note is the exhortation at the end of the Introduction: 'Guard the truth that has been entrusted to you': now the apostolic teaching has been completed and constitutes a 'deposit', that is a treasure entrusted to the successors of the Apostles, which must be preserved by them and handed on to future generations. Revelation is thus not entrusted solely to the written word (Holy Scripture) but also to oral teaching (Tradition) handed on by the Apostles to those who carry on their work.

136 Introduction (1, 1-14)

[1] Paul, an apostle of Christ Jesus by the will of God according to the promise of the life which is in Christ Jesus,

[2] To Timothy, my beloved child:

Grace, mercy, and peace from God the Father and Christ Jesus our Lord.

³ I thank God whom I serve with a clear conscience, as did my fathers, when I remember you constantly in my prayers. ⁴ As I remember your tears, I long night and day to see you, that I may be filled with joy. ⁵ I am reminded of your sincere faith, a faith that dwelt first in your grandmother Lois and your mother Eunice and now, I am sure, dwells in you. ⁶ Hence I remind you to rekindle the gift of God that is within you through the laying on of my hands; ⁷ for God did not give us a spirit of timidity but a spirit of power and love and self-control.

⁸ Do not be ashamed then of testifying to our Lord, nor of me his prisoner, but take your share of suffering for the gospel in the power of God, ⁹ who saved us and called us with a holy calling, not in virtue of our works but in virtue of his own purpose and the grace which he gave us in Christ Jesus ages ago, ¹⁰ and now has manifested through the appearing of our Saviour Christ Jesus, who abolished death and brought life and immortality to light through the gospel. ¹¹ For this gospel I was appointed a preacher and apostle and teacher, ¹² and therefore I suffer as I do. But I am not ashamed, for I know whom I have believed, and I am sure that he is able to guard until that Day what has been entrusted to me. ¹³ Follow the pattern of the sound words which you have heard from me, in the faith and love which are in Christ Jesus; ¹⁴ guard the truth that has been entrusted to you by the Holy Spirit who dwells within us.

137 Tradition and Holy Scripture
(3, 10-17)

¹⁰ Now you have observed my teaching, my conduct, my aim in life, my faith, my patience, my love, my steadfastness, ¹¹ my persecutions, my sufferings, what befell me at Antioch, at Iconium, and at Lystra, what persecutions I endured; yet from them all the Lord rescued me. ¹² Indeed all who desire to live a godly life in Christ Jesus will be persecuted, ¹³ while evil men and impostors will go on from bad to worse, deceivers and

deceived. [14] But as for you, continue in what you have learned and have firmly believed, knowing from whom you learned it [15] and how from childhood you have been acquainted with the sacred writings which are able to instruct you for salvation through faith in Christ Jesus. [16] All scripture is inspired by God and profitable for teaching, for reproof, for correction, and for training in righteousness, [17] that the man of God may be complete, equipped for every good work.

Timothy was the son of a Jewess who had become a Christian (see No. 45) In the previous section, 136, St Paul praises his mother, Eunice, and also his grandmother, Lois. From them Timothy had learnt from his earliest years the Sacred History of the Old Testament.

Here St Paul records the common teaching of all the Apostles, based on Jesus' attitude to the Sacred Books of the Jews: they are 'inspired' by God and intended to lead men to salvation. St Peter too gives the same teaching (see No. 156). The 'inspiration' of the Sacred Books implies that their human writers (prophets, wise men, historians) were God's instruments to make known to the religious community (Israel and later the Church) his will and his plans for salvation.

The sacred writers did not write in ecstasy or under divine dictation but were inspired by God in conceiving and writing their works. Therefore Holy Scripture is 'veracious', that is, it contains without error those truths which God wished to convey for the salvation of men.

Holy Scripture attains its maximum value when it is read in the milieu of the Church, in the light of the apostolic teaching handed on by the Tradition (see No. 137 above) to which St Paul refers in the words 'continue in what you have learned and firmly believed, knowing from whom you have learned it'.

138 Spiritual testament (4, 1-8)

[1] I charge you in the presence of God and of Christ Jesus who is to judge the living and the dead, and by his appearing and his kingdom: [2] preach the word, be urgent in season and out of season, convince, rebuke, and exhort, be unfailing in patience and in teaching. [3] For the time is coming when people

will not endure sound teaching, but having itching ears they will accumulate for themselves teachers to suit their own likings, ⁴ and will turn away from listening to the truth and wander into myths. ⁵ As for you, always be steady, endure suffering, do the work of an evangelist, fulfil your ministry.

⁶ For I am already on the point of being sacrificed; the time of my departure has come. ⁷ I have fought the good fight, I have finished the race, I have kept the faith. ⁸ Henceforth there is laid up for me the crown of righteousness, which the Lord, the righteous judge, will award to men on that Day, and not only to me but also to all who have loved his appearing.

As in the first letter so also in the last, the thought of Christ's 'glorious coming' or 'Parousia' at the end of time, is present and paramount (see Nos. 55 and 58).

St Paul feels that death is near and thinks of it as the last act of a sacrifice. Libation consisted of pouring wine from a goblet on to the altar: similarly St Paul thinks of his life as being poured out in fighting and striving entirely and solely for the Lord. He fears neither death nor his meeting with Christ as Judge, for he looks for his reward as the 'crown' which is awarded to victors.

139 Latest news
(4, 9-22)

⁹ Do your best to come to me soon. ¹⁰ For Demas, in love with this present world, has deserted me and gone to Thessalonica; Crescens has gone to Galatia, Titus to Dalmatia. ¹¹ Luke alone is with me. Get Mark and bring him with you; for he is very useful in serving me. ¹² Tychicus I have sent to Ephesus. ¹³ When you come, bring the cloak that I left with Carpus at Troas, also the books, and above all the parchments. ¹⁴ Alexander the coppersmith did me great harm; the Lord will requite him for his deeds. ¹⁵ Beware of him yourself, for he strongly opposed our message. ¹⁶ At my first defence no one took my part; all deserted me. May it not be charged against them! ¹⁷ But the Lord stood by me and gave me strength to proclaim

the word fully, that all the Gentiles might hear it. So I was rescued from the lion's mouth. [18] The Lord will rescue me from every evil and save me for his heavenly kingdom. To him be the glory for ever and ever. Amen.

[19] Greet Prisca and Aquila, and the household of Onesiphorus. [20] Erastus remained at Corinth: Trophimus I left ill at Miletus. [21] Do your best to come before winter. Eubulus sends greetings to you, as do Pudens and Linus and Claudia and all the brethren.

[22] The Lord be with your spirit. Grace be with you.

St Paul had been arrested at Troas; in his unforeseen forced departure he had not been able to take his few possessions with him. He wants his books and above all his precious 'parchments' on which the Bible was written: he also thinks of his cloak, for winter is approaching. The law suit against Paul has already begun; the people who have not come forward to take his part are not his disciples, who indeed are all far away, but influential people, powerful friends who have feared to compromise themselves. St Paul knows that only the Lord can save him: yet he will not save him in this world, but rather 'in his heavenly kingdom'.

II. The Letter to the Hebrews

The beginning of the Letter to the Hebrews in the Vatican Codex (fourth century).

Note that the letter begins abruptly like a theological treatise without the usual headings in which the names of Paul and the recipients appear in the other letters. The very elegant style of this letter also differs considerably from that of St Paul's letters. For these reasons the question of the authorship of this letter has been raised from the earliest centuries. Since it was always copied as an appendix to St Paul's thirteen letters, it could be said to belong to St Paul in some sense, in that he vouches for the writing and supports it with his own authority. It is thought that the author was a disciple of St Paul and his companion in the apostolate who, adding his own reflexions to the teaching of the master, put together in agreement with him a truly original work. He did not dare to put it forward under his own name, or under that of the master who was particularly hated by the Jews and disliked by some Judaizing Christians. Thus, and although the recipients knew whence the letter came and who supported it with his authority, these particulars were not included in the writing itself. The letter came from Italy, that is apparently from Rome, when St Paul was there in 63-64 A.D.

The Hebrews to whom this letter is addressed are Christians of Jewish origin probably belonging to the Palestinian communities. They have in fact suffered persecution from their fellow-citizens and are feeling the appeal of the old Jewish cult. This letter was therefore written before the Jewish War (66-70 A.D.) and probably after the murder of St James (62 A.D.), which showed that it was becoming more and more difficult for Christians to co-exist in the midst of the Jewish national community.

The doctrinal points dealt with in this letter are those most useful for the purpose of detaching the Jewish Christians from the cult still in force in the Jerusalem Temple:

1) Christ is the Son of God, superior to the Angels, the guarantor of the prophets and so superior even to Moses. Consequently, the Christians have a greater responsibility and a more pressing duty to be faithful to God's word.

2) Christ is the High Priest of the New Covenant. The New Covenant is superior to the old and Christ's priesthood is far superior to that of Aaron and the Levites.

3) The worship introduced by Christ is the reality, of which the worship in the Old Testament is only a 'shadow' or illustration.

4) In particular, Christ's sacrifice on the cross is the only sacrifice which can truly expiate for sins, once and for ever.

To this doctrinal exposition are added exhortations to the practice of the virtues, specially those of perseverance in the faith and fortitude under persecutions for the love of Christ.

140 Prologue: Christ is the Son of God (1, 1-4)

[1] In many and various ways God spoke of old to our fathers by the prophets; [2] but in these last days he has spoken to us by a Son, whom he appointed the heir of all things, through whom also he created the world. [3] He reflects the glory of God and bears the very stamp of his nature, upholding the universe by his word of power. When he had made purification for sins, he sat down at the right hand of the Majesty on high, [4] having become as much superior to angels as the name he has obtained is more excellent than theirs.

141 Christ the High Priest (4, 14-16; 5, 1-10; 7, 26-28)

4, [14] We have a great high priest who has passed through the heavens, Jesus, the Son of God; let us hold fast our confession.

[15] For we have not a high priest who is unable to sympathize with our weaknesses, but one who in every respect has been tempted as we are, yet without sinning. [16] Let us then with confidence draw near to the throne of grace, that we may receive mercy and find grace to help in time of need.

5, [1] For every high priest chosen from among men is appointed to act on behalf of men in relation to God, to offer gifts and sacrifices for sins. [2] He can deal gently with ignorant and wayward, since he himself is beset with weakness. [3] Because of this he is bound to offer sacrifice for his own sins as well as for those of the people. [4] And one does not take the honour upon himself, but he is called by God, just as Aaron was.

[5] So also Christ did not exalt himself to be made a high priest, but was appointed by him who said to him,

"Thou art my Son,
today I have begotten thee;"
[6] as he says also in another place,
"Thou art a priest for ever,
after the order of Melchizedek."

[7] In the days of his flesh, Jesus offered up prayers and supplications, with loud cries and tears, to him who was able to save him from death, and he was heard for his godly fear. [8] Although he was a Son, he learned obedience through what he suffered; [9] and being made perfect he became the source of eternal salvation to all who obey him, [10] being designated by God a high priest after the order of Melchizedek.

7, [26] For it was fitting that we should have such a high priest, holy, blameless, unstained, separated from sinners, exalted above the heavens. [27] He has no need, like those high priests, to offer sacrifices daily, first for his own sins and then for those of the people; he did this once for all when he offered up himself. [28] Indeed, the law appoints men in their weakness as high priests, but the word of the oath, which came later than the law, appoints a Son who has been made perfect for ever.

In its relations with God, mankind always needs a mediator, the priest; this was specially true in the Old Testament. Christ has not abolished the priesthood, but has gathered together in himself all the positive aspects of the priesthood, while abolishing those that are negative.

In particular: 1) He is a man among men and therefore knows how to sympathize with human

The present-day city of Nablus, near the ancient Shechem, is still the centre of the religious life of the Samaritans. Today they represent no more than a small ethnic group which is still inspired by the ancient Mosaic law. In the photograph is an old Samaritan priest reading Holy Scripture.

weaknesses; 2) he was chosen by God; 3) he is the Mediator, interceding and pleading for us; 4) but, in contrast to the former priests, he is without personal sin; 5) therefore he has offered sacrifice for the sins of others and not for his own; 6) he was the Son of God (quotation from Psalm 2, 7); his sacrifice was quite sufficient to save men and has

no need to be repeated like the former sacrifices, which could only atone in a symbolic manner. The mention of Melchizedek (derived from Psalm 109, 4) recalls that the ancient priest-king of this name blessed Abraham (Genesis 14, 17-20) and so showed himself superior to Aaron and the Levites who were Abraham's descendants 142.

142 Christ is the mediator of the new covenant
(9, 11-15 - 24, 28)

[11] But when Christ appeared as a high priest of the good things that have come, then through the greater and more perfect tent (not made with hands, that is, not of this creation) [12] he entered once for all into the Holy Place, taking not the blood of goats and calves but his own blood, thus securing an eternal redemption. [13] For if the sprinkling of defiled persons with the blood of goats and bulls and with the ashes of a heifer sanctifies for the purification of the flesh, [14] how much more shall the blood of Christ, who through the eternal Spirit offered himself without blemish to God, purify your conscience from dead works to serve the living God.

[15] Therefore he is the mediator of a new covenant, so that those who are called may receive the promised eternal inheritance, since a death has occurred which redeems them from the transgression under the first covenant.

[24] For Christ has entered, not into a sanctuary made with hands, a copy of the true one, but into heaven itself, now to appear in the presence of God on our behalf. [25] Nor was it to offer himself repeatedly, as the high priest enters the Holy Place yearly with blood not his own; [26] for then he would have had to suffer repeatedly since the foundation of the world. But as it is, he has appeared once for all at the end of the age to put

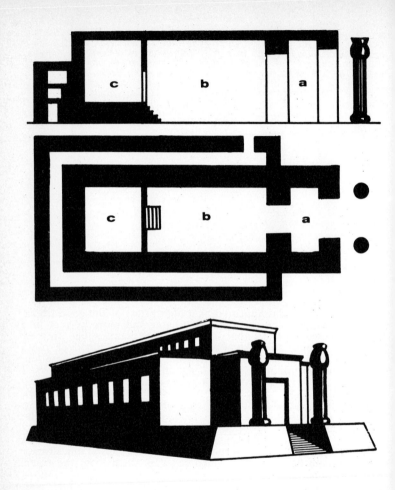

Section, plan and reconstruction of Solomon's Temple on the basis of Father de Vaux's studies. There can be seen: (a) the Vestibule, (b) the Holy Place, and (c) the Holy of Holies.

away sin by the sacrifice of himself. [27] And just as it is appointed for men to die once, and after that comes judgment, [28] so Christ, having been offered once to bear the sins of many, will appear a second time, not to deal with sin but to save those who are eagerly waiting for him.

The former sacrifice expressed the duty of giving worship to God, recognizing him as the sovereign creator and giver of all good. In particular the 'sacrifice of atonement' offered by the Jews specially on the Day of Atonement, to ask for pardon and purification for all the sins of the people committed during the year, expressed the need of reconciliation and the impossibility of entering into relationship with God so long as the state of sin remained. The blood of the victim played an important part in atonement sacrifices; blood was the symbol of life: sprinkling with blood signified the return to life since sin, which alienates us from God, is death. Jesus Christ has offered his death on the cross as an atonement sacrifice, and as the only act capable of atoning for all the sins of the world. The High Priest first slew the victims, that is the expiatory bullock and goat, in the Temple Court, and then entered the Sanctuary (called also Tabernacle or Tent). He went through it and passed beyond the veil of the Holy of Holies carrying the blood of the victims in a basin. He sprinkled it in front of himself in the place which symbolized the mysterious presence of God. So Jesus was first slain on the cross, as Priest and Victim, then was raised from the dead, and passed through (the veil) to present himself to God, offering for us atonement and reconciliation, won by means of his blood, poured out for love of men and in obedience to the Father.

Christ's sacrifice is unique, for all men of all times, and, unlike the former sacrifices, has no need of repetition. The Holy Mass is rightly called a sacrifice for it makes the Christian communities, of all ages and all places on earth, sharers in that unique sacrifice.

143 Suffering in the life of the christian (12, 1-11)

¹ Therefore, since we are surrounded by so great a cloud of witnesses, let us also lay aside every weight and sin which clings so closely, and let us run with perseverance the race that is set before us, ² looking to Jesus the pioneer and perfecter of our faith, who for the joy that was set before him endured the cross, despising the same, and is seated at the right hand of the throne of God.

³ Consider him who endured from sinners such hostility against himself, so that you may not grow weary or fainthearted. ⁴ In your struggle against sin you have not yet resisted to the point of shedding your blood. ⁵ And have you forgotten the exhortation which addressed you as sons?—

"My son, do not regard lightly the discipline of the Lord, nor lose courage when you are punished by him.

⁶ For the Lord disciplines him whom he loves, and chastises every son whom he receives."

⁷ It is for discipline that you have to endure. God is treating you as sons; for what son is there whom his father does not discipline? ⁸ If you are left without discipline, in which all have participated, then you are illegitimate children and not sons. ⁹ Besides this, we have had earthly fathers to discipline us and we respected them. Shall we not much more be subject to the Father of spirits and live? ¹⁰ For they disciplined us for a short time at their pleasure, but he disciplines us for our good, that we may share his holiness. ¹¹ For the moment all discipline seems painful rather than pleasant; later it yields the peaceful fruit of righteousness to those who have been trained by it.

The Christian life is a struggle, specially in times of persecution; the author of the letter makes use of a sporting metaphor, of a race watched by thousands of 'witnesses', the spirits of the saints who have struggled before us. He quotes the example of Christ who has faced a most painful and humiliating death. Then, quoting a passage of the book of Proverbs (3, 11-12), he shows that suffering is a sign of God's love towards us. He is like a father who, desirous of the true wellbeing of his children, does not spare them hard but salutary lessons.

144 Various counsels
(13, 1-21)

¹ Let brotherly love continue. ² Do not neglect to show hospitality to strangers, for thereby some have entertained angels unawares. ³ Remember those who are in prison, as though in prison with them; and those who are illtreated, since you also are in the body. ⁴ Let marriage be held in honour among all, and let the marriage bed be undefiled; for God will judge the immoral and adulterous. ⁵ Keep your life free from love of money, and be content with what you have; for he has said, "I will never fail you nor forsake you." ⁶ Hence we can confidently say,

"The Lord is my helper,
I will not be afraid;
what can man do to me?"

⁷ Remember your leaders, those who spoke to you the word of God; consider the outcome of their life, and imitate their faith. ⁸ Jesus Christ is the same yesterday and today and for ever. ⁹ Do not be led away by diverse and strange teachings; for it is well that the heart be strengthened by grace, not by foods, which have not benefited their adherents. ¹⁰ We have an altar from which those who serve the tent have no right to eat. ¹¹ For the bodies of those animals whose blood is brought into the sanctuary by the high priest as a sacrifice for sin are burned outside the camp. ¹² So Jesus also suffered outside the gate in order to sanctify the people through his own blood. ¹³ Therefore let us go forth to him outside the camp, bearing abuse for him. ¹⁴ For here we have no lasting city, but we seek the city which is to come. ¹⁵ Through him then let us continually offer up a sacrifice of praise to God, that is, the fruit of lips that acknowledge his name. ¹⁶ Do not neglect to do good and to share what you have, for such sacrifices are pleasing to God.

¹⁷ Obey your leaders and submit to them; for they are keeping watch over your souls, as men who will have to give account. Let them do this joyfully, and not sadly, for that would be of no advantage to you.

[18] Pray for us, for we are sure that we have a clear conscience, desiring to act honourably in all things. [19] I urge you the more earnestly to do this in order that I may be restored to you the sooner.

[20] Now may the God of peace who brought again from the dead our Lord Jesus, the great shepherd of the sheep, by the blood of the eternal covenant, [21] equip you with everything good that you may do his will, working in you that which is pleasing in his sight, through Jesus Christ; to whom be glory for ever and ever. Amen.

Among the various counsels we note the exhortation to cease from taking part in the sacred banquets of the Jews, banquets which were a part of the peace offering (or communion). In these sacrifices only a small part of the victim was burnt on the altar, the rest was divided between the priest and the donor, with his family and friends. The Letter to the Hebrews contrasts this sacrificial banquet with the Eucharist, at the altar from which those who persist in the religion of the Old Testament may not eat. He also distinguishes between the 'sacrifice of praise', i.e. prayer offered through Christ, and works of charity which are like 'sacrifices which are pleasing to God'. One detail is worthy of notice: in the sacrifices of atonement for the sins of all the people and of the priests, the body of the victim could not be eaten, once the blood of the victim had been taken into the Sanctuary for the ritual sprinklings. It was taken 'outside the camp', that is outside the town, and there it was burnt.

The author of the letter sees in this ceremony of the ancient cult a figure of Christ who, as a victim for atonement, was crucified outside the city; and from this he proceeds to make a touching appeal to go 'outside the camp', that is away from the Jewish community, and for the love of Christ to face the contempt of their own fellow countrymen.

III. The other Apostles' seven Letters, called Catholic

The seven Letters which were not written by St Paul but by other Apostles were called 'Catholic', i.e. 'universal' or 'general', because they seem to be addressed to the Church in general and not to one community or person in particular. To be sure, the two last Letters of St John have a particular destination but as they are so very short, they were considered appendices of his first Letter.

From St James's Letter

The beginning of St James's Letter in the Vatican Codex (fourth century).

The first of the Catholic Letters was written by that James who is also called 'the Lord's brother', that is Jesus' cousin, who ruled the Christian community at Jerusalem for a long time (see Nos. 42, 86, 87, 101) after the departure of St Peter in 42 or 43 A.D. (see No. 33). He is generally (but not by all) identified with James called the Less, one of the twelve Apostles. He had been granted a special appearance of the risen Jesus (see No. 80). He was a man considerably respected even by many Jews, but was murdered by certain fanatics in the year 62 when, on the death of the Procurator Festus (see Nos. 107 and 108) there supervened a short period of freedom from Roman control in Judea.

Letter of St James

This Letter was written to Christians of Jewish origin (symbolized as the twelve tribes) who lived in the Dispersion (or Diaspora) outside Palestine. According to some it may have been composed even before St Paul's missionary journeys but it was more probably written in St James's last years, between 55 and 62.

This is a work of hortatory and moral character, similar in style to the Wisdom literature of the Old Testament, specially to Proverbs and Ecclesiasticus, but it is pervaded by the spirit of the Gospel and recalls Jesus' teaching in the Sermon on the Mount (St Matthew, 5-7). The subjects follow each other at random, forming twelve sections in which the following ideas prevail: 1) trials and temptations, 2) the right use of the word; 3) against favouritism; 4) faith and works; 5) mastery of the tongue; 6) true and false wisdom; 7) against greed for worldly wealth; 8) against judging one's neighbour; 9) the frailty of human life; 10) against the selfishness of the rich; 11) patience and perseverance; 12) various counsels, varieties of prayer, the anointing of the sick, brotherly aid in spiritual difficulties.

145 Introduction
(1, 1-4)

¹ James, a servant of God and of the Lord Jesus Christ,
To the twelve tribes in the Dispersion:
Greeting.
² Count it all joy, my brethren, when you meet various trials, ³ for you know that the testing of your faith produces steadfastness. ⁴ And let steadfastness have its full effect, that you may be perfect and complete, lacking in nothing.

146 Doers of the word
(1, 22-27)

²² But be doers of the word, and not hearers only, deceiving yourselves. ²³ For if any one is a hearer of the word and not a doer, he is like a man who observes his natural face in a mirror; ²⁴ for he observes himself and goes away and at once

forgets what he was like. ²⁵ But he who looks into the perfect law, the law of liberty, and perseveres, being no hearer that forgets but a doer that acts, he shall be blessed in his doing. ²⁶ If any one thinks he is religious, and does not bridle his tongue but deceives his heart, this man's religion is vain. ²⁷ Religion that is pure and undefiled before God and the Father is this: to visit orphans and widows in their affliction, and to keep oneself unstained from the world.

The perfect law of liberty is the Gospel which influences behaviour from within, in contrast to the Old Testament which threatened physical sanctions from without. One looks at oneself in a mirror in order to tidy oneself; so we must look at the reflection of our conduct in the law of the Gospel in order to be made right and perfect in accordance with the divine teaching.

147 Faith and works
(2, 14-24 and 26)

¹⁴ What does it profit, my brethren, if a man says he has faith but has not works? Can his faith save him? ¹⁵ If a brother or sister is ill-clad and in lack of daily food, ¹⁶ and one of you says to them, "Go in peace, be warmed and filled," without giving them the things needed for the body, what does it profit? ¹⁷ So faith by itself, if it has no works, is dead.
¹⁸ But some one will say, "You have faith and I have works." Show me your faith apart from your works, and I by my works will show you my faith. ¹⁹ You believe that God is one; you do well. Even the demons believe—and shudder. ²⁰ Do you want to be shown, you foolish fellow, that faith apart from works is barren? ²¹ Was not Abraham our father justified by works, when he offered his son Isaac upon the altar? ²² You see that faith was active along with his works, and faith was completed by works, ²³ and the scripture was fulfilled which says, "Abraham believed God, and it was reckoned to him as

righteousness"; and he was called the friend of God. ²⁴ You see that a man is justified by works and not by faith alone. ²⁶ For as the body apart from the spirit is dead, so faith apart from works is dead.

St James, like St Paul, quotes the words of Genesis 15, 6, on the faith of Abraham. But whereas St Paul teaches that justification comes from faith and not from works (see No. 95), St James asserts that faith without works does not save. The contradiction is no more than apparent. St Paul is speaking of the way of obtaining justification, that is forgiveness of sins and restoration of innocence. St James on the other hand is speaking of the person who has already obtained faith (and so is already justified) and has the duty of translating his faith into practical life with good works. St Paul is treating a deeper problem: the works of the Law by themselves, not inspired by faith, cannot save us, first of all because we are all sinners (and therefore condemned by the Law) and next because our good works are out of proportion to the supernatural blessings which God gives by grace (that is, freely) to those who have faith in the redemptive work of Christ: works cannot save without faith (St Paul) but faith cannot save if it remains without works (St James).

148 Social injustices bring divine punishment (5, 1-6)

¹ Come now, you rich, weep and howl for the miseries that are coming upon you. ² Your riches have rotted and your garments are moth-eaten. ³ Your gold and silver have rusted, and their rust will be evidence against you and will eat your flesh like fire. You have laid up treasure for the last days. ⁴ Behold, the wages of the labourers who mowed your fields, which you kept back by fraud, cry out; and the cries of the harvesters have reached the ears of the Lord of hosts. ⁵ You have lived on the earth in luxury and in pleasure; you have fattened your hearts in a day of slaughter. ⁶ You have condemned, you have killed the righteous man; he does not resist you.

From these words which need no comment, the Catechism has deduced one of the 'sins which cry to God for vengeance' and that is 'defrauding the workman of his just wages'.

149 Anointing of the sick and intercessory prayer (5, 14-19)

[14] Is any among you sick? Let him call for the elders of the church, and let them pray over him, anointing him with oil in the name of the Lord; [15] and the prayer of faith will save the sick man, and the Lord will raise him up; and if he has committed sins, he will be forgiven. [16] Therefore confess your sins to one another, and pray for one another, that you may be healed. The prayer of a righteous man has great power in its effects. [17] Elijah was a man of like nature with ourselves and he prayed fervently that it might not rain, and for three years and six months it did not rain on the earth. [18] Then he prayed again and the heaven gave rain, and the earth brought forth its fruit.

[19] My brethren, if any one among you wanders from the truth and some one brings back a sinner from the error of his way will save his soul from death and will cover a multitude of sins.

From this passage the Church has always derived the proof not only that the anointing of the sick is a very ancient rite of apostolic origin but also that it is a true sacrament. It is in fact an external rite which signifies corporal and spiritual medicine; anointing with oil (the matter of the sacrament) is accompanied by a prayer (the form of the sacrament) and has, for effects, divine grace, forgiveness of sins and a physical or moral strengthening. The ministers of this sacrament are the 'elders', (see Nos. 131 and 134) that is, the priests.

According to the words of the letter and the practice of the early Church, the Ritual foresees cases in which it is opportune for more priests to take part, and when the administration of the sacrament is the concern of a wider circle of the parochial community.

This passage shows also the value of intercession when prayer is offered for a brother in the faith and the subject of the prayer commends himself to the prayers of the brethren, revealing to them his need of God's forgiveness (public confession).

Pictorial reconstruction of the apse of Constantine's Basilica in Rome, on the ruins of which the Basilica of St Peter stands today. In the centre of the ikonostasis can be seen the marble monument which — as archaeological excavations attest — held the remains of St Peter's tomb.

From St Peter's First Letter

The beginning of St Peter's First Letter in the Vatican Codex (fourth century).

The Apostle St Peter was in Rome about the year 63 or 64 when he wrote this letter to the Christians (he calls them 'chosen', that is chosen by God, and 'exiles' because they are on their way to their heavenly country), scattered among the pagans in the various districts of Asia Minor. His assistant in the drafting of the letter was that Silvanus who had been with St Paul on his second journey (see No. 54) and is called Silas in the book of the Acts (see Nos. 43, 44, 46, 48 and 51). The letter was prompted by the difficult position in which those Christian communities were placed. It was not a question of official persecution (which was to break out suddenly at the end of 64) but of continual opposition and hostility, of attacks both underhand and open, on the part of the pagan populations in the midst of whom these young Christian communities lived. The beginning, here reproduced, contains a summary of the whole theme of the letter which is then developed in three sections. The first part is a fervent plea for holiness, and an account of its duties and motives, of its essential characteristic which is brotherly love, and its supreme example, Jesus Christ. In the second part the writer passes in review the duties of the Christian with regard to established authority, family relations, and the persecutions. The Christians are repeatedly urged to patience and perseverance, in expectation of divine justice on the occasion of the 'manifestation', that is, the second coming of Christ. The third part contains admonitions to the 'elders' (see No. 131), to the young and to all the faithful; sobriety, watchfulness, firmness in the faith and endurance of persecutions are the virtues which lead to our eternal reward.

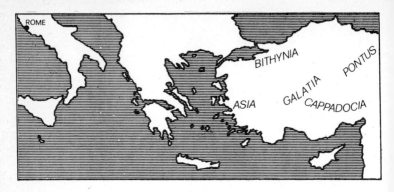

Rome and the Churches of Asia Minor.

150 The call to salvation (1, 1-12)

¹ Peter, an apostle of Jesus Christ, — To the exiles of the Dispersion in Pontus, Galatia, Cappadocia, Asia, and Bithynia, ² chosen and destined by God the Father and sanctified by the Spirit for obedience to Jesus Christ and for sprinkling with his blood:

May grace and peace be multiplied to you.

³ Blessed be the God and Father of our Lord Jesus Christ! By his great mercy we have been born anew to a living hope through the resurrection of Jesus Christ from the dead, ⁴ and to an inheritance which is imperishable, undefiled, and unfading, kept in heaven for you, ⁵ who by God's power are guarded through faith for a salvation ready to be revealed in the last time. ⁶ In this you rejoice, though now for a little while you may have to suffer various trials, ⁷ so that the genuineness of your faith, more precious than gold which though perishable is tested by fire, may redound to praise and glory and honour at the revelation of Jesus Christ. ⁸ Without having seen him you love him; though you do not now see him you believe in him and rejoice with unutterable and exalted joy. ⁹ As the outcome of your faith you obtain the salvation of your souls.

¹⁰ The prophets who prophesied of the grace that was to be yours searched and inquired about this salvation; ¹¹ they inquired what person or time was indicated by the Spirit of Christ within them when predicting the sufferings of Christ and the subsequent glory. ¹² It was revealed to them that they were serving not themselves but you, in the things which have now been announced to you by those who preached the good news to you through the Holy Spirit sent from heaven, things into which angels long to look.

151 The people of God
(2, 1-10)

¹ So put away all malice and all guile and insincerity and envy and all slander. ² Like newborn babes, long for the pure spiritual milk, that by it you may grow up to salvation; ³ for you have tasted the kindness of the Lord.

⁴ Come to him, to that living stone, rejected by men but in God's sight chosen and precious; ⁵ and like living stones be yourselves built into a spiritual house, to be a holy priesthood, to offer spiritual sacrifices acceptable to God through Jesus Christ. ⁶ For it stands in scripture:

"Behold, I am laying in Zion a stone, a cornerstone chosen
    and precious,
and he who believes in him will not be put to shame."

⁷ To you therefore who believe, he is precious, but for those who do not believe,

"The very stone which the builders rejected
has become the head of the corner,"

⁸ and

"A stone that will make men stumble,
a rock that will make them fall;" (1)

for they stumble because they disobey the word, as they were destined to do.

⁹ But you are a chosen race, a royal priesthood, a holy nation, God's own people, that you may declare the wonderful deeds of him who called you out of darkness into his marvellous light. ¹⁰ Once you were no people but now you are God's people; once you had not received mercy but now you have received mercy.

(1) Isaiah 28,10; Psalm 117,22; Isaiah 8,14.

Shechem. A sheep market in the Samaritan plain at the foot of Mount Gerizim. The largely pastoral environment of ancient Palestine is apparent in the frequent biblical use of referennces to the shepherd and his flock.

'You were straying like sheep, but have now returned to the Shepherd and Guardian of your souls' (1 Peter 2,25).

The preceding passage (No. 150) contains the assertion that Baptism has regenerated us, that is, has caused us to be reborn to a new life. Here the image of new birth is continued and the requirements of the new life are expounded: spiritual milk, that is, the food of God's word, and the Eucharist to which Psalm 33, 8, refers: 'O taste and see that the Lord is good'. Baptism incorporates us into the people of God who have inherited the privileges of the people of the Old Covenant, according to Exodus 19, 5-6: 'a chosen race' (referring to redemption), a royal 'priesthood' (sharing in the dignity of Christ, the priest-king) 'a holy nation' (that is consecrated to God's service and pledged to reflect the Lord's holiness in daily life). The mysterious reality of the 'people of God' is explained with the metaphor of a 'spiritual building', i.e. the Temple, made up of 'living stones' (individual Christians) built on the foundation stone of Jesus Christ. The metaphor of the building was also used by St Paul (see Nos. 71 and 126).*

152 Suffering after the example of Christ
(2, 19-25)

[19] For one is approved if, mindful of God, he endures pain while suffering unjustly. [20] For what credit is it, if when you do wrong and are beaten for it you take it patiently? But if when you do right and suffer for it you take it patiently, you have God's approval. [21] For to this you have been called, because Christ also suffered for you, leaving you an example, that you should follow in his steps. [22] He committed no sin; no guile was found on his lips. [23] When he was reviled, he did not revile in return; when he suffered, he did not threaten; but he trusted to him who judges justly. [24] He himself bore our sins in his body on the tree, that we might die to sin and live to righteousness. By his wounds you have been healed. [25] For you were straying like sheep, but have now returned to the Shepherd and Guardian of your souls.

The Christians to whom St Peter is speaking were suffering persecution because of their faith and good life, which was in contrast to their surroundings. *There is nothing to be surprised at in this! To do good and receive evil is the natural state of Christians. Moreover Christ was the first to suffer, the just for the*

367

QVESTA É LA COLONNA DOVE STANDO
LEGATI SS·APOSTOLI PIETRO E PAOLO
CONVERTIRNO I SS·MARTIRI PROCESSO
E MARTINIANO CVSTODI DELLE CARCERI ET
ALTRI XLVII ALLA FEDE DI CRISTO QVALI
BEZZORNO COLL'ACQVA DI QVESTO
FONTE SCATVRITA MIRACOLOSAMENTE

Rome. The interior of the Mamertime Prison where legend has it that the Apostles Peter and Paul were imprisoned before their martyrdom.

unjust, in fact truly for us. St Peter here quotes the famous Chapter 53 of Isaiah where the Messiah is described as 'bearing our sins in his body', so that, 'by his wounds we have been healed'.

153 Persecution has broken out
(4, 12-19)

[12] Beloved, do not be surprised at the fiery ordeal which comes upon you to prove you, as though something strange were happening to you. [13] But rejoice in so far as you share Christ's sufferings, that you may also rejoice and be glad when his glory is revealed. [14] If you are reproached for the name of Christ, you are blessed, because the spirit of glory and of God rests upon you. [15] But let none of you suffer as a murderer, or a thief, or a wrongdoer, or a mischief-maker; [16] yet if one suffers as a Christian, let him not be ashamed, but under that name let him glorify God. [17] For the time has come for judgment to begin with the household of God; and if it begins with us, what will be the end of those who do not obey the gospel of God? [18] And
> "If the righteous man is scarcely saved, where will the impious and sinner appear?"
[19] Therefore let those who suffer according to God's will do right and entrust their souls to a faithful Creator.

These words refer to the first mutterings of a widespread persecution. St Peter describes the sufferings of the righteous ('the household of God'), as the beginning of God's judgment which will cleanse the world of all sinners in the last days. Persecution then must be a call to sanctify one's own conduct more and more.

154 Epilogue
(5, 8-14)

[8] Be sober, be watchful. Your adversary the devil prowls around like a roaring lion, seeking some one to devour. [9] Resist

him, firm in your faith, knowing that the same experience of suffering is required of your brotherhood throughout the world. [10] And after you have suffered a little while, the God of all grace, who has called you to his eternal glory in Christ, will himself restore, establish, and strengthen you. [11] To him be the dominion for ever and ever. Amen.

[12] By Silvanus, a faithful brother as I regard him, I have written briefly to you, exhorting and declaring that this is the true grace of God; stand fast in it. [13] She who is at Babylon, who is likewise chosen, sends you greetings; and so does my son Mark. [14] Greet one another with the kiss of love.

Peace to all of you that are in Christ.

Here 'Babylon' is not the very ancient city of Mesopotamia but is a symbolic name used by the Christians to mean Rome, as it is repeatedly in the Apocalypse (see No. 176). St Peter writes therefore from Rome and adds to his own greetings those of the whole Christian community living in Rome. Silvanus is the scribe and he probably also rewrote the letter in good Greek (see the introduction to No. 150). Mark is that John Mark who as a young man accompanied St Paul and St Barnabas on the first missionary journey (see Nos. 35 and 36) and later parted from them (see No. 44). But later still he is found again at St Paul's side when he is a prisoner in Rome (see Nos. 123 and 129). He is the author of the second gospel, which bears his name. According to tradition he was St Peter's interpreter in Rome and later became the first Bishop of Alexandria in Egypt. The 'kiss of love' was already a normal rite in the liturgical assemblies of the Christian community.

From St Peter's Second Letter

The beginning of St Peter's Second Letter the Vatican Codex (fourth century).

St Peter's second Letter was written towards the end of his life (about 67 A.D.) by a scribe other than Silvanus: hence the different style. This scribe also made use of St Jude's Letter which was directed against the same false teachers with whom this letter deals, though the circumstances were different; heretics had infiltrated among those to whom it was addressed, spreading religious doctrines very different from the simplicity and austerity of the Gospel. Further, they denied the Parousia, i.e. the coming of Christ as Judge at the end of the world. Thus the letter is of a controversial nature. In the first part it expounds the greatness of the divine gifts and the necessity of continual spiritual progress; in the second it denounces the presence of false teachers and foretells their punishment; in the third it expresses certainty about the Parousia and gives reasons for its apparent delay.

The passage given here, right at the beginning of the letter, contains a perfect description of the revelation of the New Testament; the state of the Christian is called a 'partaking of the divine nature'. It is what St Paul frequently calls 'being in Christ' or 'having put on Christ' or again 'having the Spirit of God', and, more commonly, St John calls 'becoming children of God'. The 'nature' of God (being what God is) is in itself incommunicable. No one can become God. But the man redeemed by Christ, regenerated (that is born into a new life) by Baptism does not remain imprisoned in his own nature but by God's grace escapes from it and enters into communication with a new power coming from God which theologians call 'sanctifying grace' (grace being a free gift) which is 'supernatural', i.e. it

371

Mount Tabor, in Galilee, rises in isolation in the Plain of Esdraelon. Perhaps because of this it was described by tradition as the 'high mountain' (see Matthew 17, 1 and parallels) on which Jesus was transfigured. It is to this episode in the life of Jesus that St Peter refers in this second Letter (see No. 156).

surpasses the needs and possibilities of human nature. This is a mysterious truth, but we know its effects, which are: to know God, to love God and to be loved by him in return, to enjoy God's presence in this life and the sight of him in life eternal, to be continually satisfied with his presence and to be transformed even bodily into the image of the glory of the risen Christ.

155 Introduction. The precious gift of faith (1, 1-11)

[1] Simon Peter, a servant and apostle of Jesus Christ.

To those who have obtained a faith of equal standing with ours in the righteousness of our God and Saviour Jesus Christ:

[2] May grace and peace be multiplied to you in the knowledge of God and of Jesus our Lord.

[3] His divine power has granted to us all things that pertain to life and godliness, through the knowledge of him who called us to his own glory and excellence, [4] by which he has granted to us his precious and very great promises, that through these you may escape from the corruption that is in the world because of passion, and become partakers of the divine nature. [5] For this very reason make every effort to supplement your faith with virtue, and virtue with knowledge, [6] and knowledge with self-control, and self-control with steadfastness, and steadfastness with godliness, [7] and godliness with brotherly affection, and brotherly affection with love. [8] For if these things are yours and abound, they keep you from being ineffective or unfruitful in the knowledge of our Lord Jesus Christ. [9] For whoever lacks these things is blind and shortsighted and has forgotten that he was cleansed from his old sins. [10] Therefore, brethren, be the more zealous to confirm your call and election, for if you do this you will never fall; [11] so there will be richly provided for you an entrance into the eternal kingdom of our Lord and Saviour Jesus Christ.

156 The inspiration of Holy Scripture (1, 16-21)

[16] For we did not follow cleverly devised myths when we made known to you the power and coming of our Lord Jesus

Christ, but we were eyewitnesses of his majesty. [17] For when he received honour and glory from God the Father and the voice was borne to him by the Majestic Glory, "This is my beloved Son, with whom I am well pleased," [18] we heard this voice borne from heaven, for we were with him on the holy mountain. [19] And we have the prophetic word made more sure. You will do well to pay attention to this as to a lamp shining in a dark place, until the day dawns and the morning star rises in your hearts. [20] First of all you must understand this, that no prophecy of scripture is a matter of one's own interpretation, [21] because no prophecy ever came by the impulse of man, but men moved by the Holy Spirit spoke from God.

St Peter records his presence at the transfiguration (St Matthew 17, 1-8; St Mark 9, 2-8; St Luke 9, 28-36). This anticipated experience of the glory of Christ is for St Peter a confirmation of the prophecies about the 'Parousia' (i.e. the second coming of Christ). From this the Apostle passes on to speak of Holy Scripture in general and of its inspiration. Men who spoke 'from God', that is, the prophets and those who wrote the 'prophecies of Scripture', did not do so of their own initiative, but were 'moved' by the Holy Spirit. They therefore spoke and wrote as God's instruments (see No. 137 for Scripture 'inspired by God'). In consequence God speaks to us also through Holy Scripture. It is indispensable, like a lamp before the sun rises. The 'morning star', that is the star which announces the imminence of the dawn, signifies the dawn of the eternal day in which we shall see truth in the splendour of God's light: then we shall have no need of the 'lamp', that is, Holy Scripture.

157 The end of the world: new heavens and a new earth (3, 3-13)

[3] First of all you must understand this, that scoffers will come in the last days with scoffing, following their own passions [4] and saying, "Where is the promise of his coming? For ever

since the fathers fell asleep, all things have continued as they were from the beginning of creation." [5] They deliberately ignore this fact, that by the word of God heavens existed long ago, and an earth formed out of water and by means of water, [6] through which the world that then existed was deluged with water and perished. [7] But by the same word the heavens and earth that now exist have been stored up for fire, being kept until the day of judgment and destruction of ungodly men.

[8] But do not ignore this one fact, beloved, that with the Lord one day is as a thousand years, and a thousand years as one day. [9] The Lord is not slow about his promise as some count slowness, but is forbearing toward you, not wishing that any should perish, but that all should reach repentance. [10] But the day of the Lord will come like a thief, and then the heavens will pass away with a loud noise, and the elements will be dissolved with fire, and the earth and the works that are upon it will be burned up.

[11] Since all these things are thus to be dissolved, what sort of persons ought you to be in lives of holiness and godliness, [12] waiting for and hastening the coming of the day of God, because of which the heavens will be kindled and dissolved, and the elements will melt with fire! [13] But according to his promise we wait for new heavens and a new earth in which righteousness dwells.

The first generation lived in expectation of the end of the world and of Christ's coming as if these events were not far away (see Nos. 57-59), although Jesus' saying about the impossibility of knowing the time of these events in advance, was well known. When St Peter wrote this letter the first generation was coming to its end; hence there was a certain anxious disappointment among some, while others made fun of their expectations. This passage replies to such difficulties with three reflexions:

1) First of all, it is not true that all things are as they were at the beginning of creation: at the beginning the earth was covered by the sea and the power of God made it emerge; later the waters of the flood inundated it; we know that the same power of God will destroy 'the heavens and the earth that now exist' with fire, so as to make 'new heavens and a new earth' according to the words of the prophet (Isaiah 65, 17 and 66, 22) and these will be the eternal dwelling of the righteous (see No. 179). We do not know whether the 'fire' which causes this catastrophe and renewal of the Universe is to be understood as a material reality or as a mere

Rome. The Crypt of St Peter: bas-relief on a sarcophagus of the fourth century depicting Christ giving the Law to the Apostles Peter and Paul.

metaphor taken from the refining of precious metals by fire (see No. 71).

2) In the second place, God does not measure time as we men do. Indeed Psalm 89, 4 says: 'A thousand years in thy sight are but as yesterday when it is past'.

3) In the third place, God is prolonging the time of waiting because he wishes all to have time to repent and be saved.

158 St Paul's Letters and the Parousia (3, 14-18)

¹⁴ Therefore, beloved, since you wait for these, be zealous to be found by him without spot or blemish, and at peace. ¹⁵ And count the forbearance of our Lord as salvation. So also our beloved brother Paul wrote to you according to the wisdom given him, ¹⁶ speaking of this as he does in all his letters. There are some things in them hard to understand, which the ignorant and unstable twist to their own destruction, as they do the other scriptures. ¹⁷ You therefore, beloved, knowing this beforehand, beware lest you be carried away with the error of lawless men and lose your own stability. ¹⁸ But grow in the grace and knowledge of our Lord and Saviour Jesus Christ. To him be the glory both now and to the day of eternity. Amen.

It is interesting to notice that, at the time when this Letter was written, there already existed a collection of St Paul's Letters and that they were counted equal to 'the other Scriptures', that is, they were considered divinely inspired books (see No. 156). We also notice the difficulty which some passages of Holy Scripture present and that some people, allowing themselves to be led astray by their own ideas and prejudices, may give these passages a 'twisted' sense which is really not theirs. Hence follows the need to read the Bible with a prudent and well-instructed guide.

From St Jude's Letter

Beginning of the Letter of St Jude Thaddaeus in the Vatican Codex (fourth century).

Jude, the author of the short Letter which bears his name, is probably the Apostle Judas

Thaddaeus. Some think, however, that he may be, like James his brother, one of Jesus' cousins, who did not believe in him at the beginning and only later on played an active part in the early Church. In that case Jude and James (see introduction to No. 145) would be different people from the Apostles who had the same names.

The purpose of the letter is to put its recipients (perhaps the Christians in Asia Minor) on guard against the errors of certain false teachers who, among other things, publicly indulged in immoral practices. To them it sternly threatens the gravest punishments recorded in Holy Scripture.

The second Letter of St Peter makes considerable use of this Letter which must therefore have preceded it: it may then have been written between 65 and 67.

159 Against false teachers
(1, 1-7 - 17-23)

¹ Jude, a servant of Jesus Christ and brother of James,
To those who are called, beloved in God the Father and kept for Jesus Christ:
² May mercy, peace, and love be multiplied to you.
³ Beloved, being very eager to write to you of our common salvation, I found it necessary to write appealing to you to

contend for the faith which was once for all delivered to the saints. [4] For admission has been secretly gained by some who long ago were designated for this condemnation, ungodly persons who pervert the grace of our God into licentiousness and deny our only Master and Lord, Jesus Christ.

[5] Now I desire to remind you, though you were once for all fully informed, that he who saved a people out of the land of Egypt, afterward destroyed those who did not believe. [6] And the angels that did not keep their own position but left their proper dwelling have been kept by him in eternal chains in the nether gloom until the judgment of the great day; [7] just as Sodom and Gomorrah and the surrounding cities, which likewise acted immorally and indulged in unnatural lust, serve as an example by undergoing a punishment of eternal fire.

[17] But you must remember, beloved, the predictions of the apostles of our Lord Jesus Christ; [18] they said to you, "In the last time there will be scoffers, following their own ungodly passions." [19] It is these who set up divisions, worldly people, devoid of the Spirit. [20] But you, beloved, build yourselves up on your most holy faith; pray in the Holy Spirit; [21] keep yourselves in the love of God; wait for the mercy of our Lord Jesus Christ unto eternal life. [22] And convince some, who doubt; [23] save some, by snatching them out of the fire; on some have mercy with fear, hating even the garment spotted by the flesh.

Ephesus. The basilica of St John was built in the sixth century by the Emperor Justinian on the site which a tradition as early as the 2nd century indicated as the tomb of the Apostle. It was one of the most famous and venerated Christian buildings of antiquity. It was believed that the heart of the great Apostle could still be felt beating through the stones of the sepulchre.

From St John's First Letter

The beginning of St John's First Letter in the Vatican Codex (fourth century).

The Apostle St John, according to trustworthy historical evidence, lived long at Ephesus where he died in the first years of the Emperor Trajan (about 104 A.D.) and where there was a very ancient basilica (now in ruins) built over his tomb. In addition to the Apocalypse written about 95 (see page 391) and the Fourth Gospel compiled about 100, St John left one longer Letter and two very short ones which were his last writings.

The first Letter bears no indication of whom it was addressed to. Probably it was to Christians of the Churches in Asia among whom St John lived. It is more than a mere letter, rather a sort of spiritual testament in which he summarizes his teaching of many long years and bids his readers beware of certain errors which are beginning to be spread by the efforts of some innovators whom the letter calls 'antichrists'. The letter is not clearly divided. Two principal themes recur in it; the first is moral: we must walk in the light (i.e. the Good shown by revelation) for love of the brethren; this is the condition for having 'communion' with God. The second part is doctrinal: faith in Christ means recognizing the mystery of the Incarnation (the 'antichrists' attributed a merely apparent humanity to Jesus Christ); it is the presence of the Holy Spirit which guarantees this mystery and creates in us true faith. The two themes alternate in the first part of the Letter (until chapter 4, verse 6) but in the second part they are treated together.

Immediately at the beginning of the Letter St John affirms the mystery of the Incarnation, using the same terms as at the beginning of the Fourth Gospel. The 'Word' (in Greek 'Logos') is the Son of God, the second Person of the Holy Trinity. He is called the Word because he is the revelation to creatures of the inaccessible essence of the Father and of his plan of creation and salvation. The Word is 'life' be-

381

cause he is the Creator of all that is, he is 'eternal life' because he communicates to men that sharing in the divine life (i.e. sanctifying grace) which death cannot interrupt and which will last in eternal glory. The Word was made visible in the Incarnation and assumed human nature in Jesus Christ.

The author of the Letter saw him and heard him, experienced his inspiring presence and his power of inner transformation and now communicates his experience to his disciples so that they also may receive communion of life and love with Christ and with the Father, and may remain in this communion.

160 Introduction. The Word has shown himself (1, 1-7)

¹ That which was from the beginning, which we have heard, which we have seen with our eyes, which we have looked upon and touched with our hands, concerning the word of life—² the life was made manifest, and we saw it, and testify to it, and proclaim to you the eternal life which was with the Father and was made manifest to us—³ that which we have seen and heard we proclaim also to you, so that you may have fellowship with us; and our fellowship is with the Father and with his Son Jesus Christ. ⁴ And we are writing this that our joy may be complete.

⁵ This is the message we have heard from him and proclaim to you, that God is light and in him is no darkness at all. ⁶ If we say we have fellowship with him while we walk in darkness, we live and do not live according to the truth; ⁷ but if we walk in the light, as he is in the light, we have fellowship with one another, and the blood of Jesus his Son cleanses us from all sin.

161 The illusions of the world (2, 12-17)

¹² I am writing to you, little children, because your sins are forgiven for his sake. ¹³ I am writing to you, fathers, because

you know him who is from the beginning. I am writing to you, young men, because you have overcome the evil one. I write to you, children, because you know the Father. ¹⁴ I write to you, fathers, because you know him who is from the beginning. I write to you, young men, because you are strong, and the word of God abides in you, and you have overcome the evil one.

¹⁵ Do not love the world or the things in the world. If any one loves the world, love for the Father is not in him. ¹⁶ For all that is in the world, the lust of the flesh and the lust of the eyes and the pride of life, is not of the Father but is of the world. ¹⁷ And the world passes away, and the lust of it; but he who does the will of God abides for ever.

The 'evil one' is the Devil (this word in Greek means the accuser, the slanderer): he has a certain power over 'the world', that is over organized mankind, which follows his suggestions. But the faithful who remain united to Christ, whether young or old, 'have overcome the evil one'. On the other hand those who follow 'the lust of the flesh', that is, immoderate pleasures, 'the lust of the eyes', that is, the desire for wealth, and 'pride' which leads to the pursuit of honours and of power over others, are estranged from the will of God, are incorporated into 'the world', and lose the fellowship of love with God.

162 The commandment of love
(3, 11-24)

¹¹ For this is the message which you have heard from the beginning, that we should love one another, ¹² and not be like Cain who was of the evil one and murdered his brother. And why did he murder him? Because his own deeds were evil and his brother's righteous. ¹³ Do not wonder, brethren, that the world hates you. ¹⁴ We know that we have passed out of death into life, because we love the brethren. He who does not love remains in death. ¹⁵ Any one who hates his brother is a murderer, and you know that no murderer has eternal life abiding in him.

¹⁶ By this we know love, that he laid down his life for us; and we ought to lay down our lives for the brethren. ¹⁷ But if any one has the world's goods and sees his brother in need, yet closes his heart against him, how does God's love abide in him? ¹⁸ Little children, let us not love in word or speech but in deed and in truth.

¹⁹ By this we shall know that we are of the truth, and reassure our hearts before him ²⁰ whenever our hearts condemn us; for God is greater than our hearts, and he knows everything. ²¹ Beloved, if our hearts do not condemn us, we hace confidence before God; ²² and we receive from him whatever we ask, because we keep his commandments and do what pleases him. ²³ And this is his commandment, that we should believe in the name of his Son Jesus Christ and love one another, just as he has commanded us. ²⁴ All who keep his commandments abide in him, and he in them. And by this we know that he abides in us, by the Spirit which he has given us.

The commandment of love, which Jesus had called 'new' and 'my commandment', had been proclaimed to the recipients of the letter at the very beginning of the call to faith. The practice of brotherly love distinguishes true from false Christians. If we really love the brethren 'we know that we have passed out of death into life', that is, that we are reconciled with God and living in his grace. This gives us faith in the use of prayer. If, in spite of our present good will, 'our heart', that is our conscience, reproaches us for some fault of our past life, 'God is greater than our hearts', that is, he knows better than we do, not only our responsibilities but also all the excuses for our weakness, and he does not wish remorse for some past mistake to paralyse our trust in his mercy. In other words, if we are kind to others we have the consolation of knowing that God is kind to us and has already forgiven us.

163 God is love
(4, 7-21)

⁷ Beloved, let us love one another; for love is of God, and he who loves is born of God and knows God. ⁸ He who does

not love does not know God; for God is love. [9] In this the love of God was made manifest among us, that God sent his only Son into the world, so that we might live through him. [10] In this is love, not that we loved God but that he loved us and sent his Son to be the expiation for our sins. [11] Beloved, if God so loved us, we also ought to love one another. [12] No man has ever seen God; if we love one another, God abides in us and his love is perfected in us.

[13] By this we know that we abide in him and he in us, because he has given us of his own Spirit. [14] And we have seen and testify that the Father has sent his Son as the Saviour of the world. [15] Whoever confesses that Jesus is the Son of God, God abides in him, and he in God. [16] So we know and believe the love God has for us. God is love, and he who abides in love abides in God, and God abides in him. [17] In this is love perfected with us, that we may have confidence for the day of judgment, because as he is so are we in this world. [18] There is no fear in love, but perfect love casts out fear. For fear has to do with punishment, and he who fears is not perfected in love. [19] We love, because he first loved us. [20] If any one says, "I love God," and hates his brother, he is a liar; for he who does not love his brother whom he has seen, cannot love God whom he has not seen. [21] And this commandment we have from him, that he who loves God should love his brother also.

This wonderful passage repeats the ideas of the preceding passage and needs no explanation; it needs only meditation and practice. Let us take note that Christian love, which also has the more usual but less expressive name 'charity', is a virtue closely associated with faith in the Trinity and in the Incarnation. In this context we may see three truths: the source of love is the Father; the Son is the Mediator who reconciles us to the Father, since he has become 'the expiation for our sins' and gives us 'life'; the Holy Spirit has been given to us by the Father to be the abiding power in us, to keep us in the fellowship of love with the Father and the Son. We do not discover the love of God through philosophy but believe in it through God's revealed word. This faith alone makes the Christian capable of copying to a heroic degree, in his own life and in his relations with the brethren, the tremendous example of the love of God which Christ offers us.

St John's Second Letter

Beginning of St John's Second Letter in the Vatican Codex (fourth century).

This very short Letter was written by St John to a Christian community personified under the name 'the elect lady', where the word 'lady' means an individual church. In fact St John uses the same term for the community in which he now is and whose greetings he sends to the recipients of the letter. The reason for the letter, which announces a forthcoming visit, is the presence of certain heretics who are spreading false ideas about the person of Jesus Christ. They deny that Jesus has 'come in the flesh', that is, that he had a genuine human nature. Probably they were fore-runners of the heresy called 'doceticism', according to which Jesus had merely an apparent body, that in fact he was not an 'Incarnation' but a 'manifestation' of God. St John sees in the presence of these heretics the realization of Jesus' prophecy about the rise of false prophets and the expectation of the 'anti-christ' which was contained in the primitive apostolic teaching (see introduction to No. 59).

164

[1] The elder to the elect lady and her children, whom I love in the truth, and not only I but also all who know the truth, [2] because of the truth which abides in us and will be with us for ever:

[3] Grace, mercy, and peace will be with us, from God the Father and from Jesus Christ the Father's Son, in truth and love.

⁴ I rejoiced greatly to find some of your children following the truth, just as we have been commanded by the Father. ⁵ And now I beg you, lady, not as though I were writing you a new commandment, but the one we have had from the beginning, that we love one another. ⁶ And this is love, that we follow his commandments; this is the commandment, as you have heard from the beginning, that you follow love. ⁷ For many deceivers have gone out into the world, men who will not acknowledge the coming of Jesus Christ in the flesh; such a one is the deceiver and the antichrist. ⁸ Look to yourselves, that you may not lose what you have worked for, but may win a full reward. ⁹ Any one who goes ahead and does not abide in the doctrine of Christ does not have God; he who abides in the doctrine has both the Father and the Son. ¹⁰ If any one comes to you and does not bring this doctrine, do not receive him into the house or give him any greeting; ¹¹ for he who greets him shares his wicked work.

¹² Though I have much to write to you, I would rather not use paper and ink, but I hope to come to see you and talk with you face to face, so that our joy may be complete.

¹³ The children of your elect sister greet you.

Ephesus. The site on which stood the Basilica of St John the Evangelist.

St John's Third Letter

Beginning of St John's Third Letter in the Vatican Codex (fourth century).

St John's third, very short, Letter is addressed to a certain Gaius, belonging to a neighbouring local church, to thank him for hospitality given to preachers of the Gospel, probably sent by St John himself, and to commend to him a certain Demetrius. Diotrephes, who is severely censured, is probably bishop of the Church where Gaius lives; he is ambitious and jealous of his own authority, and this impels him to keep the aged and authoritative St John at a distance and to ill treat anyone he dislikes. This letter gives us a glimpse of the organization of the Church at the end of the first century. The local churches have their own hierarchy; the Apostles, by virtue of their office missionaries and responsible for many churches, are now dead and in every church there has been appointed a resident bishop, while there still exist itinerant missionaries who depend on the charity of the Christians. St John is now the last survivor with the unquestioned authority of an Apostle, which nonetheless arouses some opposition in practical matters.

165

[1] The elder to the beloved Gaius, whom I love in the truth. [2] Beloved, I pray that all may go well with you and that you may be in health; I know that it is well with your soul. [3] For I greatly rejoiced when some of the brethren arrived and

testified to the truth of your life, as indeed you do follow the truth. ⁴ No greater joy can I have than this, to hear that my children follow the truth.

⁵ Beloved, it is a loyal thing you do when you render any service to the brethren, especially to strangers, ⁶ who have testified to your love before the church. You will do well to send them on their journey as befits God's service. ⁷ For they have set out for his sake and have accepted nothing from the heathen. ⁸ So we ought to support such men, that we may be fellow workers in the truth.

⁹ I have written something to the church; but Diotrephes, who likes to put himself first, does not acknowledge my authority. ¹⁰ So if I come, I will bring up what he is doing, prating against me with evil words. And not content with that, he refuses himself to welcome the brethren, and also stops those who want to welcome them and puts them out of the church.

¹¹ Beloved, do not imitate evil but imitate good. He who does good is of God; he who does evil has not seen God. ¹² Demetrius has testimony from every one, and from the truth itself; I testify to him too, and you know my testimony is true.

¹³ I had much to write to you, but I would rather not write with pen and ink; ¹⁴ I hope to see you soon, and we will talk together face to face.

¹⁵ Peace be to you. The friends greet you. Greet the friends, every one of them.

Patmos, now Patmo, the rocky island in the Sporades where John, in exile there, wrote the Apocalypse.

IV. The Apocalypse of St John

'Apocalypse' means Revelation, that is the removal of the veil which hides future events. The book called the Apocalypse is presented by its author as a 'prophecy' in the sense of the prophetic books of the Old Testament, which were primarily exhortations uttered in the name of God and often containing the description of visions which the prophet had seen. This is the only prophetic book of the New Testament, although the primitive instruction contained a number of predictions of future persecutions and of events connected with the end of the world; in addition to Jesus' discourse on this subject (Matthew 24, Mark 13, Luke 21) this teaching appears particularly in the Letters to the Thessalonians (see Nos. 57 and 59) and in the first Letter to the Corinthians (see No. 80). The Apocalypse falls into this line of catechetical teaching but is based on visions seen by the author. Hence its characteristic features which are completely new in relation to the other books of the New Testament, while they approximate to the literary form of Daniel and parts of Ezekiel and Zecchariah. These characteristics are the constant use of visions and of symbolical descriptions as well as of symbolical numbers, and frequent references to the ministry of the Angels. The author of the Apocalypse is possibly St John, the same who wrote the fourth Gospel and the three Letters which bear his name. He wrote it when in exile on the small island of Patmos, in the Aegean Sea, now included in the

The position of Patmos

Dodecanese. Its time of composition was about 95 A.D. during Domitian's persecution.

The purpose of the Apocalypse is primarily to encourage and console the Christians, cruelly persecuted by Domitian as they had been years before by Nero. Its visions show that the Roman Empire, inspired by Satan and upheld by the political advantages of the pagan cult of the deified emperor, could very well fight the Church and inflict martyrdom on the Christians, but its fall was already determined by divine decree, while the martyrs' triumph would precede the last events of human history. Yet pagan Rome is the type or symbolical image of every persecuting power which from time to time has arisen, and will in the future arise, in the history of Christianity. The message of the Apocalypse is therefore always up to date and pertinent to the persecuted, pilgrim Church throughout the centuries, sustaining her with certainty of Christ's ultimate victory and exhorting her to remain faithful unto death to her mission of witnessing to Christ in the face of the powers of this world. The Apocalypse, in addition to the Prologue (No. 166) and the Epilogue (No. 180) contains three parts:

1) The Present. After an initial vision follow seven Letters to the seven churches of Asia, revealing their spiritual condition and exhorting them to be faithful (Chapters 1-3, see Nos. 166-173).

2) The Future. After a general vision which takes us into heaven, where the destinies of history are controlled and revealed, we can distinguish two stages:

a) First Stage. It contains four sequences of seven—7 seals, 7 trumpet-blasts, 7 miraculous signs and 7 goblets out of which are poured as many scourges (Chapters 6-16). It is not a case of successive events, but of a review in each septet of the same things seen from different points of view. These future events are first presented in divine decrees (7 seals); then they are proclaimed (7 trumpet-blasts); they are described by means of symbolic personages (7 signs), and finally they take place (7 scourges). After every sixth element there is set by way of interlude a vision which marks a pause, while the seventh element introduces the following sequence.

b) Second Stage. The preceding sequences all lead to the fall of Rome (Chapters 17 and 18) and to Christ's victory (Ch. 19) followed by a symbolical millenium of the reign of the saints (20, 1-6). After this follows the last war against the church, the resurrection of the dead and the final judgment.

3) Eternity: Under the image of the heavenly Jerusalem is described the eternal blessedness of the elect (Chaps. 21 and 22).

Beginning of the Book of the
Apocalypse of St John in the
Vatican Codex.

166 Prologue and initial vision
(1, 1-20)

¹ The revelation of Jesus Christ, which God gave him to show to his servants what must soon take place; and he made it known by sending his angel to his servant John, ² who bore witness to the word of God and to the testimony of Jesus Christ, even to all that he saw. ³ Blessed is he who reads aloud the words of the prophecy, and blessed are those who hear, and who keep what is written therein; for the time is near.

⁴ John to the seven churches that are in Asia:

Grace to you and peace from him who is and who was and who is to come, and from the seven spirits who are before his throne, ⁵ and from Jesus Christ the faithful witness, the first-born of the dead, and the ruler of kings on earth.

To him who loves us and has freed us from our sins by his blood ⁶ and made us a kingdom, priests to his God and Father, to him be glory and dominion for ever and ever. Amen. ⁷ Behold, he is coming with the clouds, and every eye will see him, every one who pierced him; and all tribes of the earth will wail on account of him. Even so. Amen.

⁸ "I am the Alpha and the Omega," says the Lord God, who is and who was and who is to come, the Almighty.

⁹ I John, your brother, who share with you in Jesus the tribulation and the kingdom and the patient endurance, was on the island called Patmos on account of the word of God and the testimony of Jesus. ¹⁰ I was in the Spirit on the Lord's day, and I heard behind me a loud voice like a trumpet ¹¹ saying, "Write what you see in a book and send it to the seven churches, to Ephesus and to Smyrna and to Pergamum and to Thyatira and to Sardis and to Philadelphia and to Laodicea."

¹² Then I turned to see the voice that was speaking to me, and on turning I saw seven golden lampstands, ¹³ and in the midst of the lampstands one like a son of man, clothed with a long robe and with a golden girdle round his breast; ¹⁴ his head and his hair were white as white wool, white as snow; his eyes were like a flame of fire, ¹⁵ his feet were like burnished bronze, refined as in a furnace, and his voice was like the sound of many waters; ¹⁶ in his right hand he held seven stars, from his mouth issued a sharp two-edged sword, and his face was like the sun shining in full strength.

¹⁷ When I saw him, I fell at his feet as though dead. But he laid his right hand upon me, saying, "Fear not, I am the first and the last, ¹⁸ and the living one; I died, and behold I am alive for evermore, and I have the keys of Death and Hades. ¹⁹ Now write what you see, what is and what is to take place hereafter. ²⁰ As for the mystery of the seven stars which you saw in my right hand, and the seven golden lampstands, the seven stars are the angels of the seven churches and the seven lampstands are the seven churches.

In the initial form of address is expressed the mystery of the Holy Trinity, and the redemptive work of Christ is summarized. 'He who is and who was and who is to come' expresses God's eternity. Alpha and Omega are the first and last letters of the Greek alphabet: they indicate that God is the beginning and end of everything. 'The first born of the dead' refers to Jesus Christ as the first of the risen. The ultimate subject of the whole book, which is the coming of Christ as judge, is already mentioned in the Prologue. The initial vision presents Jesus Christ with attributes full of symbolical meaning. 'Son of man' recalls the vision of Daniel 7 and is the Messianic title which Jesus preferred; the robe is priestly, the girdle regal; the hair, white as snow, expresses eternal pre-existence; the sword which issues from his mouth indicates the authority of the supreme Judge. Christ is pictured in the midst of his churches and passes them in review with a judgment which still leaves time for repentance.

167 To the Church at Ephesus
2, 1-7)

[1] "To the angel of the church in Ephesus write: 'The words of him who holds the seven stars in his right and, who walks among the seven golden lampstands.
[2] " 'I know your works, your toil and your patient endurance, and how you cannot bear evil men but have tested those who call themselves apostles but are not, and found them to be false; [3] I know you are enduring patiently and bearing up for my name's sake, and you have not grown weary. [4] But I have this against you, that you have abandoned the love you had at first. [5] Remember and do the works you did at first. If not, I will come to you and remove your lampstand from its place, unless you repent. [6] Yet this you have, you hate the works of the Nicolaitans, which I also hate. [7] He who has an ear, let him hear what the Spirit says to the churches. To him who conquers I will grant to eat of the tree of life, which is in the paradise of God.' "

Ephesus (now in ruins near the village of Ayasoluk) was the chief city of the Roman province of Asia (see No. 63) and the usual home of St John. This letter provides the plan for all the others: 1) presentation of Christ with different symbolical attributes, 2) proclamation of judgment, and exhortation, 3) promise of eternal reward in symbolical terms.

The angel of each church is generally interpreted as the bishop, who bears responsibility for the whole community as well as for himself, for which reason he is regarded as a symbolical expression of the spirit which animates his church, rather than as an individual person.

The Nicolaitans mentioned here and later were a Christian sect named after Nicolaus, one of the seven deacons of Jerusalem (see No. 16); holding heretical doctrine, they also defended immoral behaviour as a way of expressing contempt for the flesh, and the superiority of the spirit; they took part in the pagan sacrificial banquets with the excuse of being immune to the dangers of idolatry.

Smyrna, present day Izmir, was a flourishing commercial city in Asia Minor. The Apocalypse addressed a letter of praise and encouragement to its Christian community.

The seven churches
of the Apocalypse.

168 To the Church at Smyrna
(2, 8-11)

[8] "And to the angel of the church in Smyrna write: 'The words of the first and the last, who died and came to life.
[9] "'I know your tribulation and your poverty (but you are rich) and the slander of those who say that they are Jews and are not, but are a synagogue of Satan. [10] Do not fear what you are about to suffer. Behold, the devil is about to throw some of you into prison, that you may be tested, and for ten days you will have tribulation. Be faithful unto death, and I will give you the crown of life. [11] He who has an ear, let him hear what the Spirit says to the churches. He who conquers shall not be hurt by the second death.'"

Smyrna is the only one of the seven churches which still survives (as Izmir); it is the seat of a Catholic archbishop. The 'second death' (see No. 178) is eternal damnation.

Roman road leading up to the ancient city of Pergamum. The Apocalypse invites the Christians of Pergamum to change their ways.

169 To the Church at Pergamum
(2, 12-17)

¹² "And to the angel of the church in Pergamum write: 'The words of him who has the sharp two-edged sword.

¹³ " 'I know where you dwell, where Satan's throne is; you hold fast my name and you did not deny my faith even in the days of Antipas my witness, my faithful one, who was killed among you, where Satan dwells. ¹⁴ But I have a few things against you: you have some there who hold the teaching of Balaam, who taught Balak to put a stumbling block before the sons of Israel, that they might eat food sacrificed to idols and practise immorality. ¹⁵ So you also have some who hold the teaching of the Nicolaitans. ¹⁶ Repent then. If not, I will come to you soon and war against them with the sword of my mouth. ¹⁷ He who has an ear, let him hear what the Spirit says to the churches. To him who conquers I will give him some of the hidden manna, and I will give him a white stone, with a new name written on the stone which no one knows except him who receives it.' "

Pergamum (today Bergama). 'Satan's throne' is probably the temple dedicated to the worship of the deified emperor (the Augusteum) or the great altar of Zeus on the Acropolis. 'Witness' means 'martyr'; Antipas was the first martyr of Asia. Balaam was the false prophet who after having blessed Israel against his will (Numbers 23, 24) advised Balak, king of the Moabites, to lead the Israelites astray by means of sacred prostitution (Numbers 31, 16). Here his name is used symbolically to indicate the Nicolaitans (see No. 167). The 'hidden manna' and the 'white stone' on which is written the 'new name' are symbols of the personal experience of Christ in eternal life.

The present day village of Akhisar which stands on the site of the ancient Thyatira on the road from Pergamum to Sardis.

170 To the Church at Thyatira
(2, 18-29)

[18] "And to the angel of the church in Thyatira write: 'The words of the Son of God, who has eyes like a flame of fire, and whose feet are like burnished bronze.
[19] "'I know your works, your love and faith and service and patient endurance, and that your latter works exceed the first. [20] But I have this against you, that you tolerate the woman Jezebel, who calls herself a prophetess and is teaching and beguiling my servants to practise immorality and to eat food sacrificed to idols. [21] I gave her time to repent, but she refuses to repent of her immorality. [22] Behold, I will throw her on a sickbed, and those who commit adultery with her I will throw into great tribulation, unless they repent of her doings; [23] and I will strike her children dead. And all the churches shall know that I am he who searches mind and heart, and I will give to each of you as your works deserve. [24] But to the rest of you in Thyatira, who do not hold this teaching, who have not learned what some call the deep things of Satan, to you I say, I do not lay upon you any other burden; [25] only hold fast what you have, until I come. [26] He who conquers and who keeps my works until the end, I will give him power over the nations, [27] and he shall rule them with a rod of iron, as when earthen pots are broken in pieces, even as I myself have received power from my Father; [28] and I will give him the morning star. [29] He who has an ear, let him hear what the Spirit says to the churches.'"

The errors of the Nicolaitans crept also into Thyatira, a small artisan community (on the site of the present Akhisar). They were spread by a self-styled prophetess, given here the symbolic name of Jezebel, the infamous wife of Ahab, king of Israel, who fostered pagan worship and opposed the prophet Elijah (1 Kings. 19, 1-2; 21, 5-23). The 'morning star' is a symbolic name meaning Jesus Christ, one who brings the light of revelation (see No. 156). The phrase from Psalm 2: 'You shall break them with a rod of iron' refers to the universal judgment exercized by Christ: the elect will share Christ's triumph over his enemies.

The ruins of Sardis, the ancient capital of Lydia. The Apocalypse addresses a stern rebuke to the Christian community at Sardis.

171 To the Church at Sardis
(3, 1-6)

¹ "And to the angel of the church in Sardis write: 'The words of him who has the seven spirits of God and the seven stars.

" 'I know your works; you have the name of being alive, and you are dead. ² Awake, and strengthen what remains and is on the point of death, for I have not found your works perfect in the sight of my God. ³ Remember then what you received and heard; keep that, and repent. If you will not awake, I will come like a thief, and you will not know at what hour I will come upon you. ⁴ Yet you have still a few names in Sardis, people who have not soiled their garments; and they shall walk with me in white, for they are worthy. ⁵ He who conquers shall be clad thus in white garments, and I will not blot his name out of the book of life; I will confess his name before my Father and before his angels. ⁶ He who has an ear, let him hear what the Spirit says to the churches.' "

Sardis was the ancient and famous capital of Lydia, already in decline in Roman times: today its name is preserved only in a modest hamlet (Sart). The church in Sardis was also completely in decline and deserved the severest rebuke.

The 'white garments' are a symbol of victory and of belonging to the race of heavenly beings.

172 To the Church at Philadelphia
(3, 7-13)

⁷ "And to the angel of the church in Philadelphia write: 'The words of the holy one, the true one, who has the key of David, who opens and no one shall shut, who shuts and no one opens.

⁸ " 'I know your works. Behold, I have set before you an open door, which no one is able to shut; I know that you have but little power, and yet you have kept my word and have not denied my name. ⁹ Behold, I will make those of the synagogue of Satan who say that they are Jews and are not, but lie—

Ruins of the old city of Philadelphia, now Alasehir. The Apocalypse praises its Christian community.

behold, I will make them come and bow down before your feet, and learn that I have loved you. [10] Because you have kept my word of patient endurance, I will keep you from the hour of trial which is coming on the whole world, to try those who dwell upon the earth. [11] I am coming soon; hold fast what you have, so that no one may seize your crown. [12] He who conquers, I will make him a pillar in the temple of my God; never shall he go out of it, and I will write on him the name of my God, and the name of the city of my God, the new Jerusalem which comes down from my God out of heaven, and my own new name. [13] He who has an ear, let him hear what the Spirit says to the churches.' "

Philadelphia is the present day Alasehir. The Letter presupposes a zealous Christianity; it was being opposed by the Jewish community but this would be converted. The 'open door' means the possibility of missionary work among the pagans.

173 To the Church at Laodicea
(3, 14-22)

[14] "And to the angel of the church in Laodicea write: 'The words of the Amen, the faithful and true witness, the beginning of God's creation.

[15] " 'I know your works: you are neither cold nor hot. Would that you were cold or hot! [16] So, because you are lukewarm, and neither cold nor hot, I will spew you out of my mouth. [17] For you say, I am rich, I have prospered, and I need nothing; not knowing that you are wretched, pitiable, poor, blind, and naked. [18] Therefore I counsel you to buy from me gold refined by fire, that you may be rich, and white garments to clothe you and to keep the shame of your nakedness from being seen, and salve to anoint your eyes, that you may see. [19] Those whom I love, I reprove and chasten; so be zealous and repent. [20] Behold, I stand at the door and knock; if any one hears my voice and opens the door, I will come in to him and eat with him, and he with me. [21] He who conquers, I will grant him to sit with me on my throne, as I myself conquered and sat down with

my Father on his throne. ²²He who has an ear, let him hear what the Spirit says to the churches.'"

Laodicea, of which a few ruins survive to the north of Denizli, was rich from the wool trade and famous for the powder with which its doctors treated eye diseases. The letter seems to allude to these characteristics. Laodicea had received the Gospel from neighbouring Colossae (see No. 123) but at the time of the Apocalypse had become lukewarm. This letter of stern reproof, but also of hope, has been used by the masters of the spiritual life to exemplify the state of 'tepidity' of the soul consecrated to God which slips into a dangerous lukewarmness, persuading itself that it is in the right way because it does not commit grave sins.

The Adoration of the Lamb. Miniature from the Gerona Apocalypse (tenth century).

174 The vision of the Lamb
(5, 6-14)

⁶ And between the throne and the four living creatures and among the elders, I law a Lamb standing, as though it had been slain, with seven horns and with seven eyes, which are the seven spirits of God sent out into all the earth; ⁷ and he went and took the scroll from the right hand of him who was seated on the throne. ⁸ And when he had taken the scroll, the four living creatures and the twenty-four elders fell down before the Lamb, each holding a harp, and with golden bowls full of incense, which are the prayers of the saints; ⁹ and they sang a new song, saying,
"Worthy are thou to take the scroll and to open its seals, for thou wast slain and by thy blood didst ransom men for God from every tribe and tongue and people and nation,
¹⁰ and hast made them a kingdom and priests to our God, and they shall reign on earth."
¹¹ Then I looked, and I heard around the throne and the living creatures and the elders the voice of many angels, numbering myriads of myriads and thousands of thousands, ¹² saying with a loud voice, "Worthy is the Lamb who was slain, to receive power and wealth and wisdom and might and honour and glory and blessing!" ¹³ And I heard every creature in heaven and on earth and under the earth and in the sea, and all therein, saying, "To him who sits upon the throne and to the Lamb be blessing and honour and glory and might for ever and ever!" ¹⁴ And the four living creatures said, "Amen!" and the elders fell down and worshipped.

The passage here quoted belongs to the background vision of the second part of the Apocalypse. The vision presents the liturgy of heaven in a symbolic fashion with the adoration of the Lamb, a symbol of Christ, and his intervention to reveal the divine decrees concerning the future of the world and of the Church. The characters described in this vision are:

1) God, seated on his throne and holding in his right hand the book sealed with seven seals, symbols of the divine decrees on history which are later to be revealed in the Apocalypse.

2) The four 'living creatures', immediately before God's throne, having respectively the appearance of a lion, an ox, a man and an eagle. Like the seraphim of Isaiah 6 they have six wings and 'never cease to sing, "Holy, holy, holy is the Lord Almighty". They are the angels of creation, because of their cosmic number (4 cardinal points, 4 elements, 4 winds) and because of their appearance as the noblest beings of the living world; they preside over the government of the universe and in the heavenly liturgy proclaim to God the adoration of all creatures.

3) The twenty-four 'elders', sitting on so many thrones, with golden crowns and, like priests, bearing in their hands, censers; they are the angels who preside over human history and offer to God the prayers of the faithful.

4) The heavenly liturgy widens in concentric circles, drawing into the hymn of praise millions of angels and the immense company of the creatures of the universe.

5) In this context appears the Lamb 'as though it had been slain', that is with the wounds of its immolation, but 'standing', that is, alive. It is Christ, slain like the Paschal lamb, a victim for redemption, but risen into glory. The seven horns symbolize divine power and the seven eyes divine omnipresence and the action of the Holy Spirit in space and time. The Lamb has the power to open the seven seals, that is to reveal the divine decrees. The whole heavenly Court and all the beings of the universe unite God and the Lamb in the same worship, thus giving liturgical expression to Christ's divinity.

Angels with cross. Mosaic of the sixth century in San Vitale at Ravenna.

175 The Woman and the dragon; the two beasts
(12, 1-12 and 17; 13, 1-18)

12, ¹And a great portent appeared in heaven, a woman clothed with the sun, with the moon under her feet, and on her head a crown of twelve stars; ²she was with child and she cried out in her pangs of birth, in anguish for delivery. ³And another portent appeared in heaven; behold, a great red dragon, with seven heads and ten horns, and seven diadems upon his heads. ⁴His tail swept down a third of the stars of heaven, and cast them to the earth. And the dragon stood before the woman who was about to bear a child, that he might devour her child when she brought it forth; ⁵she brought forth a male child, one who is to rule all the nations with a rod of iron, but her child was caught up to God and to his throne, ⁶and the woman fled into the wilderness, where she has a place prepared by God, in which to be nourished for one thousand two hundred and sixty days.

⁷Now war arose in heaven, Michael and his angels fighting against the dragon; and the dragon and his angels fought, ⁸but they were defeated and there was no longer any place for them in heaven. ⁹And the great dragon was thrown down, that ancient serpent, who is called the Devil and Satan, the deceiver of the whole world—he was thrown down to the earth, and his angels were thrown down with him. ¹⁰And I heard a loud voice in heaven, saying, "Now the salvation and the power and the kingdom of our God and the authority of his Christ have come, for the accuser of our brethren has been thrown down, who accuses them day and night before our God. ¹¹And they have conquered him by the blood of the Lamb and by the word of their testimony, for they loved not their lives even unto death. ¹²Rejoice then, O heaven and you that dwell therein! But woe to you, O earth and sea, for the devil has come down to you in great wrath, because he knows that his time is short!"

¹⁷Then the dragon was angry with the woman, and went off to make war on the rest of her offspring, on those who keep the commandments of God and bear testimony to Jesus. And he stood on the sand of the sea.

13, ¹And I saw a beast rising out of the sea, with ten horns and seven heads, with ten diadems upon its horns and a blasphemous name upon its heads. ²And the beast that I saw was like a leopard, its feet were like a bear's, and its mouth was like a lion's mouth. And to it the dragon gave his power and his throne and great authority. ³One of its heads seemed to have a mortal wound, but its mortal wound was healed, and the whole earth followed the beast with wonder. ⁴Men worshipped the dragon, for he had given his authority to the

The struggle of the Dragon against the Woman, described in the Apocalypse. Miniature from the Liber Floridus of Lambert at St Omer (twelfth century).

beast, and they worshipped the beast, saying, "Who is like the beast, and who can fight against it?"

⁵ And the beast was given a mouth uttering haughty and blasphemous words, and it was allowed to exercise authority for forty-two months; ⁶ it opened its mouth to utter blasphemies against God, blaspheming his name and his dwelling, that is, those who dwell in heaven. ⁷ Also it was allowed to make war on the saints and to conquer them. And authority was given it over every tribe and people and tongue and nation, ⁸ and all who dwell on earth will worship it, every one whose name has not been written before the foundation of the world in the book of life of the Lamb that was slain...

¹¹ Then I saw another beast which rose out of the earth; it had two horns like a lamb and it spoke like a dragon. ¹² It exercises all the authority of the first beast in its presence, and makes the earth and its inhabitants worship the first beast, whose mortal wound was healed. ¹³ It works great signs, even making fire come down from heaven to earth in the sight of men; ¹⁴ and by the signs which it is allowed to work in the presence of the beast, it deceives those who dwell on earth, bidding them make an image for the beast which was wounded by the sword and yet lived; ¹⁵ and it was allowed to give breath to the image of the beast so that the image of the beast should even speak, and to cause those who would not worship the image of the beast to be slain. ¹⁶ Also it causes all, both small and great, both rich and poor, both free and slave, to be marked on the right hand or the forehead, ¹⁷ so that no one can buy or sell unless he has the mark, that is, the name of the beast or the number of its name. ¹⁸ This calls for wisdom: let him who has understanding reckon the number of the beast, for it is a human number, its number is six hundred and sixty-six.

The seven seals, opened in turn, reveal, in the form of visions, all future events because they are already present in the divine decrees. Then the seven trumpet blasts present the same events as proclaimed and imminent.

The passage here quoted (with some omissions) follows; in it, under the form of miraculous signs appearing in heaven, are reviewed the actors in the future drama and, still in symbolic language, the basic lines of Satan's struggle against the Church.

1) The Woman is the personification of the people of God, the Church in the Old and New Testaments, bearing in her womb the Messiah, descended from Abraham and David, and bringing him forth into the light. The birth-pangs symbolize the sufferings of the Passion and Death of Christ, out of which is born the new man, the risen Christ, first-born of the new creation of the redeemed. Mary, she who was mother of the Messiah in both the physical and moral sense,

through her willing co-operation in the divine plan of the birth and Passion of Jesus, not only offers an image of the Church, but is also herself the conscious expression of the whole Church and the entire human race at the moments of the conception, birth and death of the Messiah. Mary whom Satan had no power to touch, has also provided the image of the inviolability of the Church which, as distinct from its children against whom the wrath of the Dragon is displayed (in the persecutions) will remain inaccessible to the powers of hell.

2) The Son is pictured with Messianic characteristics (Psalm 2, 'He will break them with a rod of iron'): he is certainly Jesus Christ of whom only the first and last events of the human life are mentioned: his birth and his ascension. He is the first object of the Dragon's hostility, though it can do nothing against him.

3) The Dragon, who wears seven diadems because, in consequence of the sins of mankind, he has become the 'prince of this world' in the words of the Gospel (St. John 12, 31; 14, 30 and 16, 11), is identified with Satan and the Serpent who deceived our first parents. The allusion to Genesis 3, 15 is clear; the same characters are on the stage: the Woman, the 'Woman's Seed' and the Serpent. The ancient hostility of the Serpent is expressed in his struggle against the Church; but his final defeat is already assured.

4) Michael and the Angels are introduced into the vision to indicate that the Dragon belongs to the angelic world, and that before Satan's struggle against Christ and the Church, he had rebelled against God (with the 'third part of the stars', i.e. with the complicity of a great number of angels) and banished from the host of the heavenly beings.

5) The Beast who comes from the sea (probably the sea means the West) and who receives power from the Dragon whom he in some ways resembles, is the Roman Empire, a power which opposes God by the claim of the emperors to receive divine worship. The Roman Empire is Satan's instrument to unleash persecution against the Christians. The Dragon has no power against Christ, he cannot destroy the Church, but he has succeeded in making war against the 'saints', making them objects of persecution. The symbolical numbers require explanation. First, the period to which the power of persecuting Christians is restricted, forty-two months. It corresponds to the time during which the Woman is free from the assaults of the Dragon, 1260 days or three and a half years. This number recurs several times in the Apocalypse and is derived from the length of Antiochus IV's persecution of the Jewish religion (168-164 B.C.). In the Apocalypse it has a symbolic value, being half of seven years. As seven is the perfect number, half of it is the symbol of something which is limited and incomplete. The other number, 666, which corresponds to the name of a person, has generally been taken to mean the numerical value of the Hebrew letters spelling the words Neron Kesar, that is Nero Caesar. The persecuting power of the Empire is thus personified in the first great persecutor.

6) The Beast which comes from the land (perhaps from the East, that is from the Asiatic coast

visible from Patmos) has a false
and seductive appearance 'like a
lamb', and is the false prophet
who personifies the religion and
ideology of emperor-worship. He
is a duplicate of the first Beast:
the former is the political power,
the State as persecutor; the latter
is the State religion, like State
ideology and science under the
totalitarian regimes. It does in
fact install a kind of totalitarian-
ism which deprives of his liveli-
hood anyone who does not share

the State religion. The two Beasts
together represent the figure of
Antichrist (see No. 59).

Thus the Apocalypse reveals the
true meaning, from God's point
of view, of the persecutions in the
story of the early Church and
also of those which were to recur
from time to time in its remote
future. In fact, by reason of their
many-sided symbolism they remain 'typical', i.e. representative
of the whole history of the
Church.

176 The fall of pagan Rome
(17, 1-6; 18, 1-5 and 21)

17, ¹ Then one of the seven angels who had the seven bowls
came and said to me, "Come, I will show you the judgment
of the great harlot who is seated upon many waters, ² with
whom the kings of the earth have committed fornication, and
with the wine of whose fornication the dwellers on earth have
become drunk." ³ And he carried me away in the Spirit into
a wilderness, and I saw a woman sitting on a scarlet beast
which was full of blasphemous names, and it had seven heads
and ten horns. ⁴ The woman was arrayed in purple and scarlet,
and bedecked with gold and jewels and pearls, holding in her
hand a golden cup full of abominations and the impurities
of her fornication; ⁵ and on her forehead was written a name
of mystery: "Babylon the great, mother of harlots and of earth's
abominations." ⁶ And I saw the woman, drunk with the blood
of the saints and the blood of the martyrs of Jesus.

18, ¹ After this I saw another angel coming down from heaven,
having great authority; and the earth was made bright with
his splendour. ² And he called out with a mighty voice,

"Fallen, fallen is Babylon the great!
It has become a dwelling place of demons,
a haunt of every foul spirit,
a haunt of every foul and hateful bird;
³ for all nations have drunk the wine of her impure passion,
and the kings of the earth have committed fornication with her,
and the merchants of the earth have grown rich with the
    wealth of her wantonness."

⁴ Then I heard another voice from heaven saying,
"Come out of her, my people,
lest you take part in her sins,
lest you share in her plagues;
⁵ for her sins are heaped high as heaven,
and God has remembered her iniquities."
²¹ Then a mighty angel took up a stone like a great millstone
and threw it into the sea, saying,
"So shall Babylon the great city be thrown down with violence,
and shall be found no more..."

The series of seven prodigies is followed by the series of seven goblets which pour out the divine scourges on the sinful and persecuting world. Then the story of future events continues in a form which is no longer cyclic but straightforward. The first event which introduces the 'last things' is the fall of Rome. This is presented with a twofold symbolism: on the Beast already mentioned as coming from the sea is seated a woman in royal raiment and with the symbolical name of Babylon, the ancient city which rose against God in the incident of the Tower of Babel and which under Nebuchadnezzar destroyed the Temple of the true God and drove God's people into exile. It has two characteristics: prostitution, i.e. idolatry, in Biblical language, and the shedding of the blood of the martyrs.

The fall of Rome is not described but is solemnly foretold in generic and figurative terms. This vague character and the symbolic value of the name Babylon give to the fall of Rome also a 'typical', i.e. exemplary, character, which expresses the final overthrow of every power which sets itself against God.

'Now war arose in heaven, Michael and his angels fighting against the Dragon' (Apocalypse 12,7). From a Byzantine miniature of the tenth century in the Menologion of Basil II.

177 The marriage of the triumphant Lamb
(19, 6-16)

⁶ Then I heard what seemed to be the voice of a great multitude, like the sound of mighty thunderpeals, crying, "Hallelujah! For the Lord our God the Almighty reigns. ⁷ Let us rejoice and exult and give him the glory, for the marriage of the Lamb has come, and his Bride has made herself ready; ⁸ it was granted her to be clothed with fine linen, bright and pure"— for the fine linen is the righteous deeds of the saints.

⁹ And the angel said to me, "Write this: Blessed are those who are invited to the marriage supper of the Lamb." And he said to me, "These are true words of God." ¹⁰ Then I fell down at his feet to worship him, but he said to me, "You must not do that! I am a fellow servant with you and your brethren who hold the testimony of Jesus. Worship God." For the testimony of Jesus is the spirit of prophecy.

¹¹ Then I saw heaven opened, and behold, a white horse! He who sat upon it is called Faithful and True, and in righteousness he judges and makes war. ¹² His eyes are like a flame of fire, and on his head are many diadems; and he has a name inscribed which no one knows but himself. ¹³ He is clad in a robe dipped in blood, and the name by which he is called is The Word of God. ¹⁴ And the armies of heaven, arrayed in fine linen, white and pure, followed him on white horses. ¹⁵ From his mouth issues a sharp sword with which to smite the nations, and he will rule them with a rod of iron; he will tread the wine press of the fury of the wrath of God the Almighty. ¹⁶ On his robe and on his thigh he has a name inscribed, King of kings and Lord of lords.

On the ruins of the persecuting Empire arises the victorious kingdom of Christ. He does not reign alone, but with his elect, the Church. So the hymn of triumph is followed by a wedding song; the Church is the Bride of Christ and the full realisation of the sovereignty of Christ is like a wedding feast. This imagery of a wedding, in which Christ is called by the affectionate name of the Lamb, is followed by a martial vision which recalls the Messianic Psalms (Psalms 2 and 109) in which the Messiah's victory over his opponents is told in the imagery of Israel's holy war of old. Christ appears like a warrior on horseback followed by a white-robed company. But the 'robe dipped in blood' reminds us that his victory was won by way of the Cross.

Christ as judge divides the sheep from the goats. A mosaic of the 6th century at Ravenna (Sant'Apollinare Nuovo). The fact, here represented symbolically, of the Last Judgment and of the eternal destiny of every man to blessedness or punishment, is clearly revealed in the whole of the Christian message, and is re-affirmed by the Apocalypse in the last pages of the New Testament.

178 The last judgment
(20, 11-15)

¹¹ Then I saw a great white throne and him who sat upon it; from his presence earth and sky fled away, and no place was found for them. ¹² And I saw the dead, great and small, standing before the throne, and books were opened. Also another book was opened, which is the book of life. And the dead were judged by what was written in the books, by what they had

done. ¹³ And the sea gave up the dead in it, Death and Hades gave up the dead in them, and all were judged by what they had done. ¹⁴ Then Death and Hades were thrown into the lake of fire. This is the second death, the lake of fire; ¹⁵ and if any one's name was not found written in the book of life, he was thrown into the lake of fire.

From this point onwards the Apocalypse proceeds to sketch with rapid strokes the course of future history.

When the persecuting power has been destroyed, then the Dragon, that is, Satan, will also be bound 'for a thousand years', during which Christ will reign with his martyrs. The number 'a thousand' is also symbolical and means a very long and indeterminate period, the whole history of the Church from the age of bloody persecutions until the final persecution just before the end of the world.

This last and most terrible persecution, instigated by Satan who will come out to deceive the nations which are at the four corners of the earth', is summar-ized in a few lines of the Apocalypse, which brings it to an end with the divine intervention on the side of the 'camp of the saints' and the 'beloved city'. So Satan will finally be thrown into the 'lake of fire and brimstone' for ever.

At this point the Apocalypse, here quoted, describes the resurrection of the dead and the universal judgment. In this description also there may be some traces of symbolism (the throne, the books, Hades, i.e. the place where the dead dwell). The 'lake of fire' is the hell of the lost; the passage in which Death and Hades, like personified beings, are cast into hell is also symbolical: in fact death is pictured in Holy Scripture as bound up with the power of sin.

179 The heavenly Jerusalem
(21, 1-11, 22-27; 22, 3-5)

21, ¹ Then I saw a new heaven and a new earth; for the first heaven and the first earth had passed away, and the sea was no more. ² And I saw the holy city, new Jerusalem, coming down out of heaven from God, prepared as a bride adorned for her husband; ³ and I heard a great voice from the throne saying, "Behold, the dwelling of God is with men. He will dwell with them, and they shall be his people, and God himself will be with them; ⁴ he will wipe away every tear from their eyes, and death shall be no more, neither shall there be mourning nor crying nor pain any more, for the former things have passed away."

⁵ And he who sat upon the throne said, "Behold, I make all things new." Also he said, "Write this, for these words are trustworthy and true." ⁶ And he said to me, "It is done! I am the Alpha and the Omega, the beginning and the end. To the thirsty I will give water without price from the fountain of the water of life. ⁷ He who conquers shall have this heritage, and I will be his God and he shall be my son. ⁸ But as for the cowardly, the faithless, the polluted, as for murderers, fornicators, sorcerers, idolaters, and all liars, their lot shall be in the lake that burns with fire and brimstone, which is the second death."

⁹ Then came one of the seven angels who had the seven bowls full of the seven last plagues, and spoke to me, saying, "Come, I will show you the Bride, the wife of the Lamb." ¹⁰ And in the Spirit he carried me away to a great, high mountain, and showed me the holy city Jerusalem coming down out of heaven from God, ¹¹ having the glory of God, its radiance like a most rare jewel, like a jasper, clear as crystal.

²² And I saw no temple in the city, for its temple is the Lord God the Almighty and the Lamb. ²³ And the city has no need of sun or moon to shine upon it, for the glory of God is its light, and its lamp is the Lamb. ²⁴ By its light shall the nations walk; and the kings of the earth shall bring their glory into it, ²⁵ and its gates shall never be shut by day—and there shall be no night there; ²⁶ they shall bring into it the glory and the honour of the nations. ²⁷ But nothing unclean shall enter it, nor any one who practises abomination or falsehood, but only those who are written in the Lamb's book of life.

22, ¹ There shall no more be anything accursed, but the throne of God and of the Lamb shall be in it, and his servants shall worship him; ⁴ they shall see his face, and his name shall be on their foreheads. ⁵ And night shall be no more; they need no light of lamp or sun, for the Lord God will be their light, and they shall reign for ever and ever.

Ravenna, San Vitale. Polychrome mosaic of the fourth century, depicting the peacock, a symbol of immortality.

The description of the universal judgment and the damnation of the lost is followed by that of the state of eternal blessedness, which we call Paradise, a word which recalls the image of a garden and of an earthly paradise. But instead the Apocalypse depicts the dwelling place of the saints in heaven as an enormous city, the heavenly Jerusalem, with which is associated the image of the Bride, that is the Church. In this long and joyful description (reproduced here with some omissions) we must distinguish between the symbolic language and the spiritual reality it expresses. Certainly the resurrection of the body, however much trans-

419

Christos pantokrator (Christ, creator of all things). Mosaic of the twelfth century in the apse of Cefalú Cathedral.
'He who testifies to these things says "Surely I am coming soon". Amen. Come Lord Jesus. The grace of the Lord Jesus be with all the saints. Amen' (Apocalypse 22,20; see No. 180).

figured and dominated by the spirit, will be accompanied not by the destruction, but by the transformation, of the material world ('a new heaven and a new earth'), but 'the dwelling of God with men' will be essentially the community of the saints, inundated so to speak, by the beatific presence of God: 'its temple is the Lord God almighty and the Lamb'.

The Apocalypse ends with the repeated statement that the coming of Jesus is near: 'Surely I am coming soon', and with the heartfelt prayer for the fulfilment of that expectation: 'Come, Lord Jesus!' This seems to contradict the fact that it is precisely the Apocalypse, by contrast with the prophecies of an imminent coming in the Gospel and in St Paul's letters, which proclaims the 'last things' in the perspective of a long historical development. But there is no contradiction here for it is a case of two different dimensions. In the dimension of time, the distance between Christ's first and second comings may be very long indeed: nearly two thousand years have already passed and as many again may

pass: we do not know. But in the dimension of spiritual reality, Christ is always on the point of coming. Therefore he has taught us to pray: 'Thy kingdom come'. The kingdom of God 'comes' in the inner history of every soul when Christ takes possession of it, and the more complete that possession is, the more truly does it come, until the moment of perfect union at the end of this present life. It also 'comes' in the history of the world, both in the form of 'judgment' against human institutions which collapse before it, like ancient Jerusalem or the Roman Empire, or in the form of a more and more widespread and profound outpouring of the Gospel over peoples and their cultures.

Until the two dimensions come together at the end of time, and until Christ's coming finally occurs, the Church continues to be on the boundary between them, so to say, sharing in both of them: therefore, it is inherent in its nature always to exist in a state of tension, looking towards a future which is both in and beyond time, in expectation of the full manifestation of its union with Christ.

180 Epilogue
(22, 12-21)

[12] "Behold, I am coming soon, bringing my recompense, to repay every one for what he has done. [13] I am the Alpha and the Omega, the first and the last, the beginning and the end."
[14] Blessed are those who wash their robes, that they may have the right to the tree of life and that they may enter the city by the gates. [15] Outside are the dogs and sorcerers and fornicators and murderers and idolaters, and every one who loves and practises falsehood.

¹⁶ "I Jesus have sent my angel to you with this testimony for the churches. I am the root and the offspring of David, the bright morning star."

¹⁷ The Spirit and the Bride say, "Come." And let him who hears say, "Come." And let him who is thirsty come, let him who desires take the water of life without price.

¹⁸ I warn every one who hears the words of the prophecy of this book: if any one adds to them, God will add to him the plagues described in this book, ¹⁹ and if any one takes away from the words of the book of this prophecy, God will take away his share in the tree of life and in the holy city, which are described in this book.

²⁰ He who testifies to these things says, "Surely I am coming soon." Amen. Come, Lord Jesus!

²¹ The grace of the Lord Jesus be with all the saints. Amen.

INDEXES

Theological index

In this index it has seemed best to follow an order which is systematic rather than alphabetical. The numbers refer not to the pages but to the numbers of the sections into which the whole book after the introduction is divided.

Subjects and sayings are classified in ten principal headings as follows: I. The Christian Religion; II. God; III. Jesus Christ; IV. The Holy Spirit; V. Redemption; VI. Justification; VII. Morality; VIII. The Church; IX. The Sacraments; X. Holy Scripture.

I. THE CHRISTIAN RELIGION

Word (of God) 10. 16. 21. 22. 30-32. 35. 37. 38. 40. 44-46. 48. 51. 63.

Word of salvation, of life, of grace 14. 38. 68. 116.

Gospel (Good News, Glad Tidings) 42. 54. 56. 72. 75. 80. 82. 83. 85-88. 94. 95. 117. 119. 120. 124. 129. 136. 153.

Promise (Prophecy) fulfilled 5. 8. 10. 18. 23. 38. 42. 47. 48. 110. 116. 156.

Universal Message (to the Jews and to the Pagans) 24. 29-31. 39. 42. 89. 110. 116. 122. 126.

Faith (that in which one believes) 16. 37. 38. 40. 45. 107.

Way (mode of living and serving God) 24. 46. 62-64. 103. 107.

"Christians" 31. 111. 153.

"Nazarenes" 107.

II. GOD

DIVINE ATTRIBUTES

One God 78. 147.

Living God 39. 131. 142.

Most High 18. 46.

Creator and Lord of the universe 10. 39. 50.

Does not dwell in material buildings 18. 50.

He who is and was and is to come 166

The Alpha and the Omega, the Beginning and the End 166. 179.

REVELATION

In nature 39. 50.

Through the prophets 94. 140. 151. 156.

In Jesus Christ 50. 124. 140. 155. 160.

THE TRINITY
  The Three Persons named together 5. 78. 90. 94. 98. 126. 150.

GOD THE FATHER
  Father 2. 54. 70. 80. 85. 120. 125. 130. 150. 156. 159. 160. 161. 163. 164.
  Father of Jesus Christ 54. 84. 119. 124. 150. 164. 166. 170. 171. 173.
  Our Father 54. 56. 85. 90. 98. 117. 119. 124. 129.

ATTRIBUTES OF THE FATHER
  God is Light 160 (see 151)
  God is Love 163 (see 98. 126)

God, rich in mercy 126 (see 99. 150).

A just God who justifies 95. 98.

God has sent his Son 90. 98. 163.

God has raised and glorified him 5. 8. 9. 14. 30. 38. 50. 82. 94. 118. 121. 125.

God has sent the Holy Spirit 90.

To God is subjected the kingdom of Christ 80.

The whole work of Redemption is to the glory of God 118. 124.

III. JESUS CHRIST

Son of God (the Father) 25. 54. 70. 80. 86. 88. 90. 94. 98. 120. 124. 140. 141. 156. 160. 162-164. 170.

Pre-existing as God 118. 120. 140. 173.

Creator 120. 140.

Author of Life 8.

Word of God 160. 177.

Foretold by the Prophets 5. 8. 10. 18. 23. 38. 42. 47. 48. 110. 116. 156.

Incarnate in time 90. 94. 118. 131. 163.

Descended from David 38. 94. 180.

"Servant" of God 8. 10.

"Son of Man" 19.

Messiah (Christ) 5. 8. 10. 21. 25. 47. 51. 62. 110.

Earthly life (details) 1. 3. 5. 8. 10. 30. 38. 63. 118.

Death on the crosss (historical fact) 5. 8. 9. 14. 30. 38.

Redemptive death (theological meaning) 68. 73. 80. 85. 95. 118. 120. 124. 142. 152. 160. 163. 166. 174.

Resurrection 2. 5. 8. 9. 14. 30. 38. 50. 80. 85. 124. 144.

Appearances when risen 2. 3. 24. 30. 80. 103. 110.

Glorification 1. 2. 5. 8. 19. 94. 118. 125. 131. 143.

Christ as "Lord" (basic passages) 5. 78. 118. 177.

Christ the Lord (as title) 19. 26. 54. 60. 70. 73-77. 80-82. 84. 85. 94. 96-98. 100. 119. 124. 125. 129. 130. 136. 138. 139. 144. 145. 155. 156. 158. 159.

Universal primacy 120. 125. 166.

Higher than the Angels 120. 121. 125. 140. 150. 175. 177. 180.

Kingdom of Christ 80. 138. 166. 174. 177.

Christ a Priest for ever 141.

Christ a Victim for atonement 95. 142. 152. 163. 174.

Mediator of the New Covenant 77. 142.

Christ the "Saviour" 9. 14. 38. 127. 136. 155. 158. 163.

Author of redemption (see V. REDEMPTION).

Intercedes for us 98. 142.

Head of the Church 120. 125.

Bridegroom of the Church 83. 127. 177.

Christ sends the Holy Spirit 5.

Christ, source of divine Life 5. 80. 121.

Mediator of saving grace 42. 88. 95.

Miracles are wrought in his name 7. 27. 46. 63.

Christ the universal Judge 30. 50. 82. 138. 178. 180.

The Parousia (second coming) of Christ 2. 8. 54. 56. 58. 59. 70. 117. 122. 138. 144. 157. 158. 166.

IV. THE HOLY SPIRIT
(Spirit of God, Spirit of Christ)

MANIFESTATION AND ATTRIBUTES

Prophesied for the Messianic age 5.

Promised by the Father and by Jesus 2.

Sent by the glorified Christ 5.

Sent by the Father 90.

"Baptism" of the Church at Pentecost 4. (see 2).

Extraordinary signs of his coming 4. 10. 22. 30. 63.

Conferred by the Apostles 22. 63.

Dwells in the Chrurch as in a Temple 71.

Confers unity on the Church 78. 126.

Dwells in the Christian as in a Temple 136.

Gift of God 5. 22-30. 42. 63.

Sign and seal of heavenly inheritance 98. 124.

Spirit of the children of God 90. 98.

EFFECTS

Power 2. 54.

Gifts and charisms 4. 10. 37. 54. 78. 99.

Joy 54.

Ability to bear witness 10. 14. 17.

PERSONAL ACTION

Has spoken through the Prophets 3. 10. 150. 156.

As Spirit of prophecy, warns the Church 167-173. 180.

Guides the Church in decisions of belief 43.

Confirms the Pastors of the Church 68.

Speaks in Stephen 17.

Speaks to Philip, to Peter 23. 30. 31.

Sends Paul and Barnabas to the apostolate 37.

Directs the apostolic journeys 45. 68.

Reveals Paul's future captivity 68. 69.

427

Speaks to the hearts of all who hear the Word. 23. 30. 36. 45. 68. 69.
Guides in the fulfilment of holy works 92. 98.

Intercedes for Christians 98.
Against him are opposed lies, trials, resistance 12. 18.
Speaks with the Father and the Son 5. 78. 90. 98. 126. 150.

V. REDEMPTION
(wrought by God)

PREPARATION

God's (saving) Justice 95. 98.
God's eternal plan 124. 136.
Election 38. 54. 98. 124. 155.

REALIZATION IN CHRIST

In the power of Christ's death 68. 73. 80. 85. 88. 95. 118. 120. 124. 142. 152. 160. 163. 166.
Forgiveness of sins 5. 8. 14. 30. 38. 85. 95. 110. 120. 121. 124. 161. 166.
Reconciliation 120.
Adoption as sons of God and heirs of divine blessings 90. 98. 124.
Victory over sin 96. 121. 161.
Liberation from the Law 89. 92. 97.

Pacification of the peoples 89. 122. 126.
Victory over death 80. 82. 136.

FULFILMENT AT THE END OF TIME

General resurrection 57. 80. 82. 105. 107. 110.
Last Judgment 30. 50. 82. 107. 138. 142. 163. 178. 180.
Wrath (punishment) 8. 58. 73. 82. 137. 153. 159. 170. 176. 178. 180.
The end of the world 157-179.
The redemption of material creation 98.
Life in eternal glory 122. 150. 153. 159. 167. 168. 178. 179.
The Kingdom of God 73. 80.

VI. JUSTIFICATION

NEGATIVE PREPARATION

Universality of sin 96.
Fall of man 95. 97.
The pagan under the power of Satan 110.
Incapability of the Law 38. 88. 95. 97.
Ineffectiveness of circumcision 41. 42. 87. 93. 121.

ENTRY INTO SALVATION

Conversion 5. 8. 31. 32. 39. 42. 50. 54. 68. 73. 110. 152. 157.
Salvation by means of faith 38. 42. 89. 95. 110. 121. 126.
Faith as a gift 46.
Sharing in Christ's death and resurrection 88. 93. 121. 126.
Grace (free communion with

God) 42. 88. 95. 96. 124. 126. 136. 155.

Children of God 89. 90. 98. 124. 178.

A new man 122.

A new creation 93.

The gift of the Spirit 90, 98. 124.

Possession of eternal life 8. 14. 31. 38. 82. 93. 96. 122. 136. 160. 162.

PROGRESS IN RIGHTEOUSNESS

Righteousness 88. 95. 96. 117. 137. 147. 152. 157.

Life according to the Spirit 88. 92. 98. 122.

Christian freedom 92.

Hope 82. 98. 136. 138. 143. 159.

Death in Christ (with Christ immediately after death) 82. 117.

OBSTACLES AND DIFFICULTIES

Tribulations 40. 56. 82. 98. 143. 145. 152. 153.

Satan as enemy 55. 84. 98. 110. 161. 168. 172. 175.

Satan as tempter 56. 59. 74. 83. 131. 154. 162. 169.

Antichrist 59. 164. 175.

Persecutions 9. 14. 15. 20. 24. 33. 38. 39. 46. 84. 102-107. 153. 166. 175.

VII. THE MORAL LIFE

Necessity of moral life 76. 126. 146.

Faith and works 147.

Charity (love of one's neighbour) 79. 92. 99. 118. 122. 144. 162. 163. 164.

Love for God 81. 98. 163.

Unity and concord 70. 71. 99.

Solidarity with those in need 81. 100. 144.

Forgiving offences 99. 122.

Domestic duties 128. 131. 133.

Slavery 128. 129.

Connubial morality 74. 127. 144.

Celibacy and virginity 74.

Work 60.

Virtues to practise (lists) 92. 99. 107. 122. 144.

Vices to avoid (lists) 73. 76. 92. 122. 161.

Divisions 71.

Presumption 72.

Social injustice 148.

Vices of the flesh 73.

Magic 22. 37. 63.

Prayer, examples of 2. 6. 10. 16. 28. 29. 54. 56. 70. 94. 117. 119. 125.

Prayer, exhortations to 99. 100. 144. 149.

Growth in Christ 91. 125.

Christian witness 15. 20. 24. 33. 68. 105. 110. 117. 136.

Apostolate 68. 70. 72. 75. 83. 84. 91. 94. 110.

Martyrdom 19. 33. 69.

VIII. THE CHURCH

ITS NATURE

People of God 151. 166. 179.

Body of Christ 78. 120.

Christ the Head of the Church 120. 125.

Bride of Christ 83. 127. 177. 180.

Spiritual building 71. 126. 151. 179.
House of God 131. 153.

MARKS OF THE CHURCH

Unity in the diversity of gifts 78. 99.
Catholicity, all discrimination being barred 24. 29-31. 39. 42. 89. 110. 116. 122. 126.
Holiness: requires conversion 5. 8. 38. 39. 50. 107.
The Christians called "saints" 24. 27. 70. 81. 94. 98. 100. 110. 117. 119. 120. 124-126. 129. 133. 159. 170.
Sanctified by means of the sacraments (see IX. THE SACRAMENTS)
Is made pure and holy by Christ 127.
Apostolicity 2. 11. 32. 87. 126.

TASKS AND POWERS

Proclamation of the Gospel 2. 3. 5. 9. 42. 54. 56. 68. 70. 72. 75. 82. 85-87. 91. 94. 95. 117.
Guardianship and defence of revelation 68. 83. 85-87. 130. 134.
Authority to decide about doctrine and discipline 41-43.
Authority to correct and excommunicate 22. 72. 85.
Extraordinary gifts:
miracles 6. 7. 13. 21. 22. 27. 39. 46. 63. 66. 114.
prophecies and charisms 32. 36. 69. 78. 99.
angelic interventions 2. 14. 23. 28. 33. 34. 113.

STRUCTURE

The Church (universal) 12. 20. 27. 33. 68. 78. 80. 86. 120. 125. 127. 131.

Local church 32. 36. 40. 41. 43. 53. 54. 68. 70. 72. 77. 123. 154. 164. 165.
Local churches 40. 45. 74. 81. 84-86. 166-173. 180.

HIERARCHY AND ORGANIZATION

In general 144.
The Apostles 1. 3. 5. 6. 11. 14. 16. 22. 41-43. 45. 72. 78. 80. 83. 86. 126. 159. 167.
The "Twelve" 5. 16. 80.
Witnesses of the resurrection 2. 3. 8. 14. 30. 38. 80. 103. 110.
They preside over the community 2. 3. 42.
They exercize authority in administration 4. 11.
They institute the deacons 16.
They confer the Holy Spirit 22. (see 63).
They institute the presbyters 40.
They control the new churches 32.
They make decisions about faith and discipline 41-43.
Peter (Cephas): his outstanding authority 3. 5. 14. 30. 31. 33. 42. 70. 71. 80. 86-88.
The Apostle (Peter) 150. 155.
The Apostle (Paul) 70. 75. 80. 85. 94. 119. 124. 130. 136.
Deputies of the Apostles 130-132. 134. 136.
Presbyters-Bishops 32. 40. 41. 43-45. 68. 101. 132. 134. 149.
Their authority is subordinate to the Apostles' 41-43. 68. 101. 132. 136.
They look after the material interests of the community 32.
Ordained by an Apostle or by his deputy 40. 131. 134.

Deacons:
They assist the poor 16.
They preach and baptize 17. 21. 22. 23.
Ordained by the Apostles or a deputy 16. 117. 131.
Widows in the Church's service 133.

ECCLESIAL LIFE
Communal worship 6. 10. 33.

Prayer with fasting 36. 40.
Sunday worship 66. 81. 166.
Administration of the sacraments (see IX. THE SACRAMENTS).
Social assistance and goods held in common 6. 11. 16. 144.
Solidarity of the local churches 32. 81. 100.

IX. THE SACRAMENTS

BAPTISM
Entrance into the church 5. 22. 23. 24. 30. 46. 63. 103.
Makes us children of God 89.
Sharing in Christ's death and resurrection 121.
Gives the forgiveness of sins 5. 103. 121.
Preceded by conversion and faith 5. 8. 22. 51. 89.
Incorporates us in the Body of Christ 78.

CONFIRMATION
Gift of the Spirit conferred by the Apostles after baptism 5. 22. 63. 124.

THE EUCHARIST
The fact of celebrating 6. 66.
Doctrinal facts and aspects, 76. 77. probably 144.

PENANCE
Public confession 149.
Possibility of penance after baptism 149. 169. 171. 173.

ANOINTING OF THE SICK 149.

ORDINATION 16. 40. 132. 136. (see VIII. CHURCH, HIERARCHY).

MATRIMONY 127.

X. HOLY SCRIPTURE

The Prophecies 5. 8. 10. 18. 23. 38. 42. 47. 48. 110. 116. 156.
The Decalogue 18. 99.

Inspiration and Interpretation 156. 158.
Inspired Scripture and Tradition 137.

Historical and geographical index

(People, places, institutions)

The names preceded by an asterisk (*) are not found in the sacred text but in the Introduction, Notes or Summaries.

The numbers refer to the 180 sections into which the whole of the biblical text (Acts, Letters and Apocalypse) is divided.

The dash "-" between two numbers means that the subject is treated in all the sections between the two numbers.

Single numbers preceded by "p." or series of numbers preceded by "pp." refer to the Introduction, Summaries or Notes.

"f" following a page number means that the subject is dealt with in the immediately following pages as well.

AARON: 18. 141.
ABRAHAM: 8. 18. 38. 84. 89. 147.
  p. 34f.
ACHAIA: 52. 54. 63. 81. 83. 99.
  p. 28.
ACHAICUS: 81.
*ACILIUS GLABRIO: p. 333.
ACTS OF THE APOSTLES: 1-53.
  61-69. 101-116. pp. 13. 27. 28.
  31. 33. 37. 40f.
ADAM: 80. 96.
ADRAMITTIUM: 112.
ADRIATIC SEA: 113.
*AEGEAN (SEA): p. 391.
AENEAS: 27.
AGABUS: 32. 69.
AGORA (FORUM): 46. 49.
AGRIPPA I (HEROD): 33. 34.
  p. 28.
AGRIPPA II: 109-111. p. 329.
AKELDAMA: 3.
*ALBINUS (LUCIUS): p. 43.
  p. 327.

ALEXANDER (OF EPHESUS): 64.
  139.
*ALEXANDER THE GREAT: p. 20.
ALEXANDER (a priest): 9.
ALEXANDRIA: 62. 112. 115.
  p. 31.
ALEXANDRIANS: 17.
*AMON: p. 21.
AMPHIPOLIS: 47.
ANANIAS (of Damascus): 24.
  103.
ANANIAS AND SAPPHIRA: 12.
ANANIAS (High Priest): 107.
  p. 329.
*ANANUS (HANAN): p. 28.
  p. 327. p. 329.
ANDREW (the Apostle): 2.
  p. 27f.
ANGELS: 14. 17. 18. 23. 28. 30.
  31. 33. 34. 72. 79. 83. 85. 91.
  98. 105. 113. 131. 140. 144. 150.
  166-174. 176. 177. 179.
ANNAS (High Priest): 9. p. 327.

ANTIOCH IN PISIDIA: 38-40, 137.
ANTIOCH IN SYRIA: 32. 36. 40. 43. 60. 88. p. 26. p. 37. p. 41. p. 116. p. 334.
ANTIPAS (martyr): 169.
ANTIPATRIS: 106.
*APHRODITE: p. 21.
APOCALYPSE: 166. p. 13. p. 333. p. 391f.
APOLLONIA: 47.
APOLLOS: 62. 63. 70. 71. 81. 135.
APOSTLE: 70. 75. 80. 85. 94. 119. 124. 130. 136. 150. 155. p. 26. p. 28. p. 31.
APOSTLES: 1. 3. 5. 6. 11. 14. 16. 22. 41-43. 45. 72. 78. 80. 83. 86. 126. 159. 167. p. 21. p. 25. pp. 26-29. p. 31. p. 37.
APPIA: 129.
*AQUAE SALVIAE: p. 33.
AQUILA: 51-53. 62. 81. 139.
ARABIA: 85.
ARABS: 4.
*ARAMAIC (language): p. 28. p. 34.
*ARATOS: p. 147.
ARCHIPPUS: 123. 129.
AREOPAGUS: 49. 50.
ARETAS: 84.
ARISTARCHUS: 63. 64. 112. 123. 129.
*ARMENIA: p. 28.
ARTEMAS: 135.
ARTEMIS: 64. p. 23.
*ASIA MINOR: p. 20. p. 27f. p. 334.
ASIA (province of): 4. 17. 45. 63-65. 67. 68. 81. 102. 107. 112. 150. 166.
ASIARCHS: 64.
ASSASSINS: 102.
ASSOS: 67.
*ASSYRIANS: p. 35.
ATHENIANS: 49. 50.
ATHENS: 48-51. 56.

*ATONEMENT (DAY OF): p. 287. p. 353.
ATTALIA: 40.
AUGUSTAN (cohort): 112.
AUGUSTUS (NERO): 109.
AZOTUS: 23.

BABYLON: 18.
BABYLON (ROME): 154. 176.
BALAK: 169.
BALAAM: 169.
BARBARIANS: 122.
BARJESUS: 37.
BARNABAS: 11. 26. 32. 35. 36-39. 41-44. 87. 88. 123. p. 31.
BARSABBAS (JOSEPH): 3.
BARSABBAS (JUDAS): 43.
BARTHOLOMEW: 2. p. 28.
*BASILICA OF ST PAUL: p. 328.
*BASILICA OF ST PETER: p. 328.
BEAUTIFUL GATE: 7.
*BEIRUT: p. 29.
BENJAMIN: 38.
BERNICE: 109. 111.
BEROEA: 48. 65.
*BETHSAIDA: p. 26. p. 28.
*BIBLE: p. 13. p. 34. p. 39. p. 139.
BISHOP(S): 117. 131. 134. p. 26. p. 28.
BITHYNIA: 45. 150.
BRETHREN AND SAINTS: 3. 26. 30. 31. 33. 41. 43-45. 53. 69. 74. 80. 81. 101. 115. 117. 139. p. 35.

CAESAR: 47. 108. 109. 111. 113. 116.
CAESAREA: 23. 26. 28. 30. 31. 33. 53. 69. 101. 106. 108. 109. p. 40.
CAIAPHAS: 9. p. 327.
*CALAMUS: p. 39.
*CALIGULA: p. 18. p. 42.
*CANA IN GALILEE: p. 28.
CANAAN: 18.
*CANAANITE (SIMON THE): p. 29.

CANDACE: 23.
*CAPERNAUM: p. 26. p. 28
  p. 40.
CAPPADOCIA: 4. 150.
CARPUS: 139.
*CATO: p. 278.
CAUDA: 113.
CEFA (PETER): 70. 71. 80. 85.
  87. 88.
CENCHREAE: 53.
CENTURION: 28. 30. 102. 104.
  106. 107. 112. 113.
*CESTIUS GALLIUS: p. 329.
CHALDEANS: 18.
CHIOS: 67.
CHLOE: 70.
*CHREON: p. 147.
*CHRISTIAN(S): 32. 111. pp. 35.
  327f. 333f.
*CHRISTIANITY: p. 40. p. 116.
CHURCH: 12. 20. 27. 33. 68. 80.
  86. 120. 125. 127. 131. p. 37.
  p. 40. p. 115 f. p. 334.
CHURCH (LOCAL): 54. 70. 72.
  77. 123. 129. 133. 149. 154.
  164. 165. 167-173. p. 328.
CHURCHES (LOCAL): 40. 45. 74.
  81. 84-86. 166. 167-173. 180.
  p. 38.
CILICIA: 17. 43. 85. 106.
CIRCUMCISED: 87. 88. 93. 121-
  123. 126. p. 34f., p. 116.
CLAUDIA: 139.
CLAUDIUS (EMPEROR): 32. 51.
  p. 18. p. 42.
CLAUDIUS LYSIAS: 106.
*CLEMENT: p. 334.
*CLETUS: p. 334.
CNIDUS: 112.
*CODEX: p. 39.
COLOSSAE, COLOSSIANS: 119.
CORINTH: 51. 63. 70. 82. 139.
CORINTHIANS: 51. 70. 82.
CORNELIUS: 28. 30.
COS: 69.

COUNCIL (APOSTOLIC): p. 25.
  p. 132 f., p. 135.
CRESCENS: 139.
CRETANS: 4.
CRETE: 112. 113. 134. p. 334.
CRISPUS: 51. 70.
*CUSPICUS FAUDUS: p. 42.
CYPRUS: 32. 37. 44. 69. 101. 112.
  p. 31. p. 334.
CYRENE: 4. 32. 36.
CYRENIANS: 17.

DALMATIA: 139.
DAMARIS: 50.
DAMASCUS: 24-26. 84. 85. 103.
  110. p. 31. p. 37.
*DANUBE: p. 28.
DAVID: 3. 5. 18. 38. 42. 94. 172.
  180.
DEACONS: 16. 117. 131.
*DEAD SEA: p. 331.
DEMAS: 123. 129. 139.
DEMETRIUS: 64. 165.
DERBE: 39. 45. 65.
DIANA: SEE ARTEMIS.
*DIASPORA: p. 24f., p. 34.
  p. 333.
DIONYSIUS THE AREOPAGITE:
  50.
DIOTREPHES: 165.
*DIVINITIAES (GRAECO - RO-
  MAN): p. 22f.
*DODECANESE: p. 392.
*DOMITIAN: p. 19. p. 44. p. 333.
  p. 392.
*DON (river): p. 28.
DRUSILLA: 107.

EASTER: 33.
EGYPT: 4. 18. p. 20.
EGYPTIANS: 18. 102.
ELAMITES: 4.
ELDER (THE) (John the Apostle):
  164-165.
*ELDERS (PRESBYTERS): p. 37.
*ELEAZAR (THE ZEALOT):
  p. 331.

ELYMAS: 37.
EPAPHRAS: 119. 123. 129.
EPHESIANS: 64. 124.
EPHESUS: 53. 62-64. 67. 68. 80.
 81. 124. 130. 139. 166. 167.
 p. 23. p. 27f.
EPICUREANS: 49.
ERASTUS: 63. 139.
*ETHIOPIA: p. 28f.
ETHIOPIAN: 23.
EUBULUS: 139.
EUNICE: 136.
EUTYCHUS: 66.
*EVARISTUS: p. 334.
EVE: 83.

FAIR HAVENS: 112.
FELIX (ANTONIUS): 106. 107.
 109. p. 43.
FESTUS (PORCIUS): 107-111.
 p. 43. p. 327.
*FLAVIA DOMITILLA: p. 333.
*FLAVIUS CLEMENS: p. 333.
FORUM (AGORA): 46. 49.
FORUM (APPIAN): 115.
FORTUNATUS: 81.

HERMES: 39. p. 23.

GAIUS (JOHN'S DISCIPLE): 165.
GAIUS (PAUL'S DISCIPLE): 64.
 65. 70.
GALATIA: 45. 81. 85. 139. 150.
GALATIANS: 85. p. 38.
*GALBA: p. 19. p. 44. p. 331.
GALILEANS: 2. 4. 15. p. 34.
GALILEE: 27. 30. 38. p. 26. p. 28.
 p. 329.
GALLIO: 52.
GAMALIEL: 14. 103. p. 33.
GAZA: 23.
GENTILES: 10. 18. 38. 42. 94. 95.
 p. 31. p. 34f.
*GESSIUS FLORUS: p. 43. p. 329.
*GODESS ROME: p. 22.

GOSPEL (GOOD NEWS): 42. 54.
 56. 72. 75. 80. 82. 83. 85-88.
 94. 95. 117. 119. 120. 124. 129.
 136. 153. p. 25. p. 35. p. 41.
*GOSPELS (BOOKS): p. 13.
 p. 28. p. 31. p. 37.
GREECE: 65. p. 20f. p. 329.
 p. 334.
GREEK (language): 102. p. 34.
GREEKS: 32. 39. 45. 48. 63. 68.
 89. 95. 102. 122. p. 21.

HAMOR: 18.
*HANAN II (ANANUS): p. 28.
 p. 327. p. 329.
HARAN: 18.
HEBREW (language): 102. p. 34.
HEBREWS: 16. 84. 140. p. 24.
 p. 34f., p. 329. p. 333.
*HELLENISM: p. 20f.
HELLENISTS: 16. 26. p. 34. p. 116.
HERA: p. 21.
HEROD (ANTIPAS): 10. 36.
HEROD (AGRIPPA I): 33. 34.
 p. 42.
HEROD (THE GREAT): 106.
HIERAPOLIS: 123.

ICONIUM: 38-40. 45. 137.
*IGNATIUS OF ANTIOCH: p. 334.
*INDIA: p. 28.
ISAAC: 18. 147. p. 34.
ISAIAH: 23. 116.
ISRAEL: 2. 5. 9. 10. 14. 18. 24.
 30. 38. 93. 116. 169.
*ISRAEL (JACOB): p. 34.
*ISRAEL (KINGDOM OF): p. 35.
ISRAELITES: 5. 8. 15. 38. 84. 102.
 p. 34.
ITALIAN (cohort): 28.
ITALY: 51. 112. p. 334.

JACOB: 8. 18. p. 34.
JAMES THE GREAT: 2. 33. p. 27f.
JAMES THE LESS: 2. 33. 42. 80.
 85. 87. 88. 101. 145. 159.
 p. 28. p. 116. p. 327. p. 329.

JASON: 47.

JERUSALEM: 2-4. 9. 13. 16. 23. 24. 26. 30-32. 35. 38. 41. 45. 67-69. 81. 85. 87. 99. 101. 103. 105. 107. 108. 110. 116. 172. 179. pp. 24-26. p. 28. p. 31. p. 33f., p. 34. p. 37. p. 40f., p. 115f., p. 327. p. 329. p. 331.

JESSE: 38.

JESUS CALLED JUSTUS: 123.

JESUS CHRIST: his name appears in almost every section of the Acts and in every page of the Letters of the Apostles: and also on p. 13. p. 21. pp. 26-28. p. 31. p. 40. p. 327. p. 329. p. 333.

JEWS: 4. 25. 30. 32. 33. 37-39. 45. 47-49. 51. 52. 63-65. 68. 69. 75. 84. 88. 89. 95. 101-103. 105-110. 116. 122. 172. p. 24. p. 34f., p. 329. p. 333.

JEWISH - CHRISTIANS: p. 40f., p. 327. p. 329.

JEWISH WAR: pp. 329-331.

JEZEBEL: 170.

JOEL: 5.

JOHN (THE APOSTLE): 7-9. 22. 33. 87. 160. 164. 166. p. 13. p. 27f., p. 333f., p. 391f.

JOHN (THE BAPTISM): 2. 30. 31. 38. 62. 63. p. 27f.

*JOHN (OF GISCALA): p. 331.

JOHN MARK: see Mark.

JOPPA: 27. 28. 30. 31.

*JORDAN: p. 329.

JOSEPH BARSABBAS: 3.

JOSEPH FLAVIUS: p. 267. p. 278.

JOSEPH (THE PATRIARCH): 18.

JOVE (ZEUS): 39. p. 21. p. 23.

*JUDAH (tribe of): p. 34.

*JUDAISM: p. 116. p. 327. p. 333.

JUDAS BARSABBAS: 43.

JUDAS OF DAMASCUS: 24.

JUDAS THE GALILEAN: 15.

JUDAS ISCARIOT: 3.

JUDAS THADDAEUS: 2. 159. p. 29.

JUDEA: 2. 4. 20. 27. 30-32. 41. 69. 85. 116. p. 20. p. 40. p. 329.

JULIUS: 112.

*JUNO: p. 21.

*JUVENAL: p. 282.

KEDRON: p. 327.

*LAKE OF GALILEE: p. 26.

LAODICEA: 123. 166. 173.

LAODICEANS: 123.

LASAE: 112.

LETTERS OF THE APOSTLES: 54-60. 70-100. 117-165. p. 13. p. 38.

LIBERTINES: 17.

LINUS: 139. p. 334.

LOIS: 136.

LUCIUS OF CYRENE: 36.

LUKE: 123. 129. 139. p. 13. p. 31. p. 137.

LYBIA: 4.

LYCAONIA: 39.

LYCIA: 112.

LYDIA: 46.

LYSIAS (CLAUDIUS): 106. 107.

LYSTRA: 39. 40. 45. 137.

MACEDONIA: 45. 46. 51. 54. 63. 65. 81. 83. 99. 130. p. 334.

MACEDONIANS: 45. 64. 112.

MADIAN: 18.

MALTA: 114.

*MAMERTIME (prison): p. 331.

MANAEN: 36.

*MARCELLUS (MARULLUS): p. 42.

MARK: 33. 35. 37. 38. 123. 129. 139. 154. pp. 13-31.

MARY (MOTHER OF JESUS): 2.

MARY (MOTHER OF MARK): 33.

*MASADA: p. 331.

MATTHEW: 2. pp. 13-28.

MATTHIAS: 3. p. 29.

MEDES: 4.

*MEDITERRANEAN SEA: pp. 14-
17. 20.
MELCHIZEDECH: 141.
MERCURY (HERMES): 39.
p. 23.
MESOPOTAMIA: 4. 18.
MESSIAH: 5. 8. 10. 25. 47. 51.
62. 110. p. 333.
MICHAEL: 175.
MILETUS: 67. 68. 139.
MNASON: 101.
MOLOCH: 18.
MOSES: 8. 17. 18. 41. 42. 76. 96.
101. 110. p. 34.
MYRA: 112.
MYSIA: 45.
MYTILENE: 67.

NATHANAEL: p. 28.
NAZARENE (JESUS): 5. 7. 9. 17.
103. 110.
NAZARENES: 107.
*NAZIRATE: p. 151. p. 264.
NEAPOLIS: 46.
*NERO: p. 18. p. 25f., p. 33. p. 43.
p. 327f., p. 329. p. 331. p. 333.
See also Caesar and Au-
gustus.
*NERVA: p. 19. p. 44. p. 334.
*NEW TESTAMENT (books):
p. 13. p. 19.
NICANOR: 16.
NICHOLAS OF ANTIOCH: 16.
NICHOLAITANS: 167. 169.
NICOPOLIS: 135.
NYMPHA: 123.

OLD TESTAMENT: p. 34. p. 333.
p. 348f.
OLIVES (MOUNT OF): 2.
*OLYMPUS: p. 21.
ONESIMUS: 123. 129.
ONESIPHORUS: 139.
*OSTIAN WAY: p. 328.
*OTTO: p. 19. p. 44. p. 331.

*PAX ROMANA: p. 25.

PAGANS: 24. 31. 38-43. 51. 69.
74. 76. 84. 86-88. 95. 101. 110.
116. 124. 126. p. 35. p. 40f.,
p. 116.
*PALESTINE: p. 14. p. 24. p. 28 f.
PAMPHYLIA: 4. 38. 40. 44. 112.
PAPHOS: 37. 38.
*PAPYRUS: p. 39.
PARCHMENT: 139. p. 39.
PARTHIANS: 4.
PATARA: 69.
PATMOS: 166. p. 27.
*PATRAS: p. 28.
PAUL (Apostle): from no. 37 to
no. 139 is the starring of the
history and the auctor of the
Letters.
And also at no. 158 and on
pp. 31. 33. 37f., 41. 116. 327f.
*PELOPONNESE: p. 28.
*PENTATEUCH: p. 35.
PENTECOST: 4. 67. 81. p. 26.
p. 28f., p. 334.
PERGA: 38. 40.
PERGAMUM: 166. 169.
*PERSIA: p. 20. p. 28.
PETER: 2. 3. 5. 7-9. 12. 22. 27-31.
33. 42. 87. 150. 155. pp. 26-28.
p. 37. p. 41. p. 116. p. 328. See
also Cephas.
PHARAOH: 18.
PHARISEES: 15. 41. 105. 110.
PHENICE: 112.
PHILADELPHIA: 166. 172.
PHILEMON: 129.
PHILIP (THE APOSTLE): 2.
p. 27f.
PHILIP (THE DEACON): 16. 21-
23. 69.
PHILIPPI: 46. 65. 117.
PHILIPPIANS: 117.
PHOENICIA: 32. 41. 69.
PHRYGIA: 4. 45. 61.
PILATE (PONTIUS): 8. 10. 38.
p. 42.
*PLINY THE YOUNGER: p. 334.

POLYTARCHS: 47.
PONTUS: 4. 51. 150.
PORCH (PORTICO) OF SOLO-
  MON: 8. 13.
PRESBYTERS: 32. 40. 41. 43. 45.
  68. 101. 132. 134. 149.
PRISCILLA (PRISCA): 51. 53. 62.
  81. 139.
PROSELYTES: 4. 16. 38. p. 34f.
PTOLEMAIS: 69.
*PTOLEMIES: p. 20.
PUBLIO (chief man of the
  Island): 114.
PUDENS: 139.
PUTEOLI: 115.

*RELIGION (GRAECO-ROMAN):
  p. 22f.
REPHAN: 18.
RHEGIUM: 115.
RHODA: 33.
RHODES: 69.
*ROMAN EMPIRE: p. 14. p. 16.
ROMANS: 4. 46. 94. 104. 106.
  109. 116. p. 21. p. 38. pp. 229-
  231.
ROME: 51. 63. 94. 105. 115. 116.
  p. 14f., p. 26. p. 33. p. 37.
  p. 328. p. 331. p. 334. See also
  BABYLON (ROME).

SADDUCEES: 9. 14. 105. p. 61.
SAINTS (THE CHRISTIANS): 24.
  27. 81. 110. p. 35.
SALAMIS: 37. p. 31.
SALMONE: 112.
SAMARIA: 2. 20-22. 27. 41.
  p. 34f., p. 40.
SAMARITANS: 22. p. 34f., p. 116.
SANHEDRIM: 9. 14. 15. 17. 105-
  107. p. 116. p. 327f.
SAMOS: 67.
SAMOTHRACIA: 46.
SAMUEL: 8. 38.
SARDIS: 166. 171.
SAUL (KING): 38.

SAUL (PAUL): 20. 24-26. 32. 35.
  36. 37. 103. 110. p. 33.
SCEVA: 63.
SCRIBES: 9. 17. 105.
*SCYTHIA: p. 28.
SCYTHIANS: 122.
SECUNDUS: 65.
SELEUCIA: 37.
*SELEUCIDS: p. 20.
SERGIUS PAULUS: 37.
SHARON: 27.
*SCROLL (VOLUME): p. 39.
SHECHEM: 18.
SIDON: 34. 112.
SILAS (SILVANUS): 43. 44. 46-
  48. 51. 54. 154.
*SIMEON BAR GHIORA: p. 331.
SIMEON NIGER: 36.
*SIMON (BISHOP OF JERUSA-
  LEM): p. 334.
SIMON MAGUS: 22.
SIMON PETER: 28. 30. 31. 155.
  See also PETER.
SIMON THE TANNER: 27. 28.
SIMON THE ZEALOT: 2. p. 29.
SINAI (MOUNT): 18.
SION: 151.
SMYRNA: 166. 168.
SOLOMON: 18.
SOLOMON'S PORCH: 8. 13.
SOPATER: 65.
SOSTHENES: 52. 70.
SPAIN: 99. p. 33.
STEPHEN: 16-20. 32. 103. p. 116.
STEPHANAS: 70. 81.
*STYLE OF THE LETTERS: p. 38.
STOICS: 49.
*SUETONIUS: p. 150.
*SYMEON PETER: 42.
SYNAGOGUE: 17. 24. 25. 37-39.
  42. 47-49. 51. 53. 62. 63. 103.
  107. 110. p. 24f.
*SYNCRETISM: p. 21.
SYRACUSE: 115.
SYRIA: 43. 45. 53. 65. 69. 85
  p. 14. p. 28. p. 329. p. 334.

439

*SYRO-MALABAR: p. 28.
SYRTES: 113.

TABITHA: 27.
*TACITUS: p. 25. p. 275. p. 328.
TARSUS: 24. 26. 32. 102. 103.
  p. 31. p. 33.
TEMPLE: 50. 59. 71. 79. 126. 172.
  179.
TEMPLE AT JERUSALEM: 6. 7. 9.
  14. 101-103. 107. 108. 110.
  p. 115. p. 327. pp. 329-331.
*TERTULLIAN: p. 333.
TERTULLUS: 107.
THEOPHILUS: 1.
THESSALONIANS: 54. 65.
THESSALONICA: 47. 54. 112.
  139.
THEUDAS: 15.
THOMAS: 2. p. 28.
*THREE FOUNTAINS: p. 33.
  p. 328.
THREE TAVERNS: 115.
THYATIRA: 46. 166. 172.
*TIBERIUS: p. 14. p. 18. p. 42.
*TIBERIUS ALEXANDER: p. 42.
TIMON: 16.
TIMOTHY: 45. 48. 51. 54. 56. 63.
  65. 72. 81. 117. 119. 129. 130.
  136.
TITIUS JUSTUS: 51.
TITUS: 87. 134. 139.

*TITUS (EMPEROR): p. 19. p. 44.
  p. 329. p. 331. p. 333.
*TRAJAN: p. 14. p. 19. p. 44
  p. 334.
TRIBUNE: 102. 104-107. 109.
TROAS: 45. 46. 65. 139. p. 33.
  p. 328.
TROGYLLIUM: 67.
TROPHIMUS: 65. 102. 139.
TWELVE (APOSTLES): 16.
  p. 115f.
TWINS: 115.
TYCHICUS: 65. 123. 135. 139.
TYRANNUS: 64.
TYRE: 34. 69.

UNLEAVENED BREAD (DAYS
  OF): 33. 65.

*VATICAN HILL: p. 328.
*VENICE: p. 31.
*VENTIDIUS CUMANUS: p. 42.
*VENUS: p. 21. p. 195.
*VESPASIAN: p. 19. p. 44.
  p. 329. p. 331.
*VITELLIUS: p. 19. p. 44. p. 331.

*WORSHIPPERS OF GOD: p. 35.

*ZEALOTS: p. 329. p. 331.
ZENAS: 135.
ZEUS (JOVE): 39. p. 21. p. 23.

Index of the illustrations

(Page numbers are given)

AIN DIRWE: 90.
AKELDAMA: 52.
ALEXANDER THE GREAT: 20.
ALTAR OF AUGUSTAN PEACE: 15.
AMPHIPOLIS: 176.
ANATOLIA: 190.
ANCYRA (ANKARA) temple of the goddess Roma: 22. 234.
ANTIOCH IN PISIDIA: 122.
ANTIOCH IN SYRIA: 108. St Peter's church: 110.
ANTIPATRIS: 272.
APOLLONIA: 156.
APPIAN WAY: 294.
ARTEMIS: 23. 174.
ASCENSION (Shrine, on the Mount of Olives): 50. 51.
ATHENS: 144. 145. 146. 149. 158.
ATTALIA: 120.
BAPTISTRY (CRUCIFORM): 310.
BEROEA: 142.
BETH SHEARIM: 74.
CAESAREA BY THE SEA: 104. 106. 276. 284.
CAESAREA IN CAPPADOCIA: 228.
CAESAREA PHILIPPI, sources of the Jordan: 280.
CANDLESTICK (seven-branched) basrelief on the Arch of Titus in Rome: 329.
CENACLE IN JERUSALEM: 56. 57.
COLOSSAE: 306.
CORFU, mosaic in the Cathedral: 420.
CORINTH, remains of the Synagogue: 25.
remains of the "Bema": 151.
site of the ancient harbour: 188.
remains of the Temple of A-pollo: 148. 194.
the stadium: 200.
DAMASCUS: traditional site of Paul's flight: 92.
wall: 94. 224.
DARDANELLES (Strait): 216.
DERBE: 128.
EMPIRE OF ALEXANDER: 21.
EPHESUS, ruins of St Luke's Tomb: 30.
ancient street: 172.
ruins of the Temple of Artemis: 174.
ancient picture of St Peter & Paul: 181.
street in the Agora: 186.
ruins: 316.
St John's Basilica: 380. 387.
EUCHARIST (early Christian mosaic): 204.
GALATIA: 240.
GEHENNA: 52.
GERONA APOCALYPSE: 406.
GISH: 32.
GRAFFITI in the Catacombs of St Sebastian in Rome: 328.
GREECE, Mount Olympus: 22.
ICONIUM: 232. 236.
JERUSALEM, seen from the South-west: 46.
Basilica of the Dormition: 54.
Interior of the Cenacle: 56.
Roman stairway: 66.
Panorama of the Temple Area: 82.
Site of St Stephen's Martyrdom: 84.
Church of St James the Great: 112.
Sepulchre of Christ: 212.
seen from the South: 260.
Greek inscription in the Temple: 265.

Site of the Antonia Tower: 266. 270.

Esplanade of the Temple: 268.

Pinnacle of the Temple: 326.

JOPPA: St Peter's Church: 98.

site of Simon's house: 100.

alley in the old city: 102.

JOVE (ZEUS): 23.

LEBONA, Valley of: 88.

LIBER FLORIDUS, struggle of the Woman with the dragon: 410.

LUKE: 12th century miniature: 36.

tomb: 30.

LYSTRA: 124. 162.

MACEDONIA: 336.

MADRAS, Tomb of St Thomas: 29.

MALTA, St Paul's Bay: 290.

MASADA: 330.

MENOLOGION OF BASIL II: 414.

MILETUS, Remains of the Roman Theatre: 180.

Ruins: 182.

MURATORIAN fragment: 37. 38.

NEAPOLIS: 138. 218.

NERO (emperor): 18.

OLIVES, Mount of: 48. 50.

PAPYRUS (2nd century B.C.): 39.

PATMOS: 332. 390.

PERGAMUM: 398.

PHILADELPHIA: 404.

PHILIPPI, St Paul's prison: 140. 305.

Agora: 300.

PUTEOLI: 292.

RAVENNA, mosaics: 408. 416. 419.

ROCK TEMPLES OF PAN: 281.

ROMAN EMPIRE, marble map of, in Via dei Trionfi, Rome: 14.

ROMAN THEATRE: 302.

ROME, Church of the Tre Fontane 33.

Forum Romanum: 246. 248. 295.

Basilica of St Paul: 296.

Reconstruction of the apse of the Vatican Basilica: 362.

Mamertime Prison: 368.

Bas-relief in the crypt of St Peter's: 376.

SAMARITAN priest: 350.

SARDIS: 402.

SELEUCIA: 130.

SHECHEM: 366.

SIDON: 286.

SILLA (near Iconium): 238.

SINAI, Oasis of Wadi Gharandel: 78.

Mountain Mass: 80.

SMYRNA: 396.

STRATO, Tower of: 284.

TABOR, Mount: 372.

TARSUS, remains of Roman Baths: 96.

TAURUS RANGE: 170.

TEMPLE AT JERUSALEM, site of the "Beautiful Gate": 62.

eastern side of the esplanade: 64.

"Golden Gate": 70. 71.

Mosque of El Aksa: 72.

section, plan and perspective: 352.

THESSALONICA: 152. 154. 164. 167.

THYATIRA: 400.

TIBERIUS (Emperor): 18.

TRAJAN (Emperor): 19.

TROAS: 178.

TURKEY, Cilician Gates: 136.

TYRE, Anchors of Phoenician Stone, 288.

VATICAN CODEX: 38. 155. 163. 187. 220. 229. 243. 245. 301. 308. 347. 357. 363. 378. 381. 386. 388. 393.

VESPASIAN (Emperor): 19.

WEAVER: 222.

in the same series ▶

is given him from heaven. You yourselves bear me witness, that I said, I am not the Christ, but I have been sent before him. He who has the bride is the bridegroom; the friend of the bridegroom who stands and hears him, rejoices greatly at the bridegroom's voice; therefore this joy of mine is now full. He must increase, but I must decrease."

The Baptist in prison, Jesus leaves Judaea
Mt. 4, 12. Mk. 4, 17. Lk. 3, 19–20. Jn. 4, 1–3

But Herod the tetrarch, who had been reproved by him for Herodias, his brother's wife, and for all the evil things that Herod had done, added this to them all, that he shut up John in prison.

Now when the Lord knew that the Pharisees had heard that Jesus was making and baptizing more disciples than John (although Jesus himself did not baptize, but only his disciples), he left Judaea and departed again to Galilee.

Jesus passes through Samaria. His talk with the Samaritan woman
Jn. 4, 4–42

He had to pass through Samaria. So he came to a city of Samaria, called Sychar, near the field that Jacob gave to his son Joseph. Jacob's well was there, and so Jesus, wearied as he was with his journey, sat down beside the well. It was about the sixth hour.

There came a woman of Samaria to draw water. Jesus said to her, "Give me a drink." For his disciples had gone away into the city to buy food. The Samaritan woman said to him, "How is it that you, a Jew, ask a drink of me, a woman of

* This expression holds all the greatness of the moral character of John. Never has he worked for his own glory but only for the glory of Another (The Messiah).

89

THE GOSPEL OF JESUS

The RSV text of the four Gospels arranged in one continuous narrative, 110 colour photographs of the Holy Land, 38 illustrations in black and white, little maps and time chart on every page. Two introductions (on the geographical-historical background and on the didactic aspect of the Gospels). Notes and references. Gaily and attractively presented and extremely useful for encouraging especially the young to read the gospels for themselves. 380 pages.

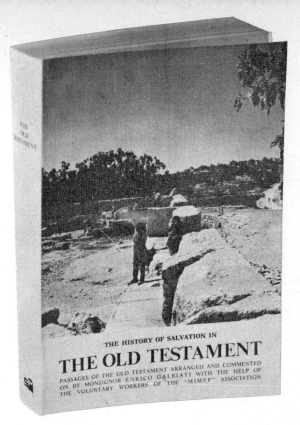

THE HISTORY OF SALVATION IN
THE OLD TESTAMENT
PASSAGES OF THE OLD TESTAMENT ARRANGED AND COMMENTED
ON BY MONSIGNOR ENRICO GALBIATI WITH THE HELP OF
THE VOLUNTARY WORKERS OF THE "MIMEP" ASSOCIATION

THE HISTORY OF SALVATION IN
THE OLD TESTAMENT

Passages from the various books of the Old Testament have been
arranged in continuous narrative form. The introduction, commentary
and notes will help the reader to understand both the themes of the
Bible and its message of salvation. The colour photographs and other
illustrations and maps, together with their captions, vividly bring home
the places mentioned in the text. 466 pages.